HEBREWS

Verse-by-Verse

The Expositor's Bible Study and Commentary

DR. MAXWELL SHIMBA

Shimba Publishing LLC

Printed in the United States of America

First Printing Edition 2024

Table of Contents

Introduction to the Book of Hebrews

Authorship and Date:

The authorship of the Book of Hebrews remains a topic of debate among scholars. Traditionally attributed to the apostle Paul, the letter's style and vocabulary differ significantly from Paul's other writings. Other suggested authors include Barnabas, Apollos, or an unknown early Christian leader. The date of composition is also uncertain, but it is generally believed to have been written between AD 60 and AD 100.

Purpose and Audience:

The letter to the Hebrews was written to encourage and exhort Jewish Christians who were facing persecution and the temptation to revert to Judaism. The author sought to strengthen their faith in Jesus Christ as the ultimate fulfillment of the Old Testament prophecies and sacrificial system.

Recipients:

The original recipients of the letter were likely Jewish Christians, possibly located in or near Jerusalem. They were familiar with Jewish customs, traditions, and the Old Testament Scriptures.

Theme:

The central theme of Hebrews is the superiority of Jesus Christ. The author presents Jesus as superior to angels, Moses, and the Levitical priesthood. He is portrayed as the ultimate high priest whose sacrifice on the cross surpasses all previous sacrifices, ushering in a new covenant between God and humanity.

Overview of the Book of Hebrews

Structure and Themes:
The Book of Hebrews can be divided into two main sections: the doctrinal section (Chapters 1-10) and the practical exhortations (Chapters 11-13). The doctrinal section establishes Jesus' superiority and explains the implications of His work, while the practical section exhorts believers to live out their faith in light of these truths.

Unique Features and Style:
Hebrews stands out for its sophisticated Greek style and its rich use of Old Testament quotations and allusions. The author employs a variety of rhetorical techniques, including argumentation, exhortation, and warning, to persuade the audience of the superiority of Christ.

Outline:
1. Introduction (1:1-4)
2. Christ's Superiority to Angels (1:5-2:18)
3. Christ's Superiority to Moses (3:1-4:13)
4. Christ's Superiority as High Priest (4:14-10:39)
   - His Appointment as High Priest (4:14-7:28)
   - The Superiority of His Priesthood (8:1-10:18)
   - The Finality of His Sacrifice (10:19-39)
5. Exhortations to Faith and Endurance (11:1-12:29)
6. Practical Exhortations (13:1-25)
   - Love and Hospitality (13:1-3)

- Respect for Leaders and Godly Living (13:7-17)
- Final Instructions and Benediction (13:18-25)

In summary, the Book of Hebrews is a profound exploration of the person and work of Jesus Christ, emphasizing His supremacy and the believer's need to persevere in faith. It combines deep theological insights with practical exhortations, making it a rich resource for understanding the Christian faith.

Titles of Jesus in Hebrews

25 titles of Jesus found in the Book of Hebrews:

1. Son of God (Hebrews 1:2)
2. Heir of All Things (Hebrews 1:2)
3. Creator of the World (Hebrews 1:2)
4. Radiance of God's Glory (Hebrews 1:3)
5. Exact Representation of God's Being (Hebrews 1:3)
6. Sustainer of All Things (Hebrews 1:3)
7. Purifier of Sins (Hebrews 1:3)
8. High Priest (Hebrews 2:17)
9. Apostle (Hebrews 3:1)
10. Author of Salvation (Hebrews 5:9)
11. Forerunner (Hebrews 6:20)
12. Anchor of the Soul (Hebrews 6:19)
13. High Priest According to the Order of Melchizedek (Hebrews 6:20)
14. Mediator of a New Covenant (Hebrews 9:15)
15. Great Shepherd of the Sheep (Hebrews 13:20)
16. Founder and Perfecter of Our Faith (Hebrews 12:2)
17. King of Righteousness (Hebrews 7:2)
18. King of Peace (Hebrews 7:2)
19. Surety of a Better Covenant (Hebrews 7:22)
20. High Priest Forever (Hebrews 7:24)
21. Minister in the Sanctuary (Hebrews 8:2)

22. Testator of the New Covenant (Hebrews 9:16)

23. Offering for Our Sins (Hebrews 10:12)

24. Author and Finisher of Our Faith (Hebrews 12:2)

25. God of Peace (Hebrews 13:20)

These titles highlight various aspects of Jesus' identity, ministry, and role in the salvation of believers, underscoring His preeminence and sufficiency in all things.

The Son is God's Revelation

Hebrews chapter 1 begins with a powerful declaration about the supremacy of Jesus Christ. Let's break down verse 1 and explore its meaning with reference to the King James Bible, interpretation, commentary, and concordance.

Verse 1 (King James Version):
> God, who at sundry times and in divers manners spake in time past unto the fathers by the prophets,

Interpretation:
This verse introduces the theme of the book of Hebrews, which is the superiority of Jesus Christ over all things, including the prophets of the Old Testament. It highlights how God communicated with His people in the past through various means, such as dreams, visions, and direct speech, as recorded in the Old Testament.

Commentary:
- "God": The mention of "God" at the beginning emphasizes the divine origin of the message that follows.
- "sundry times and in divers manners": This phrase indicates that God's communication was not limited to one specific time or method but occurred repeatedly and in various ways throughout history.
- "spake in time past unto the fathers by the prophets": God communicated with the forefathers of the Jewish people (Abraham, Isaac, Jacob, etc.) through the prophets, who served as His messengers. This communication is recorded in the Old Testament.

Concordance:
- The phrase "in time past unto the fathers" suggests that God's communication was directed to the patriarchs of Israel, including Abraham, Isaac, and Jacob.
- The phrase "by the prophets" refers to the various prophets in the Old Testament who spoke on behalf of God, such as Moses, Isaiah, Jeremiah, and others.

This verse sets the stage for the rest of Hebrews, showing that while God spoke through the prophets in the past, He has now spoken through His Son, Jesus Christ, who is the ultimate revelation of God to humanity.

Verse 2 (King James Version):
> Hath in these last days spoken unto us by his Son, whom he hath appointed heir of all things, by whom also he made the worlds;

Interpretation:

This verse continues the theme of God's communication, contrasting the past ways of speaking through prophets with His present method of speaking through His Son, Jesus Christ. It emphasizes Jesus' unique role as the heir of all things and the creator of the universe.

Commentary:

- "Hath in these last days spoken unto us by his Son": This highlights the new and final revelation of God through Jesus Christ, emphasizing the present time as the culmination of God's communication with humanity.

- "whom he hath appointed heir of all things": Jesus is not only the Son of God but also the heir of all things, indicating His supreme authority and inheritance over the entire universe.

- "by whom also he made the worlds": This phrase underscores Jesus' role as the agent of creation, affirming His divine nature and participation in the creation of the universe.

Concordance:

- The phrase "in these last days" suggests that Jesus' coming marks the end of an era and the beginning of a new age, fulfilling the prophecies of the Old Testament.

- The phrase "by his Son" emphasizes the direct and intimate relationship between God the Father and Jesus Christ, highlighting Jesus' unique position as the revealer of God's will.

- The phrase "heir of all things" echoes passages in the New Testament that affirm Jesus' sovereignty and dominion over all creation.

- The phrase "by whom also he made the worlds" reinforces the idea of Jesus' preexistence and active role in the creation of the universe, aligning with other New Testament passages that affirm His divine nature and creative power.

This verse reinforces the central message of Hebrews, emphasizing the superiority of Jesus Christ as the final and ultimate revelation of God to humanity, the heir of all things, and the creator of the universe.

Verse 3 (King James Version):
> Who being the brightness of his glory, and the express image of his person, and upholding all things by the word of his power, when he had by himself purged our sins, sat down on the right hand of the Majesty on high;

Interpretation:
This verse further elaborates on the nature and role of Jesus Christ, emphasizing His divine attributes and actions. It describes Jesus as the radiance of God's glory, the exact representation of God's being, the sustainer of all things, the one who purifies sins, and the one who is exalted at the right hand of God.

Commentary:
- "Who being the brightness of his glory": This phrase highlights Jesus' role as the visible manifestation of God's glory, indicating His divine nature and the radiance of His being.

- "and the express image of his person": This phrase emphasizes that Jesus is the exact representation or imprint of God's nature, indicating His perfect correspondence with the Father in essence and character.

- "and upholding all things by the word of his power": This phrase underscores Jesus' role as the sustainer and preserver of the universe, indicating His power and authority over all creation.

- "when he had by himself purged our sins": This phrase refers to Jesus' sacrificial death on the cross, where He, by His own actions, cleansed humanity from sin, highlighting His role as the Savior of mankind.

- "sat down on the right hand of the Majesty on high": This phrase signifies Jesus' exaltation and enthronement at the right hand of God, indicating His authority, power, and glory.

Concordance:

- The phrase "the brightness of his glory" echoes similar descriptions of Jesus in the New Testament, highlighting His divine radiance and glory.

- The phrase "the express image of his person" emphasizes the unique and perfect representation of God's nature that Jesus embodies.

- The phrase "upholding all things by the word of his power" suggests Jesus' ongoing role in sustaining and maintaining the universe, aligning with other passages that affirm His divine sovereignty and control.

- The phrase "sat down on the right hand of the Majesty on high" indicates Jesus' exaltation and reign at the right hand of God, fulfilling prophecies and affirming His authority and majesty.

This verse further emphasizes the supremacy of Jesus Christ, highlighting His divine nature, role in creation, work of redemption, and exaltation to the highest position of authority and honor.

Verse 4 (King James Version):

> Being made so much better than the angels, as he hath by inheritance obtained a more excellent name than they.

Interpretation:

This verse compares Jesus Christ to angels, emphasizing His superiority over them. It highlights that Jesus has inherited a more excellent name than the angels, indicating His preeminence and divine status.

Commentary:
- "Being made so much better than the angels": This phrase emphasizes that Jesus, though fully human, is superior to angels in His nature, role, and authority, highlighting His unique status as the Son of God.
- "as he hath by inheritance obtained a more excellent name than they": This phrase suggests that Jesus' superiority over angels is not by nature but by inheritance, indicating His divine status and the honor bestowed upon Him by God the Father.

Concordance:
- The phrase "made so much better than the angels" highlights Jesus' superiority over angels, a theme that is developed further in the following verses and throughout the book of Hebrews.
- The phrase "by inheritance obtained a more excellent name" suggests that Jesus' status and authority are based on His divine inheritance as the Son of God, indicating His unique relationship with the Father.
- This verse contrasts with the belief prevalent in some Jewish circles at the time that angels played a significant role in mediating between God and humanity. The author of Hebrews is asserting Jesus' superiority over angels and reinforcing His central role in God's plan of salvation.

This verse reinforces the theme of Jesus' superiority over angels, highlighting His unique status as the Son of God and the heir of a name that is above all others. It serves as a foundation for the author's argument for the supremacy of Jesus Christ in the rest of the chapter and the book of Hebrews.

Verse 5 (King James Version):
> For unto which of the angels said he at any time, Thou art my Son, this day have I begotten thee? And again, I will be to him a Father, and he shall be to me a Son?

Interpretation:
This verse quotes two Old Testament passages (Psalm 2:7 and 2 Samuel 7:14) to emphasize the uniqueness of Jesus' relationship with God the Father. It highlights that God never spoke to any angel in the same way He spoke to Jesus, affirming Jesus' divine sonship and special status.

Commentary:
- "For unto which of the angels said he at any time": This rhetorical question emphasizes the point that God has never addressed any angel in the manner described in the following verses, highlighting the uniqueness of Jesus' relationship with God.
- "Thou art my Son, this day have I begotten thee": This phrase quotes Psalm 2:7, a messianic psalm that speaks of the special relationship between God and the Messiah. It emphasizes Jesus' divine sonship and His unique status as the Son of God.
- "And again, I will be to him a Father, and he shall be to me a Son": This phrase quotes 2 Samuel 7:14, a promise made to King David regarding his descendant, who would be the Messiah. It further emphasizes the special relationship between God and the Messiah, indicating that Jesus fulfills this messianic prophecy.

Concordance:

- The quote "Thou art my Son, this day have I begotten thee" is a direct reference to Psalm 2:7, a psalm that was understood messianically and is quoted several times in the New Testament in reference to Jesus (Acts 13:33; Hebrews 5:5).

- The quote "I will be to him a Father, and he shall be to me a Son" is a direct reference to 2 Samuel 7:14, where God promises to establish the throne of David forever through his descendants, ultimately fulfilled in Jesus Christ.

This verse highlights the unique relationship between Jesus Christ and God the Father, contrasting it with the relationship between God and angels. It emphasizes Jesus' divine sonship and His fulfillment of messianic prophecies, further establishing His superiority over angels.

Verse 6 (King James Version):

> And again, when he bringeth in the firstbegotten into the world, he saith, And let all the angels of God worship him.

Interpretation:

This verse quotes another Old Testament passage (Deuteronomy 32:43, LXX) to highlight the worship that is due to Jesus Christ. It emphasizes Jesus' exalted status and the reverence that all angels are commanded to show Him.

Commentary:

- "And again, when he bringeth in the firstbegotten into the world": This phrase refers to Jesus' incarnation, emphasizing His preeminence and the significance of His entry into the world.

- "he saith, And let all the angels of God worship him": This phrase quotes Deuteronomy 32:43 in the Septuagint (LXX)

8

translation, which commands all the angels to worship the Lord. Here, it is applied to Jesus, indicating His divine nature and the worship that is rightfully His.

Concordance:
- The quote "And let all the angels of God worship him" is a reference to Deuteronomy 32:43 in the Septuagint (LXX), where God is exalted and all the angels are called to worship Him. In Hebrews, this verse is applied to Jesus, indicating His divine status and the worship due to Him.
- This verse reinforces the theme of Jesus' superiority over angels, highlighting His divine nature and the worship that is rightfully His.

This verse further emphasizes the exalted status of Jesus Christ and the worship that is due to Him, highlighting His superiority over angels and His divine nature. It underscores the central theme of Hebrews, which is the supremacy of Jesus Christ over all creation.

Verse 7 (King James Version):
> And of the angels he saith, Who maketh his angels spirits, and his ministers a flame of fire.

Interpretation:
This verse contrasts the nature and role of angels with that of Jesus Christ. It describes angels as spirits and ministers who serve God's purposes, highlighting their subordinate role compared to the exalted status of Jesus.

Commentary:

- "And of the angels he saith": This phrase introduces a quotation from Psalm 104:4, which describes the nature and role of angels.

- "Who maketh his angels spirits, and his ministers a flame of fire": This phrase describes angels as spiritual beings who serve as messengers and ministers of God, highlighting their ethereal nature and their function in carrying out God's will.

Concordance:

- The quote "Who maketh his angels spirits, and his ministers a flame of fire" is a reference to Psalm 104:4, which praises God for His creation and provision for all living creatures, including angels. It emphasizes the ethereal and spiritual nature of angels, highlighting their role as ministers of God's will.

This verse emphasizes the subordinate role of angels compared to the exalted status of Jesus Christ. It highlights the ethereal and ministerial nature of angels, contrasting it with the divine and sovereign nature of Jesus. This serves to further establish Jesus' superiority over angels and His unique status as the Son of God.

Verse 8 (King James Version):
> But unto the Son he saith, Thy throne, O God, is for ever and ever: a sceptre of righteousness is the sceptre of thy kingdom.

Interpretation:
This verse directly addresses Jesus Christ as the Son and quotes from Psalm 45:6-7, where the king is addressed as God. It emphasizes the eternal nature of Jesus' throne and the righteousness of His rule.

Commentary:

- "But unto the Son he saith": This phrase introduces a direct quotation addressed to Jesus Christ, highlighting His unique status as the Son of God.

- "Thy throne, O God, is for ever and ever": This phrase quotes from Psalm 45:6, where the king is addressed as God, emphasizing the divine nature of Jesus Christ and the eternal nature of His reign.

- "a sceptre of righteousness is the sceptre of thy kingdom": This phrase emphasizes that Jesus' rule is characterized by righteousness and justice, highlighting His perfect and just reign over His kingdom.

Concordance:

- The quote "Thy throne, O God, is for ever and ever" is a reference to Psalm 45:6, where the king is addressed as God, emphasizing the eternal and divine nature of the king's reign. In Hebrews, this verse is applied to Jesus Christ, highlighting His divine nature and eternal rule.

- The phrase "a sceptre of righteousness is the sceptre of thy kingdom" emphasizes the just and righteous rule of Jesus Christ, indicating that His kingdom is characterized by righteousness and justice.

This verse further establishes the divine nature and eternal reign of Jesus Christ. It highlights His unique status as the Son of God and the righteousness of His rule, contrasting it with the temporary and imperfect rule of earthly kings.

Verse 9 (King James Version):
> Thou hast loved righteousness, and hated iniquity; therefore God, even thy God, hath anointed thee with the oil of gladness above thy fellows.

Interpretation:

This verse describes the character of Jesus Christ, highlighting His love for righteousness and His hatred for iniquity. It also emphasizes God's response to Jesus' righteousness, which is to anoint Him with the oil of gladness, signifying His exaltation and joy.

Commentary:
- "Thou hast loved righteousness, and hated iniquity": This phrase emphasizes Jesus' moral perfection and His complete alignment with God's will, highlighting His perfect righteousness.
- "therefore God, even thy God, hath anointed thee with the oil of gladness above thy fellows": This phrase indicates that God has rewarded Jesus' righteousness by exalting Him and anointing Him with the oil of gladness, a symbol of joy and honor. This exaltation sets Jesus apart from His companions, indicating His unique status and relationship with God.

Concordance:
- The quote "Thou hast loved righteousness, and hated iniquity" is a reference to Psalm 45:7, where the king's love for righteousness and hatred for wickedness are praised. In Hebrews, this verse is applied to Jesus Christ, emphasizing His perfect righteousness and moral perfection.
- The phrase "God, even thy God, hath anointed thee with the oil of gladness above thy fellows" emphasizes God's response to Jesus' righteousness, indicating His exaltation and honor above all others.

This verse further highlights the moral perfection and exaltation of Jesus Christ. It emphasizes His perfect alignment with God's will and His unique status as the Son of God. It also underscores the joy and honor that result from living a life of righteousness and obedience to God.

Verse 10 (King James Version):
> And, Thou, Lord, in the beginning hast laid the foundation of the earth; and the heavens are the works of thine hands:

Interpretation:
This verse continues to emphasize the supremacy of Jesus Christ by quoting from Psalm 102:25-27, which attributes the creation of the heavens and the earth to the Lord. In the context of Hebrews, this passage is applied to Jesus, highlighting His role as the Creator and sustainer of the universe.

Commentary:
- "Thou, Lord, in the beginning hast laid the foundation of the earth": This phrase attributes the creation of the earth to the Lord, emphasizing His role as the Creator and foundation of all things.
- "and the heavens are the works of thine hands": This phrase extends the scope of creation to include the heavens, emphasizing the Lord's sovereignty and creative power over the entire universe.

Concordance:
- The quote "Thou, Lord, in the beginning hast laid the foundation of the earth" is a reference to Psalm 102:25, where the Lord is praised as the Creator of the earth. In Hebrews, this verse is applied to Jesus Christ, highlighting His role as the Creator and foundation of the earth.
- The phrase "and the heavens are the works of thine hands" emphasizes the Lord's creative power over the heavens, indicating His sovereignty and authority over all creation.

This verse further establishes the divine nature and creative power of Jesus Christ. It highlights His role as the Creator and sustainer of the universe, emphasizing His supremacy over all creation.

Verse 11 (King James Version):
> They shall perish; but thou remainest; and they all shall wax old as doth a garment;

Interpretation:
This verse contrasts the temporary nature of the created world with the eternal nature of Jesus Christ. It emphasizes that while the heavens and the earth will perish and grow old, Jesus will remain unchanged and eternal.

Commentary:
- "They shall perish; but thou remainest": This phrase highlights the impermanence of the created world compared to the eternal nature of Jesus Christ. It emphasizes His unchanging and eternal existence.
- "and they all shall wax old as doth a garment": This phrase further emphasizes the transitory nature of the created world, likening it to a garment that wears out over time.

Concordance:
- The quote "They shall perish; but thou remainest" echoes the sentiments expressed in Psalm 102:26, which contrasts the temporary nature of creation with the eternal nature of God. In Hebrews, this verse is applied to Jesus Christ, emphasizing His unchanging and eternal nature.
- The phrase "and they all shall wax old as doth a garment" reinforces the idea of the created world's transience, highlighting its eventual decay and obsolescence.

This verse underscores the eternal and unchanging nature of Jesus Christ, contrasting it with the temporary and decaying nature of the created world. It emphasizes His supremacy and eternal existence, highlighting His role as the unchanging foundation of all things.

Verse 12 (King James Version):
> And as a vesture shalt thou fold them up, and they shall be changed: but thou art the same, and thy years shall not fail.

Interpretation:
This verse continues the theme of the eternal nature of Jesus Christ, contrasting His unchanging nature with the changing and temporary nature of the created world. It uses imagery of clothing being folded up and changed to emphasize the transience of the world compared to the eternal nature of Jesus.

Commentary:
- "And as a vesture shalt thou fold them up, and they shall be changed": This phrase uses metaphorical language to describe the temporary nature of the created world, likening it to clothing that can be folded up and changed. This imagery emphasizes the transitory and changing nature of the world.
- "but thou art the same, and thy years shall not fail": This phrase contrasts the changing nature of the world with the eternal and unchanging nature of Jesus Christ. It emphasizes that Jesus remains the same throughout eternity and His years will never end.

Concordance:
- The quote "And as a vesture shalt thou fold them up, and they shall be changed" echoes the imagery of changing and folding up clothing, similar to Isaiah 51:6, which speaks of the heavens being rolled

up like a scroll. In Hebrews, this verse is applied to Jesus Christ, emphasizing His eternal nature compared to the changing world.

- The phrase "but thou art the same, and thy years shall not fail" emphasizes the unchanging and eternal nature of Jesus Christ. It echoes passages like Psalm 102:27, which speaks of God's unchanging nature and eternal existence.

This verse reinforces the eternal and unchanging nature of Jesus Christ, contrasting it with the changing and temporary nature of the created world. It emphasizes His supremacy and eternal existence, highlighting His role as the unchanging foundation of all things.

Verse 13 (King James Version):
> But to which of the angels said he at any time, Sit on my right hand, until I make thine enemies thy footstool?

Interpretation:
This verse continues to emphasize the superiority of Jesus Christ over angels by highlighting the unique relationship between Jesus and God the Father. It quotes from Psalm 110:1 to demonstrate that God never said to any angel to sit at His right hand, a position of honor and authority.

Commentary:
- "But to which of the angels said he at any time": This phrase emphasizes the rhetorical question regarding God's communication with angels, highlighting that God has never made a statement like the one described in the following verse to any angel.
- "Sit on my right hand, until I make thine enemies thy footstool": This phrase quotes Psalm 110:1, where the Lord invites the

Messiah to sit at His right hand, indicating the exalted position of the Messiah and His authority over His enemies.

Concordance:

- The quote "Sit on my right hand, until I make thine enemies thy footstool" is a reference to Psalm 110:1, which was understood messianically and is quoted several times in the New Testament in reference to Jesus (Matthew 22:44; Acts 2:34-35). In Hebrews, this verse is applied to Jesus Christ, highlighting His exalted status and authority over all things.

- This verse reinforces the theme of Jesus' superiority over angels, highlighting His unique relationship with God the Father and His exalted position at the right hand of God.

This verse further establishes the supremacy of Jesus Christ over angels, highlighting His unique relationship with God the Father and His exalted position of authority. It emphasizes that Jesus occupies a position of honor and power that is above all angels, indicating His divine nature and role in God's plan of redemption.

Verse 14 (King James Version):
> Are they not all ministering spirits, sent forth to minister for them who shall be heirs of salvation?

Interpretation:
This verse emphasizes the role of angels as ministering spirits who serve and assist those who are heirs of salvation. It contrasts the temporary nature of angels' ministry with the eternal salvation that believers receive through Jesus Christ.

Commentary:

- "Are they not all ministering spirits": This phrase highlights the nature of angels as servants who minister to the needs of God's people. It emphasizes their role as messengers and agents of God's will.

- "sent forth to minister for them who shall be heirs of salvation": This phrase indicates the purpose of angels' ministry, which is to serve and assist those who are heirs of salvation. It emphasizes that angels are sent by God to care for and protect believers.

Concordance:

- The phrase "ministering spirits" emphasizes the role of angels as servants who carry out God's will. This concept is found in other parts of the Bible, such as Psalm 104:4 and Acts 7:53.

- The phrase "heirs of salvation" refers to believers who have received salvation through faith in Jesus Christ. This concept is found throughout the New Testament, emphasizing the inheritance that believers receive as children of God.

This verse highlights the role of angels as servants who minister to the needs of believers. It emphasizes that while angels serve an important role in God's plan, their ministry is temporary and secondary to the eternal salvation that believers receive through Jesus Christ.

CHAPTER 2
The role of Christ in salvation

Verse 1 (King James Version):
> Therefore we ought to give the more earnest heed to the things which we have heard, lest at any time we should let them slip.

Interpretation:
This verse serves as an exhortation to pay close attention to the teachings and truths that have been heard, particularly those concerning salvation through Jesus Christ. It warns against neglecting or drifting away from these truths.

Commentary:
- "Therefore we ought to give the more earnest heed to the things which we have heard": This phrase emphasizes the importance of paying close attention to the teachings of the Gospel, indicating that

the truths of salvation through Jesus Christ are of utmost importance and should not be taken lightly.

- "lest at any time we should let them slip": This phrase warns against neglecting or drifting away from the truths of the Gospel. It emphasizes the danger of forgetting or becoming indifferent to these truths, which can lead to spiritual decline and loss of faith.

Concordance:
- The phrase "we ought to give the more earnest heed" underscores the importance of paying careful attention to the Gospel message. This theme is echoed in other parts of the New Testament, such as Hebrews 4:1 and 2 Peter 1:19.
- The phrase "lest at any time we should let them slip" highlights the danger of neglecting or forgetting the truths of the Gospel. This warning is consistent with other passages in the New Testament that caution against falling away from the faith, such as Hebrews 3:12-13 and 2 Peter 3:17.

This verse emphasizes the importance of remaining steadfast in the faith and not allowing the truths of the Gospel to slip away or be forgotten. It encourages believers to pay close attention to the teachings of the Gospel and to hold fast to their faith in Jesus Christ.

Verse 2 (King James Version):
> For if the word spoken by angels was stedfast, and every transgression and disobedience received a just recompence of reward;

Interpretation:
This verse introduces a comparison between the message delivered by angels (referring to the Law given through angels) and the message of salvation through Jesus Christ. It suggests that just as the

Law delivered by angels was reliable and carried consequences for disobedience, so too is the message of salvation through Christ.

Commentary:

- "For if the word spoken by angels was stedfast": This phrase refers to the Law given to Moses on Mount Sinai, which tradition holds was mediated by angels. It suggests that the Law was reliable and trustworthy.

- "and every transgression and disobedience received a just recompence of reward": This phrase indicates that under the Law, disobedience and transgression were met with just punishment or retribution, highlighting the seriousness of violating God's commandments.

Concordance:

- The phrase "word spoken by angels" refers to the Law given to Moses, as traditionally believed by Jewish scholars and mentioned in Acts 7:53 and Galatians 3:19.

- The phrase "every transgression and disobedience received a just recompence of reward" underscores the principle of retribution under the Law, where disobedience was met with punishment, as seen in examples throughout the Old Testament.

This verse sets the stage for the contrast between the Law and the message of salvation through Jesus Christ that is developed in the following verses. It suggests that if the Law, delivered by angels, was steadfast and carried consequences for disobedience, then the message of salvation through Jesus Christ, which is superior to the Law, should be even more carefully heeded.

Verse 3 (King James Version):

> How shall we escape, if we neglect so great salvation; which at the first began to be spoken by the Lord, and was confirmed unto us by them that heard him;

Interpretation:

This verse warns against neglecting the great salvation offered through Jesus Christ. It emphasizes the seriousness of ignoring or disregarding this salvation, which was first proclaimed by Jesus Himself and confirmed by those who heard Him.

Commentary:

- "How shall we escape, if we neglect so great salvation": This phrase highlights the dire consequences of neglecting or disregarding the salvation offered through Jesus Christ. It suggests that there is no escape from judgment if one rejects this salvation.

- "which at the first began to be spoken by the Lord, and was confirmed unto us by them that heard him": This phrase emphasizes the authoritative nature of the message of salvation, which was first proclaimed by Jesus Himself during His earthly ministry and then confirmed by His apostles and disciples who heard Him.

Concordance:

- The phrase "so great salvation" underscores the magnitude and importance of the salvation offered through Jesus Christ, highlighting its superiority and significance.

- The phrase "at the first began to be spoken by the Lord" emphasizes the origin of the message of salvation, which was first proclaimed by Jesus Himself during His ministry on earth.

This verse serves as a warning against neglecting or disregarding the salvation offered through Jesus Christ. It emphasizes the authoritative nature of this salvation, which was first proclaimed by Jesus and then confirmed by His followers. It highlights the seriousness of rejecting this salvation and the need to heed the message of salvation through Jesus Christ.

Verse 4 (King James Version):
> God also bearing them witness, both with signs and wonders, and with divers miracles, and gifts of the Holy Ghost, according to his own will?

Interpretation:
This verse highlights how God confirmed the message of salvation through Jesus Christ with signs, wonders, miracles, and gifts of the Holy Spirit. It emphasizes that these manifestations were according to God's will and served as a testimony to the truth of the message.

Commentary:
- "God also bearing them witness": This phrase indicates that God provided evidence to confirm the message of salvation preached by the apostles and early believers.
- "both with signs and wonders, and with divers miracles, and gifts of the Holy Ghost": This phrase describes the various ways in which God confirmed the message, including miraculous signs, wonders, and spiritual gifts bestowed upon believers by the Holy Spirit.
- "according to his own will": This phrase emphasizes that these manifestations were in accordance with God's sovereign purpose and plan.

Concordance:
- The phrase "God also bearing them witness" emphasizes that God provided evidence to confirm the message of salvation, a theme

seen throughout the New Testament (Acts 14:3; Romans 15:18-19; 1 Corinthians 2:4-5).

- The phrase "signs and wonders, and with divers miracles, and gifts of the Holy Ghost" highlights the variety of ways in which God confirmed the message, including miraculous signs, wonders, and spiritual gifts (Acts 2:22; 1 Corinthians 12:4-11).

- The phrase "according to his own will" underscores that these manifestations were not arbitrary but were in accordance with God's sovereign will and purpose (1 Corinthians 12:11).

This verse emphasizes the supernatural confirmation of the message of salvation through Jesus Christ. It highlights the various ways in which God bore witness to the truth of this message, confirming it with signs, wonders, miracles, and gifts of the Holy Spirit. These manifestations served as a testimony to the truth of the Gospel and the power of God at work in the early church.

Verse 5 (King James Version):
> For unto the angels hath he not put in subjection the world to come, whereof we speak.

Interpretation:
This verse emphasizes that the world to come, which is the subject of the writer's discussion (likely referring to the age of the Messiah and the kingdom of God), is not subjected to angels. Instead, it is under the authority of Jesus Christ.

Commentary:
- "For unto the angels hath he not put in subjection the world to come": This phrase highlights that the future kingdom, ruled by the

Messiah, is not under the authority of angels. It contrasts the limited authority of angels with the supreme authority of Jesus Christ.

- "whereof we speak": This phrase indicates that the writer is discussing this future kingdom and the authority of Jesus Christ over it.

Concordance:

- The phrase "the world to come" refers to the future age of the Messiah and the kingdom of God, a theme found in other New Testament passages (Matthew 12:32; Ephesians 1:21-22; Hebrews 6:5).

- The phrase "hath he not put in subjection the world to come" emphasizes that the future kingdom is not under the authority of angels but under the authority of Jesus Christ, aligning with other passages that affirm the exalted status and authority of Christ (Ephesians 1:20-22; Philippians 2:9-11).

This verse reinforces the supremacy of Jesus Christ over angels and emphasizes His authority over the future kingdom. It highlights that the world to come is under the rule of Jesus Christ, not angels, underscoring His unique status and authority as the Son of God and the promised Messiah.

Verse 6 (King James Version):

> But one in a certain place testified, saying, What is man, that thou art mindful of him? or the son of man, that thou visitest him?

Interpretation:

This verse quotes from Psalm 8:4-6, where the psalmist marvels at the greatness of God's creation and wonders why God would be mindful of humanity. It is used here to emphasize the exalted position that God has given to humanity, despite their frailty and insignificance.

Commentary:

- "But one in a certain place testified, saying": This phrase introduces a quotation from the Old Testament, indicating that the writer is quoting from a specific passage to make a point.

- "What is man, that thou art mindful of him? or the son of man, that thou visitest him?": This phrase quotes from Psalm 8:4-6, where the psalmist reflects on the greatness of God's creation and marvels at the special attention that God gives to humanity, despite their seemingly insignificant status.

Concordance:

- The quote "What is man, that thou art mindful of him?" is from Psalm 8:4, where the psalmist marvels at the fact that God is mindful of humanity, despite their smallness in comparison to the vastness of creation.

- The quote "or the son of man, that thou visitest him?" is from the same passage in Psalm 8:4, where the psalmist questions why God would visit or care for humanity, given their seemingly lowly status.

This verse serves to emphasize the special attention and care that God has for humanity, despite their frailty and insignificance. It is used here to underscore the exalted position that God has given to humanity, as seen in the context of the writer's discussion of the supremacy of Jesus Christ and His role in the redemption of humanity.

Verse 7 (King James Version):

> Thou madest him a little lower than the angels; thou crownedst him with glory and honour, and didst set him over the works of thy hands:

Interpretation:

This verse continues the quotation from Psalm 8:5-6, emphasizing that God made humanity (referring to Adam) a little lower than the angels but crowned them with glory and honor, giving them dominion over the works of His hands.

Commentary:

- "Thou madest him a little lower than the angels": This phrase reflects the psalmist's reflection on the creation of humanity, acknowledging that God made humanity lower than the angels in terms of their status or rank in creation.

- "thou crownedst him with glory and honour, and didst set him over the works of thy hands": This phrase emphasizes that despite humanity's lower position than angels, God crowned them with glory and honor, giving them authority over the works of His hands, which includes the earth and its creatures.

Concordance:

- The phrase "Thou madest him a little lower than the angels" is a direct quote from Psalm 8:5, where the psalmist reflects on the status of humanity in relation to angels, acknowledging humanity's lower position.

- The phrase "thou crownedst him with glory and honour, and didst set him over the works of thy hands" is also from Psalm 8:5-6, where the psalmist praises God for the exalted position and authority that He has given to humanity.

This verse highlights the exalted status and authority that God has given to humanity, despite their lower position than angels. It emphasizes that God has crowned humanity with glory and honor, giving them dominion over His creation. This underscores the special place that humanity holds in God's creation and His care and concern for them.

Verse 8 (King James Version):

> Thou hast put all things in subjection under his feet. For in that he put all in subjection under him, he left nothing that is not put under him. But now we see not yet all things put under him.

Interpretation:

This verse continues the quotation from Psalm 8:6, emphasizing that God has subjected all things to humanity, giving them dominion over creation. However, the writer acknowledges that this dominion is not yet fully realized, as there are still aspects of creation that are not yet under humanity's control.

Commentary:

- "Thou hast put all things in subjection under his feet": This phrase reiterates the idea that God has subjected all things to humanity, symbolized by putting them under their feet, which is a symbol of dominion and authority.

- "For in that he put all in subjection under him, he left nothing that is not put under him": This phrase emphasizes that God has subjected all aspects of creation to humanity's authority, leaving nothing outside of their dominion.

- "But now we see not yet all things put under him": This phrase acknowledges that while God has given humanity dominion over creation, this dominion is not yet fully realized, as there are still aspects of creation that remain outside of humanity's control.

Concordance:

- The phrase "Thou hast put all things in subjection under his feet" is a direct quote from Psalm 8:6, where the psalmist reflects on

God's dominion over creation and the exalted status that He has given to humanity.

- The phrase "But now we see not yet all things put under him" reflects the writer's acknowledgment that while God has given humanity dominion over creation, this dominion is not yet fully realized, a theme echoed in other New Testament passages (Romans 8:19-21).

This verse emphasizes the authority and dominion that God has given to humanity over creation, echoing the sentiments expressed in Psalm 8. However, it also acknowledges that this dominion is not yet fully realized, pointing to the future fulfillment of God's plan for humanity and creation.

Verse 9 (King James Version):
> But we see Jesus, who was made a little lower than the angels for the suffering of death, crowned with glory and honour; that he by the grace of God should taste death for every man.

Interpretation:
This verse focuses on Jesus Christ, highlighting His incarnation and sacrificial death. It emphasizes that although Jesus was made lower than the angels and experienced death, He was crowned with glory and honor because He tasted death for every person, fulfilling God's plan of salvation.

Commentary:
- "But we see Jesus, who was made a little lower than the angels for the suffering of death": This phrase refers to Jesus' incarnation, where He took on human form and was made lower than the angels, subjecting Himself to the human experience, including suffering and death.

- "crowned with glory and honour": This phrase emphasizes the exaltation of Jesus after His death and resurrection, highlighting that He was crowned with glory and honor as a result of His obedience and sacrifice.

- "that he by the grace of God should taste death for every man": This phrase explains the purpose of Jesus' suffering and death, emphasizing that He tasted death for every person, experiencing the full extent of death's consequences on behalf of humanity, as an act of grace from God.

Concordance:
- The phrase "who was made a little lower than the angels" echoes the language of Psalm 8:5, where humanity is described as being made a little lower than the angels, emphasizing Jesus' identification with humanity in His incarnation.

- The phrase "crowned with glory and honour" reflects the exaltation of Jesus after His death and resurrection, a theme found in other New Testament passages (Philippians 2:9-11; Hebrews 1:3).

This verse highlights the central message of the Gospel, emphasizing Jesus' incarnation, sacrificial death, and subsequent exaltation. It underscores that Jesus, through His suffering and death, tasted death for every person, offering salvation to all through His grace.

Verse 10 (King James Version):
> For it became him, for whom are all things, and by whom are all things, in bringing many sons unto glory, to make the captain of their salvation perfect through sufferings.

Interpretation:

This verse emphasizes that it was fitting for God, the creator and sustainer of all things, to bring many people to glory (salvation) through the suffering of Jesus Christ. It suggests that Jesus, as the captain or pioneer of salvation, was made perfect through His suffering, fulfilling God's plan for redemption.

Commentary:

- "For it became him, for whom are all things, and by whom are all things": This phrase emphasizes that it was fitting and appropriate for God, who is the source and sustainer of all things, to bring many people to salvation through Jesus Christ.

- "in bringing many sons unto glory": This phrase refers to the salvation and glorification of believers, emphasizing that God's plan of redemption includes bringing many people into a state of glory and honor.

- "to make the captain of their salvation perfect through sufferings": This phrase describes Jesus Christ as the pioneer or leader of salvation, who was made perfect or complete through His suffering and death. This does not imply moral imperfection in Jesus, but rather the completion of His mission and the fulfillment of God's plan through His suffering.

Concordance:

- The phrase "bringing many sons unto glory" reflects the idea of believers being brought into a state of glory and honor through salvation, a theme found in other New Testament passages (Romans 8:29-30; 2 Corinthians 3:18).

- The phrase "the captain of their salvation" describes Jesus as the leader or pioneer of salvation, emphasizing His role in leading believers to salvation and glory (Hebrews 12:2).

This verse emphasizes the centrality of Jesus Christ in God's plan of salvation. It highlights that Jesus, as the pioneer of salvation, was made perfect through His suffering, fulfilling God's plan to bring many people to glory. It underscores the redemptive work of Jesus and His role as the leader of salvation for believers.

Verse 11 (King James Version):
> For both he that sanctifieth and they who are sanctified are all of one: for which cause he is not ashamed to call them brethren,

Interpretation:
This verse highlights the unity between Jesus Christ, who sanctifies (sets apart for a holy purpose), and those who are sanctified (made holy). It emphasizes that Jesus and believers share a common nature or origin, which is why Jesus is not ashamed to call them brothers and sisters.

Commentary:
- "For both he that sanctifieth and they who are sanctified are all of one": This phrase emphasizes the unity between Jesus, who sanctifies believers through His sacrifice, and believers themselves, who are made holy through Him. It suggests that there is a shared nature or origin between Jesus and believers.
- "for which cause he is not ashamed to call them brethren": This phrase highlights the close relationship between Jesus and believers, emphasizing that Jesus is not ashamed to call believers His brothers and sisters, indicating a deep and intimate bond.

Concordance:
- The phrase "he that sanctifieth" refers to Jesus Christ, who sanctifies believers through His sacrifice (Hebrews 10:10).

- The phrase "they who are sanctified" refers to believers who are made holy through the sacrifice of Jesus Christ (Hebrews 10:14).

This verse emphasizes the close relationship between Jesus Christ and believers. It highlights that Jesus and believers share a common nature or origin, which is why Jesus is not ashamed to call them brothers and sisters. It underscores the intimate bond between Jesus and believers, emphasizing the depth of His love and care for them.

Verse 12 (King James Version):
> Saying, I will declare thy name unto my brethren, in the midst of the church will I sing praise unto thee.

Interpretation:
This verse quotes from Psalm 22:22, where the psalmist expresses his intention to declare God's name to his brothers and sisters and to praise God in the midst of the assembly. The writer of Hebrews uses this verse to show that Jesus fulfills this prophecy by declaring God's name to His followers and praising God among them.

Commentary:
- "Saying, I will declare thy name unto my brethren": This phrase indicates the intention of the speaker (David in the context of Psalm 22, but applied here to Jesus) to proclaim God's name to His brothers and sisters, referring to believers.
- "in the midst of the church will I sing praise unto thee": This phrase describes the act of praising God in the assembly of believers, indicating a public declaration of God's greatness and glory.

Concordance:

- The quote "I will declare thy name unto my brethren" is from Psalm 22:22, where David expresses his intention to proclaim God's name to his brothers and sisters, a prophecy that is seen as being fulfilled in Jesus Christ.

- The phrase "in the midst of the church will I sing praise unto thee" emphasizes the public nature of the praise, indicating that it will be done in the assembly of believers, which is consistent with the practice of worship in the early Christian church.

This verse highlights Jesus' role as the one who declares God's name to believers and praises God among them. It emphasizes the intimate relationship between Jesus and believers, portraying Him as a faithful and loving brother who proclaims God's name and leads His followers in worship.

Verse 13 (King James Version):
> And again, I will put my trust in him. And again, Behold I and the children which God hath given me.

Interpretation:
This verse quotes from Isaiah 8:17-18, where Isaiah expresses his trust in God and identifies himself and the people as children whom God has given him. The writer of Hebrews uses this verse to show that Jesus, like Isaiah, puts His trust in God and identifies with His followers as children given to Him by God.

Commentary:
- "And again, I will put my trust in him": This phrase indicates the speaker's (Isaiah's in the context of Isaiah 8, but applied here to Jesus) trust in God, indicating a deep reliance on God's faithfulness and protection.

- "And again, Behold I and the children which God hath given me": This phrase emphasizes the relationship between the speaker (Isaiah or Jesus) and the people, portraying them as children given to Him by God, indicating a close and intimate bond.

Concordance:
- The quote "I will put my trust in him" is from Isaiah 8:17, where Isaiah expresses his trust in God's protection and salvation, a sentiment that is also seen in Jesus' trust in God the Father.
- The quote "Behold I and the children which God hath given me" is from Isaiah 8:18, where Isaiah identifies himself and the people as children given to Him by God, a concept that is applied to Jesus and His followers in the New Testament (Hebrews 2:13; John 17:6).

This verse emphasizes Jesus' trust in God and His identification with His followers as children given to Him by God. It highlights the deep and intimate relationship between Jesus and His followers, portraying Him as a faithful and loving leader who puts His trust in God and cares for His followers as a loving shepherd cares for His flock.

Verse 14 (King James Version):
> Forasmuch then as the children are partakers of flesh and blood, he also himself likewise took part of the same; that through death he might destroy him that had the power of death, that is, the devil;

Interpretation:
This verse explains that since human beings (the children) are made of flesh and blood, Jesus also became human ("took part of the same") so that through His death, He might destroy the devil, who has the power of death.

Commentary:

- "Forasmuch then as the children are partakers of flesh and blood": This phrase acknowledges that humans are made of flesh and blood, emphasizing their physical and mortal nature.

- "he also himself likewise took part of the same": This phrase indicates that Jesus also became human, taking on a physical body and sharing in the human experience.

- "that through death he might destroy him that had the power of death, that is, the devil": This phrase explains the purpose of Jesus' incarnation and death—to defeat the devil, who holds the power of death, and to conquer sin and death through His sacrifice.

Concordance:

- The phrase "he also himself likewise took part of the same" emphasizes Jesus' full participation in human life and experience, a concept also found in Philippians 2:7, which describes Jesus as taking on the form of a servant and being made in human likeness.

- The phrase "that through death he might destroy him that had the power of death, that is, the devil" underscores the victory of Jesus over the devil and the power of death, a theme found in other New Testament passages (Colossians 2:15; 1 John 3:8).

This verse highlights the significance of Jesus' incarnation and death. It emphasizes that by becoming human and dying on the cross, Jesus defeated the devil and the power of death, providing salvation and eternal life for humanity. It underscores the importance of Jesus' sacrifice in the redemption of humanity and the defeat of evil.

Verse 15 (King James Version):
> And deliver them who through fear of death were all their lifetime subject to bondage.

Interpretation:

This verse explains that Jesus came to deliver those who, because of their fear of death, lived in bondage or slavery throughout their lives. His sacrifice offers freedom from the fear of death and the bondage it brings.

Commentary:

- "And deliver them who through fear of death were all their lifetime subject to bondage": This phrase describes the condition of those who, because of their fear of death, lived in a state of bondage or slavery, being held captive by the fear of what comes after death.

Concordance:

- The phrase "through fear of death were all their lifetime subject to bondage" highlights the oppressive nature of the fear of death, which can lead to a life of bondage or slavery, a concept also found in Romans 8:15, where Paul describes believers as having been freed from the spirit of bondage to fear.

This verse emphasizes the liberating power of Jesus' sacrifice. It highlights that through His death and resurrection, Jesus offers freedom from the fear of death and the bondage it brings. Believers no longer need to fear death, for Jesus has conquered it and offers eternal life to all who believe in Him.

Verse 16 (King James Version):

> For verily he took not on him the nature of angels; but he took on him the seed of Abraham.

Interpretation:

This verse emphasizes that Jesus did not take on the nature of angels but rather took on the human nature descended from Abraham.

This highlights Jesus' identification with humanity and His role as the fulfillment of God's promise to Abraham.

Commentary:
- "For verily he took not on him the nature of angels": This phrase emphasizes that Jesus did not take on the nature of angels, indicating that His incarnation was not to become an angelic being but rather a human being.
- "but he took on him the seed of Abraham": This phrase highlights that Jesus took on the human nature descended from Abraham, indicating His identification with humanity and His role as the fulfillment of God's promise to Abraham to bless all nations through his offspring (Genesis 22:18).

Concordance:
- The phrase "the nature of angels" refers to the angelic nature, indicating that Jesus did not become an angel but rather a human being (Hebrews 1:4-5).
- The phrase "the seed of Abraham" emphasizes Jesus' descent from Abraham, highlighting His identification with humanity and His role as the fulfillment of God's promise to bless all nations through Abraham's offspring (Galatians 3:16).

This verse underscores Jesus' humanity and His role in fulfilling God's plan of redemption. It emphasizes that Jesus became human, not angelic, and that He was descended from Abraham, highlighting His identification with humanity and His role as the promised Messiah.

Verse 17 (King James Version):
> Wherefore in all things it behoved him to be made like unto his brethren, that he might be a merciful and faithful high priest in

things pertaining to God, to make reconciliation for the sins of the people.

Interpretation:

This verse explains that Jesus needed to be made like His brothers and sisters in every way so that He could serve as a merciful and faithful high priest in matters related to God. He did this to make reconciliation for the sins of the people.

Commentary:

- "Wherefore in all things it behoved him to be made like unto his brethren": This phrase indicates that it was necessary for Jesus to be fully human, sharing in the human experience, in order to fulfill His role as high priest and mediator between God and humanity.

- "that he might be a merciful and faithful high priest in things pertaining to God": This phrase describes the qualities of Jesus as a high priest—merciful, showing compassion and understanding, and faithful, being trustworthy and reliable in His role as mediator between God and humanity.

- "to make reconciliation for the sins of the people": This phrase explains the purpose of Jesus' role as high priest—to make reconciliation or atonement for the sins of the people, bridging the gap between humanity and God through His sacrifice.

Concordance:

- The phrase "it behoved him to be made like unto his brethren" emphasizes the necessity of Jesus' humanity in fulfilling His role as high priest and mediator (Philippians 2:7; Hebrews 4:15).

- The phrase "to make reconciliation for the sins of the people" underscores the central role of Jesus' sacrifice in reconciling humanity to God and providing forgiveness for sins (2 Corinthians 5:18-19; Colossians 1:20).

This verse highlights the unique role of Jesus Christ as the high priest who is both fully human and fully divine. It emphasizes that Jesus needed to be like His brothers and sisters in every way to serve as a merciful and faithful high priest, making reconciliation for the sins of the people through His sacrificial death.

Verse 18 (King James Version):
> For in that he himself hath suffered being tempted, he is able to succour them that are tempted.

Interpretation:
This verse explains that because Jesus Himself suffered and was tempted, He is able to help and support those who are also tempted.

Commentary:
- "For in that he himself hath suffered being tempted": This phrase emphasizes that Jesus experienced suffering and temptation during His earthly life, making Him empathetic and understanding towards those who face similar challenges.
- "he is able to succour them that are tempted": This phrase indicates that because of His own experiences, Jesus is able to provide assistance, comfort, and support to those who are tempted, offering them strength and guidance to overcome temptation.

Concordance:
- The phrase "he himself hath suffered being tempted" highlights the humanity of Jesus and His experience of suffering and temptation, a theme also found in Hebrews 4:15, which describes Jesus as being tempted in every way, yet without sin.

- The phrase "he is able to succour them that are tempted" underscores Jesus' ability to help and support those who are tempted, a concept also expressed in 1 Corinthians 10:13, which assures believers that God will provide a way out of temptation.

This verse emphasizes the compassion and understanding of Jesus towards those who face temptation and suffering. It highlights that because Jesus Himself experienced temptation and suffering, He is able to offer meaningful help and support to those who are struggling, providing them with the strength and guidance they need to overcome temptation.

CHAPTER 3
Christ Superior to Moses

Verse 1 (King James Version):
> Wherefore, holy brethren, partakers of the heavenly calling, consider the Apostle and High Priest of our profession, Christ Jesus;

Interpretation:
This verse urges believers to consider Jesus Christ as both the Apostle (sent one) and High Priest of their confession of faith. Believers are described as holy brethren who share in the heavenly calling.

Commentary:
- "Wherefore, holy brethren, partakers of the heavenly calling": This phrase addresses believers as holy (set apart) brethren who share in the heavenly calling, which refers to their divine invitation to salvation and eternal life in Christ.

- "consider the Apostle and High Priest of our profession, Christ Jesus": Believers are encouraged to carefully consider or contemplate Jesus Christ as both the Apostle, meaning the one sent by God with a message, and the High Priest, who intercedes on behalf of believers before God.

Concordance:
- The phrase "holy brethren" emphasizes the sanctified and familial relationship among believers, highlighting their shared status as God's chosen people (1 Peter 2:9).
- The term "partakers of the heavenly calling" underscores believers' participation in the divine invitation to salvation and eternal life through Jesus Christ (Ephesians 1:4-5).

This verse encourages believers to reflect on the unique roles of Jesus Christ as the Apostle and High Priest. As the Apostle, He is the authoritative messenger sent by God, and as the High Priest, He is the mediator between God and humanity, offering salvation and interceding for believers.

Verse 2 (King James Version):
> Who was faithful to him that appointed him, as also Moses was faithful in all his house.

Interpretation:
This verse compares the faithfulness of Jesus Christ to the faithfulness of Moses. Jesus was faithful to God, who appointed Him, just as Moses was faithful in leading the Israelites, referred to as God's "house."

Commentary:

- "Who was faithful to him that appointed him": This phrase emphasizes Jesus' faithfulness to God the Father, who appointed Him for His redemptive mission.
- "as also Moses was faithful in all his house": This phrase compares Jesus' faithfulness to Moses' faithfulness in leading the people of Israel, often referred to as God's "house" or people.

Concordance:
- The statement "Who was faithful to him that appointed him" highlights Jesus' faithfulness to God the Father, a theme emphasized throughout the New Testament (John 4:34; Philippians 2:8).
- The comparison to Moses being faithful in all his house refers to Moses' role in leading and guiding the people of Israel, a theme discussed in Hebrews 3:5-6.

This verse underscores Jesus' faithfulness to God and compares it to the faithfulness of Moses. It suggests that just as Moses was faithful in his leadership, Jesus was faithful in fulfilling His role as the Savior and High Priest appointed by God.

Verse 3 (King James Version):
> For this man was counted worthy of more glory than Moses, inasmuch as he who hath builded the house hath more honour than the house.

Interpretation:
This verse explains that Jesus is considered more glorious than Moses because the builder of a house (Jesus) is honored more than the house (Moses).

Commentary:

- "For this man was counted worthy of more glory than Moses": This phrase highlights that Jesus is considered more glorious than Moses, indicating His superior status and honor.

- "he who hath builded the house hath more honour than the house": This phrase uses an analogy to explain Jesus' superiority over Moses. In this analogy, Jesus is likened to the builder of a house, and Moses is likened to the house itself. The builder is considered more honorable than the house he builds, emphasizing Jesus' superiority over Moses.

Concordance:
- The statement "For this man was counted worthy of more glory than Moses" emphasizes Jesus' superiority over Moses, a theme that is also discussed in Hebrews 3:5-6.
- The analogy of the builder and the house is used to illustrate Jesus' superiority, highlighting the idea that the one who builds something is honored more than the thing that is built.

This verse emphasizes Jesus' superiority over Moses. It uses the analogy of a builder and a house to illustrate this point, suggesting that Jesus, as the builder, is honored more than Moses, who is likened to the house. It underscores Jesus' preeminence in the Christian faith.

Verse 4 (King James Version):
> For every house is builded by some man; but he that built all things is God.

Interpretation:
This verse emphasizes that every house is built by someone, but the one who built all things is God. It highlights God's role as the ultimate creator and builder of everything.

Commentary:

- "For every house is builded by some man": This phrase acknowledges that every physical house or structure is built by someone, emphasizing the human role in construction and creation.

- "but he that built all things is God": This phrase contrasts human builders with God, emphasizing that God is the ultimate builder and creator of all things, including the universe and everything in it.

Concordance:

- The statement "but he that built all things is God" reflects the biblical teaching that God is the creator and sustainer of the universe (Genesis 1:1; Psalm 102:25; Colossians 1:16).

- This verse emphasizes the greatness and sovereignty of God as the ultimate builder and creator, highlighting His role in the creation and maintenance of the world.

This verse underscores the divine role of God as the creator and builder of all things. It contrasts human builders with God, emphasizing God's sovereignty and greatness as the ultimate creator of the universe.

Verse 5 (King James Version):

> And Moses verily was faithful in all his house, as a servant, for a testimony of those things which were to be spoken after;

Interpretation:

This verse acknowledges Moses' faithfulness in leading the people of Israel, referring to him as a servant in God's house. Moses' faithful service was a testimony to the future revelation of God's plan through Jesus Christ.

Commentary:

- "And Moses verily was faithful in all his house": This phrase reaffirms Moses' faithfulness in leading the people of Israel, indicating that he fulfilled his role as a servant of God's people.

- "as a servant": This phrase describes Moses' role as a servant of God, emphasizing his obedience and dedication in carrying out God's commands.

- "for a testimony of those things which were to be spoken after": This phrase suggests that Moses' faithful service was a testimony or foreshadowing of the future revelation of God's plan through Jesus Christ, indicating that Moses' actions pointed forward to the coming of the Messiah.

Concordance:

- The statement "Moses verily was faithful in all his house" acknowledges Moses' faithfulness as a leader and servant of God's people (Numbers 12:7).

- This verse highlights Moses' role as a faithful servant and leader, whose actions and obedience foreshadowed the coming of Jesus Christ as the ultimate fulfillment of God's plan.

This verse affirms Moses' faithfulness as a servant of God and leader of His people. It acknowledges Moses' obedience and dedication in leading the Israelites and suggests that his actions were a foreshadowing of the future revelation of God's plan through Jesus Christ.

Verse 6 (King James Version):

> But Christ as a son over his own house; whose house are we, if we hold fast the confidence and the rejoicing of the hope firm unto the end.

Interpretation:

This verse contrasts Moses, who served as a faithful servant in God's house, with Christ, who is described as a son over His own house. Believers are considered part of Christ's house if they maintain their confidence and hope in Him until the end.

Commentary:

- "But Christ as a son over his own house": This phrase contrasts Moses' role as a servant in God's house with Christ's role as the Son over His own house. It emphasizes Christ's authority and preeminence over the household of faith.

- "whose house are we, if we hold fast the confidence and the rejoicing of the hope firm unto the end": This phrase indicates that believers are considered part of Christ's house if they continue to hold firmly to their confidence and hope in Him until the end. It emphasizes the importance of perseverance in the Christian faith.

Concordance:

- The statement "But Christ as a son over his own house" highlights Christ's authority and position as the Son of God, who rules over His household (Matthew 16:18; Ephesians 2:19-22).

- The condition "if we hold fast the confidence and the rejoicing of the hope firm unto the end" underscores the importance of perseverance in the Christian faith, a theme found in other New Testament passages (Hebrews 10:23; Revelation 3:11).

This verse emphasizes Christ's authority over His household of faith and underscores the importance of perseverance in the Christian life. It encourages believers to hold firmly to their confidence and hope in Christ until the end, reminding them of their identity as part of Christ's household.

Verse 7 (King James Version):
> Wherefore (as the Holy Ghost saith, To day if ye will hear his voice,

Interpretation:
This verse introduces a quotation from Psalm 95, which is used to exhort the readers to listen to God's voice and not harden their hearts, as the Israelites did in the wilderness.

Commentary:
- "Wherefore (as the Holy Ghost saith": This phrase introduces a quotation from the Old Testament, indicating that the words are inspired by the Holy Spirit.
- "To day if ye will hear his voice": This phrase emphasizes the importance of listening to God's voice and obeying His commands, highlighting the immediacy and urgency of responding to God's call.

Concordance:
- The reference to the Holy Ghost speaking indicates the divine inspiration of Scripture (2 Peter 1:21).
- The quotation "To day if ye will hear his voice" is from Psalm 95:7, where the psalmist exhorts the Israelites to listen to God's voice and not harden their hearts, as their ancestors did in the wilderness.

This verse serves as an introduction to a quotation from Psalm 95, which is used to exhort the readers to heed God's voice and not harden their hearts. It emphasizes the importance of obedience and responsiveness to God's call, highlighting the need to listen and respond to Him without delay.

Verse 8 (King James Version):
> Harden not your hearts, as in the provocation, in the day of temptation in the wilderness:

Interpretation:
This verse warns against hardening one's heart, as the Israelites did during the time of provocation and temptation in the wilderness, referring to the events described in Exodus and Numbers.

Commentary:
- "Harden not your hearts": This phrase is a warning against stubbornness and unbelief, urging the readers to maintain a soft and receptive heart towards God.
- "as in the provocation, in the day of temptation in the wilderness": This phrase refers to the time when the Israelites provoked God by their unbelief and disobedience during their journey through the wilderness, as described in Exodus and Numbers.

Concordance:
- The warning against hardening one's heart is a recurring theme in the Bible, emphasizing the importance of humility, obedience, and faithfulness (Psalm 95:8; Hebrews 4:7).
- The reference to the provocation and temptation in the wilderness alludes to the events recorded in Exodus 17 and Numbers 14, where the Israelites rebelled against God and refused to trust in His promises.

This verse serves as a cautionary reminder to the readers not to repeat the mistakes of the Israelites by hardening their hearts in unbelief. It highlights the consequences of disobedience and unfaithfulness, urging believers to maintain a soft and receptive heart towards God's word and His leading.

Verse 9 (King James Version):
> When your fathers tempted me, proved me, and saw my works forty years.

Interpretation:
This verse recalls the actions of the Israelites in the wilderness, where they tested and tempted God despite witnessing His works over a period of forty years.

Commentary:
- "When your fathers tempted me, proved me": This phrase describes the actions of the Israelites, who tested and tempted God by questioning His provision and guidance despite His faithfulness and miracles.
- "and saw my works forty years": This phrase refers to the period of forty years during which the Israelites witnessed God's miraculous works, including the manna, the parting of the Red Sea, and other provisions in the wilderness.

Concordance:
- The reference to the Israelites tempting and proving God recalls their actions in the wilderness, where they repeatedly tested God's patience and faithfulness (Exodus 17:2; Numbers 14:22).
- The mention of forty years alludes to the duration of the Israelites' journey through the wilderness before entering the promised land (Numbers 14:33-34).

This verse serves as a reminder of the Israelites' unbelief and rebellion during their time in the wilderness. Despite witnessing God's miraculous works over a period of forty years, they continued to test and provoke God. It serves as a warning to believers to learn from the mistakes of the past and to trust in God's faithfulness and provision.

Verse 10 (King James Version):
> Wherefore I was grieved with that generation, and said, They do alway err in their heart; and they have not known my ways.

Interpretation:
This verse explains that God was grieved with the generation of Israelites who wandered in the wilderness because they consistently went astray in their hearts and did not understand or follow God's ways.

Commentary:
- "Wherefore I was grieved with that generation": This phrase expresses God's sorrow and disappointment with the Israelites who wandered in the wilderness, indicating His displeasure with their persistent disobedience and unbelief.
- "and said, They do alway err in their heart": This phrase describes the Israelites' continual straying from God's ways in their hearts, indicating a deeper issue of unbelief and disobedience.
- "and they have not known my ways": This phrase indicates that the Israelites did not understand or follow God's ways, suggesting a lack of relationship and intimacy with God.

Concordance:
- The statement "I was grieved with that generation" reflects God's response to the Israelites' disobedience and unbelief, a theme found throughout the Old Testament (Numbers 14:29; Psalm 95:11).

- The phrase "They do alway err in their heart" highlights the root cause of the Israelites' disobedience, which was a heart issue of unbelief and rebellion (Psalm 78:8).

This verse highlights the consequences of the Israelites' disobedience and unbelief during their time in the wilderness. It emphasizes God's sorrow over their continual straying from His ways and serves as a warning to believers to remain faithful and obedient to God's will.

Verse 11 (King James Version):
> So I sware in my wrath, They shall not enter into my rest.)

Interpretation:
This verse recounts God's response to the generation of Israelites who disobeyed and rebelled against Him in the wilderness. Because of their unbelief and disobedience, God swore in His wrath that they would not enter into His rest, referring to the promised land.

Commentary:
- "So I sware in my wrath": This phrase indicates that God made a solemn oath in His anger and displeasure towards the rebellious Israelites.
- "They shall not enter into my rest": This phrase declares God's judgment on the disobedient Israelites, stating that they would not be allowed to enter the promised land and experience the rest and blessings that God had prepared for them.

Concordance:
- The statement "I sware in my wrath" reflects God's judgment on the rebellious Israelites, a consequence of their persistent unbelief and disobedience (Numbers 14:23; Psalm 95:11).

- The phrase "They shall not enter into my rest" underscores the significance of entering God's rest as a symbol of receiving His blessings and promises, a concept also found in Hebrews 4:3.

This verse serves as a sobering reminder of the consequences of disobedience and unbelief. It highlights God's judgment on the rebellious Israelites, who were denied entry into the promised land because of their persistent disobedience. It serves as a warning to believers to remain faithful and obedient to God's commands in order to enter into His rest and receive His blessings.

Verse 12 (King James Version):
> Take heed, brethren, lest there be in any of you an evil heart of unbelief, in departing from the living God.

Interpretation:
This verse warns believers to be careful and vigilant, lest any of them develop a heart of unbelief that leads them to turn away from the living God.

Commentary:
- "Take heed, brethren": This phrase is a warning to believers to be cautious and attentive, indicating the seriousness of the following exhortation.
- "lest there be in any of you an evil heart of unbelief": This phrase warns against the danger of developing a heart characterized by unbelief, which can lead to a turning away from God and His ways.
- "in departing from the living God": This phrase describes the consequence of an evil heart of unbelief—turning away from the living God, indicating a loss of faith and relationship with Him.

Concordance:

- The exhortation to "take heed" is a recurring theme in the Bible, emphasizing the importance of vigilance and spiritual awareness (Matthew 24:4; 1 Corinthians 10:12).

- The warning against developing an "evil heart of unbelief" highlights the danger of allowing doubt and unbelief to take root in one's heart, leading to a departure from God (Psalm 95:8; Hebrews 4:1).

This verse serves as a warning to believers to guard against developing a heart of unbelief that can lead to a departure from God. It emphasizes the importance of maintaining faith and trust in God, and of staying vigilant against the influences of doubt and unbelief.

Verse 13 (King James Version):
> But exhort one another daily, while it is called To day; lest any of you be hardened through the deceitfulness of sin.

Interpretation:
This verse encourages believers to regularly encourage and support each other in their faith, emphasizing the importance of doing so daily. This practice is necessary to prevent anyone from being hardened by the deceitfulness of sin.

Commentary:
- "But exhort one another daily": This phrase urges believers to regularly encourage and uplift each other, emphasizing the communal nature of the Christian faith and the importance of mutual support.
- "while it is called To day": This phrase emphasizes the urgency of the exhortation, suggesting that believers should not delay in encouraging one another but should do so promptly and consistently.

- "lest any of you be hardened through the deceitfulness of sin": This phrase warns against the hardening effect of sin, which can deceive individuals into believing that their actions are acceptable and lead them away from God.

Concordance:
- The exhortation to "exhort one another daily" underscores the importance of mutual encouragement and support in the Christian community (1 Thessalonians 5:11; Hebrews 10:24-25).
- The warning against being "hardened through the deceitfulness of sin" highlights the danger of sin in deceiving individuals and leading them away from God's truth and righteousness (Jeremiah 17:9; Ephesians 4:22).

This verse emphasizes the importance of mutual encouragement and support among believers to prevent the hardening effects of sin. It underscores the need for regular and consistent exhortation within the Christian community to maintain a steadfast faith and guard against the deceitfulness of sin.

Verse 14 (King James Version):
> For we are made partakers of Christ, if we hold the beginning of our confidence stedfast unto the end;

Interpretation:
This verse explains that believers are made partakers of Christ if they remain steadfast in their faith and confidence in Him until the end.

Commentary:

- "For we are made partakers of Christ": This phrase indicates that believers share in the benefits and blessings of Christ's salvation and redemption.

- "if we hold the beginning of our confidence stedfast unto the end": This phrase emphasizes the condition for being partakers of Christ, which is to remain firm and unwavering in faith and confidence in Him until the end of life.

Concordance:

- The statement "we are made partakers of Christ" reflects the biblical teaching that believers share in Christ's redemption and inheritance (Romans 8:17; Ephesians 3:6).

- The condition "if we hold the beginning of our confidence stedfast unto the end" underscores the importance of perseverance in the Christian faith, a theme found throughout the New Testament (Hebrews 10:36; Revelation 2:10).

This verse emphasizes the need for believers to persevere in their faith and confidence in Christ until the end of their lives. It highlights the assurance that believers share in the blessings and benefits of Christ's salvation if they remain steadfast in their faith.

Verse 15 (King James Version):
> While it is said, To day if ye will hear his voice, harden not your hearts, as in the provocation.

Interpretation:
This verse reiterates the warning from Psalm 95:7-8, emphasizing the importance of not hardening one's heart against God's voice and instruction.

Commentary:

- "While it is said, To day if ye will hear his voice": This phrase refers to the ongoing call of God to His people to listen and respond to His voice.

- "harden not your hearts, as in the provocation": This phrase reminds believers of the Israelites' disobedience and rebellion in the wilderness, warning against following their example by hardening their hearts against God's word and leading.

Concordance:

- The reference to Psalm 95:7-8 emphasizes the continuity of God's call to His people to listen and respond to Him without hardening their hearts.

- The warning against hardening one's heart echoes the theme found throughout Scripture, highlighting the danger of unbelief and disobedience (Psalm 95:8; Hebrews 3:8).

This verse serves as a reminder to believers to heed God's voice and instruction without hardening their hearts. It warns against the danger of unbelief and disobedience, urging believers to remain receptive and obedient to God's leading.

Verse 16 (King James Version):
> For some, when they had heard, did provoke: howbeit not all that came out of Egypt by Moses.

Interpretation:
This verse acknowledges that while some of the Israelites who came out of Egypt with Moses provoked God through their unbelief and disobedience, not all of them did so.

Commentary:

- "For some, when they had heard, did provoke": This phrase refers to those Israelites who, after hearing God's voice and witnessing His works, still provoked Him through their unbelief and disobedience.

- "howbeit not all that came out of Egypt by Moses": This phrase indicates that not all of the Israelites who came out of Egypt with Moses provoked God. Some remained faithful and obedient.

Concordance:

- The reference to the Israelites provoking God recalls the events described in Exodus and Numbers, where the Israelites rebelled against God despite His miraculous deliverance and provision (Numbers 14:22; Psalm 95:8).

- The statement "not all that came out of Egypt by Moses" highlights the distinction between those Israelites who provoked God and those who remained faithful, underscoring the importance of individual faith and obedience.

This verse acknowledges the mixed response of the Israelites to God's call and leading. While some provoked God through their unbelief and disobedience, not all of them did so. It serves as a reminder that faith and obedience are individual choices, and that not everyone responds to God's call in the same way.

Verse 17 (King James Version):
> But with whom was he grieved forty years? was it not with them that had sinned, whose carcases fell in the wilderness?

Interpretation:
This verse reflects on the forty years of wandering in the wilderness and points out that God was grieved with those who sinned, as evidenced by their deaths in the wilderness.

Commentary:

- "But with whom was he grieved forty years?": This phrase questions the group of people with whom God was grieved during the forty years of wandering in the wilderness.

- "was it not with them that had sinned": This phrase suggests that God was grieved with those who sinned against Him during their time in the wilderness.

- "whose carcases fell in the wilderness": This phrase refers to those who died in the wilderness due to their sin and disobedience.

Concordance:

- The reference to God's grief during the forty years in the wilderness highlights the consequences of sin and disobedience (Numbers 14:29-34; Psalm 95:10).

- The mention of "carcases" falling in the wilderness recalls the judgment that came upon the rebellious Israelites, emphasizing the seriousness of sin and its consequences (Numbers 14:32-33).

This verse emphasizes the consequences of sin and disobedience, highlighting the judgment that came upon the rebellious Israelites during their time in the wilderness. It serves as a warning to believers about the seriousness of sin and the importance of obedience to God's commands.

Verse 18 (King James Version):
> And to whom sware he that they should not enter into his rest, but to them that believed not?

Interpretation:

This verse refers to God's oath that the unbelieving Israelites would not enter into His rest, highlighting the consequence of their lack of faith.

Commentary:
- "And to whom sware he that they should not enter into his rest": This phrase refers to God's oath or declaration that the unbelieving Israelites would not enter into the promised land, which was seen as a rest from their wandering in the wilderness.
- "but to them that believed not": This phrase specifies that it was those among the Israelites who did not believe in God's promises and provision who were excluded from entering the promised land.

Concordance:
- The reference to God's oath reflects His judgment on the unbelieving Israelites, emphasizing the consequences of their lack of faith (Numbers 14:22-23; Psalm 95:11).
- The mention of "enter into his rest" alludes to the promised land as a symbol of rest and blessing, which the unbelieving Israelites were denied because of their lack of faith (Joshua 1:13; Hebrews 4:1-11).

This verse underscores the importance of faith in God's promises and provision. It highlights the consequences of unbelief, emphasizing that those who do not believe will not enter into God's rest or experience His blessings. It serves as a warning to believers to maintain faith and trust in God, lest they fall into the same disobedience and unbelief as the Israelites in the wilderness.

Verse 19 (King James Version):
> So we see that they could not enter in because of unbelief.

Interpretation:

This verse summarizes the reason why the unbelieving Israelites could not enter the promised land—they lacked faith in God's promises and provision.

Commentary:

- "So we see that they could not enter in": This phrase indicates the outcome of the Israelites' lack of faith—they were unable to enter the promised land.

- "because of unbelief": This phrase specifies that the reason for their inability to enter was their lack of faith in God's promises and ability to fulfill them.

Concordance:

- The statement "because of unbelief" emphasizes the importance of faith in God's promises and provision (Numbers 14:11, 23; Psalm 78:22).

- The reference to the Israelites' inability to enter the promised land serves as a warning to believers about the consequences of unbelief and disobedience (Numbers 14:30; Hebrews 4:6).

This verse concludes the discussion on the Israelites' lack of faith and its consequences. It highlights the importance of faith in God's promises and the danger of unbelief. It serves as a reminder to believers to trust in God and His promises, lest they fall into the same fate as the unbelieving Israelites.

C H A P T E R 4
The promise of rest

Verse 1 (King James Version):
> Let us therefore fear, lest, a promise being left us of entering into his rest, any of you should seem to come short of it.

Interpretation:
This verse exhorts believers to have a reverent fear or caution, lest any of them should fail to attain the promise of entering into God's rest.

Commentary:
- "Let us therefore fear": This phrase suggests that believers should have a reverent fear or caution, recognizing the seriousness of the promise of entering God's rest.

- "lest, a promise being left us of entering into his rest": This phrase refers to the promise of entering into God's rest, which is still available to believers.

- "any of you should seem to come short of it": This phrase warns against falling short of attaining the promised rest, emphasizing the need for diligence and faithfulness.

Concordance:

- The exhortation to "fear" reflects the biblical theme of reverent fear or awe towards God, recognizing His holiness and sovereignty (Psalm 2:11; Proverbs 1:7).

- The mention of "entering into his rest" alludes to the promised land as a symbol of rest and blessing, which believers are encouraged to enter through faith (Joshua 1:13; Hebrews 3:11-19).

This verse urges believers to take seriously the promise of entering into God's rest and to strive diligently to attain it. It emphasizes the need for faithfulness and perseverance in the Christian life, lest anyone should fail to receive the promised rest due to unbelief or disobedience.

Verse 2 (King James Version):

> For unto us was the gospel preached, as well as unto them: but the word preached did not profit them, not being mixed with faith in them that heard it.

Interpretation:

This verse contrasts the Israelites in the wilderness with the believers to whom the gospel was preached. The gospel was preached to both groups, but it did not benefit the Israelites because they did not have faith.

Commentary:

- "For unto us was the gospel preached, as well as unto them": This phrase indicates that both the Israelites in the wilderness and the believers to whom the author is writing heard the gospel preached.

- "but the word preached did not profit them": This phrase explains that the gospel did not benefit the Israelites in the wilderness.

- "not being mixed with faith in them that heard it": This phrase clarifies why the gospel did not benefit the Israelites—it was not accompanied by faith on their part.

Concordance:

- The reference to the gospel being preached to both groups emphasizes the continuity of God's message of salvation throughout history (Romans 1:16; 1 Peter 1:10-12).

- The statement "not being mixed with faith" underscores the importance of faith in receiving the benefits of the gospel (Hebrews 11:6; James 1:6-7).

This verse highlights the essential role of faith in receiving the benefits of the gospel. It contrasts the Israelites in the wilderness, who did not benefit from the gospel due to their lack of faith, with believers who are urged to have faith in order to enter into God's rest and receive His promises.

Verse 3 (King James Version):
> For we which have believed do enter into rest, as he said, As I have sworn in my wrath, if they shall enter into my rest: although the works were finished from the foundation of the world.

Interpretation:

This verse declares that those who believe enter into God's rest, as promised in Scripture. It also mentions that God's works were completed from the foundation of the world.

Commentary:
- "For we which have believed do enter into rest": This phrase emphasizes that believers enter into God's rest through their faith in Him and His promises.
- "as he said, As I have sworn in my wrath, if they shall enter into my rest": This phrase refers to God's oath that those who do not believe will not enter into His rest, highlighting the importance of faith.
- "although the works were finished from the foundation of the world": This phrase suggests that God's works, including the promise of rest, were completed before the world was created, emphasizing His sovereignty and foreknowledge.

Concordance:
- The statement "we which have believed do enter into rest" echoes the theme of faith leading to rest and salvation (Hebrews 4:10; Hebrews 11:6).
- The mention of God's works being finished from the foundation of the world emphasizes His eternal plan and purpose (Ephesians 1:4; Revelation 13:8).

This verse emphasizes the connection between faith and entering into God's rest. It highlights the certainty of God's promises and His sovereignty over all things. It encourages believers to trust in God and His promises, knowing that He has already completed His works from the foundation of the world.

Verse 4 (King James Version):

> For he spake in a certain place of the seventh day on this wise, And God did rest the seventh day from all his works.

Interpretation:

This verse refers to God's rest on the seventh day after completing His creation, as described in the book of Genesis. It connects God's rest on the seventh day with the concept of entering into His rest.

Commentary:

- "For he spake in a certain place of the seventh day on this wise": This phrase indicates that the author is referring to a specific passage in Scripture that describes God's rest on the seventh day.

- "And God did rest the seventh day from all his works": This phrase refers to God's cessation of work on the seventh day after completing His creation, as described in Genesis 2:2-3.

Concordance:

- The reference to God's rest on the seventh day alludes to the creation account in Genesis, highlighting the significance of the Sabbath rest (Genesis 2:2-3; Exodus 20:11).

- The connection between God's rest on the seventh day and the concept of entering into His rest emphasizes the spiritual rest that believers can experience through faith in Christ (Hebrews 4:9-10; Matthew 11:28-29).

This verse emphasizes the connection between God's rest on the seventh day of creation and the concept of entering into His rest. It highlights the spiritual rest that believers can experience through faith in Christ, likening it to God's rest after His creative work.

Verse 5 (King James Version):

> And in this place again, If they shall enter into my rest.

Interpretation:
This verse reiterates the concept of entering into God's rest, emphasizing the invitation and opportunity for believers to experience His rest.

Commentary:
- "And in this place again": This phrase indicates that the author is referring to another passage of Scripture that speaks about entering into God's rest.
- "If they shall enter into my rest": This phrase emphasizes the conditional nature of entering into God's rest, highlighting the importance of faith and obedience.

Concordance:
- The reference to entering into God's rest echoes the theme found throughout Hebrews 3-4, emphasizing the need for faith and obedience to enter into God's rest (Hebrews 4:1-11).
- The conditional statement "If they shall enter into my rest" underscores the importance of faithfulness and obedience in experiencing God's rest, as exemplified by the Israelites' failure to enter the promised land due to their unbelief (Hebrews 3:18-19).

This verse reinforces the theme of entering into God's rest through faith and obedience. It highlights the invitation and opportunity for believers to experience God's rest, emphasizing the need for faithfulness and obedience to enter into His rest.

Verse 6 (King James Version):

> Seeing therefore it remaineth that some must enter therein, and they to whom it was first preached entered not in because of unbelief:

Interpretation:
This verse acknowledges that despite the Israelites' failure to enter God's rest due to unbelief, there remains a promise of rest for some to enter into, implying that the promise is still available to believers.

Commentary:
- "Seeing therefore it remaineth that some must enter therein": This phrase suggests that despite the Israelites' failure to enter God's rest, there remains a promise of rest that some will enter into.
- "and they to whom it was first preached entered not in because of unbelief": This phrase refers to the Israelites who initially heard the promise of rest but did not enter into it due to their lack of faith.

Concordance:
- The mention of "some must enter therein" suggests that there is a group of people who will enter into God's rest, emphasizing the certainty of God's promise (Hebrews 4:11; Revelation 14:13).
- The reference to the Israelites' failure to enter God's rest due to unbelief highlights the consequences of unbelief and the importance of faith in experiencing God's rest (Hebrews 3:18-19; Hebrews 4:3).

This verse underscores the promise of rest that remains available to believers, contrasting the Israelites' unbelief with the faith required to enter into God's rest. It encourages believers to remain faithful and obedient, knowing that God's promise of rest is certain for those who believe.

Verse 7 (King James Version):

> Again, he limiteth a certain day, saying in David, To day, after so long a time; as it is said, To day if ye will hear his voice, harden not your hearts.

Interpretation:

This verse references a passage from Psalms (likely Psalm 95) where David speaks about the urgency of hearing God's voice and not hardening one's heart. It underscores the importance of responding to God's call without delay.

Commentary:

- "Again, he limiteth a certain day": This phrase suggests that God has appointed a specific time or day for people to respond to His call.

- "saying in David, To day, after so long a time": This phrase refers to David's words in the Psalms, emphasizing the long-standing nature of God's call to His people.

- "as it is said, To day if ye will hear his voice, harden not your hearts": This phrase quotes from Psalm 95, highlighting the urgency of responding to God's voice and the danger of hardening one's heart.

Concordance:

- The reference to God "limiteth a certain day" suggests that there is a specific time or opportunity for people to respond to God's call (Hebrews 3:7-8; Hebrews 4:5).

- The quotation from Psalm 95 underscores the continuity of God's call to His people to listen and respond to Him without hardening their hearts (Hebrews 3:15; Hebrews 4:3).

This verse emphasizes the urgency of responding to God's call and the danger of hardening one's heart. It encourages believers to listen to God's voice and respond in faith without delay, knowing that God's call is continuous and that the opportunity to enter into His rest is available today.

Verse 8 (King James Version):
> For if Jesus had given them rest, then would he not afterward have spoken of another day.

Interpretation:
This verse suggests that if Joshua had truly given the Israelites the ultimate rest that God promised, there would have been no need for the author of Hebrews to speak of another day of rest.

Commentary:
- "For if Jesus had given them rest": The name "Jesus" here refers to Joshua, the leader who brought the Israelites into the promised land.
- "then would he not afterward have spoken of another day": This phrase indicates that if Joshua had truly given the Israelites the ultimate rest that God promised, there would have been no need for the author to speak of another day of rest.

Concordance:
- The reference to Joshua providing rest for the Israelites alludes to the historical account of Joshua leading the Israelites into the promised land (Joshua 21:44; Hebrews 3:16-19).
- The mention of "another day" suggests that there is a future and ultimate rest that believers are still awaiting, which is fulfilled in Christ (Hebrews 4:9-10; Revelation 21:1-4).

This verse contrasts the rest that Joshua provided for the Israelites with the ultimate rest that believers are still awaiting. It emphasizes that the rest Joshua provided was only a foreshadowing of the rest that is fulfilled in Christ.

Verse 9 (King James Version):
> There remaineth therefore a rest to the people of God.

Interpretation:
This verse declares that a Sabbath rest remains for the people of God, emphasizing the promise of rest that believers can enter into through faith in Christ.

Commentary:
- "There remaineth therefore a rest to the people of God": This phrase emphasizes that a Sabbath rest remains available for the people of God, indicating a rest from works and a rest in Christ.

Concordance:
- The statement "a rest to the people of God" echoes the theme of entering into God's rest through faith, emphasizing the promise of rest that believers can experience in Christ (Hebrews 3:11; Hebrews 4:3).
- The concept of rest in this verse refers to a spiritual rest in Christ, where believers cease from their own works and trust in Christ's finished work for salvation (Hebrews 4:10; Matthew 11:28-29).

This verse emphasizes the promise of rest that remains available for believers. It encourages believers to enter into God's rest through faith in Christ, ceasing from their own works and trusting in His finished work for salvation.

Verse 10 (King James Version):
> For he that is entered into his rest, he also hath ceased from his own works, as God did from his.

Interpretation:
This verse explains that entering into God's rest involves ceasing from one's own works, just as God ceased from His works of creation on the seventh day.

Commentary:
- "For he that is entered into his rest": This phrase refers to the person who has entered into God's rest, which is a rest from striving to earn salvation through works.
- "he also hath ceased from his own works": This phrase indicates that entering into God's rest involves ceasing from relying on one's own efforts for salvation.
- "as God did from his": This phrase compares the believer's rest from works to God's rest from His works of creation on the seventh day.

Concordance:
- The statement "he also hath ceased from his own works" emphasizes the cessation of reliance on works for salvation and the importance of faith in Christ's finished work (Ephesians 2:8-9; Romans 4:5).
- The comparison to God's rest from His works of creation highlights the spiritual rest that believers can experience in Christ, where they cease from striving to earn salvation and trust in God's grace (Genesis 2:2-3; Hebrews 4:4).

This verse explains the nature of entering into God's rest, emphasizing that it involves ceasing from one's own works for salvation and trusting in Christ's finished work. It underscores the contrast between works-based righteousness and faith-based salvation, highlighting the sufficiency of Christ's work for salvation.

Verse 11 (King James Version):
> Let us labour therefore to enter into that rest, lest any man fall after the same example of unbelief.

Interpretation:
This verse encourages believers to strive earnestly to enter into God's rest, emphasizing the need to avoid falling into the same pattern of unbelief as the Israelites in the wilderness.

Commentary:
- "Let us labour therefore to enter into that rest": This phrase urges believers to make every effort to enter into God's rest, emphasizing the importance of diligent pursuit of faith and obedience.
- "lest any man fall after the same example of unbelief": This phrase warns against falling into the same pattern of unbelief as the Israelites in the wilderness, emphasizing the consequences of unbelief and disobedience.

Concordance:
- The exhortation to "labour...to enter into that rest" underscores the effort and diligence required in the Christian life, including faithfulness, obedience, and perseverance (Philippians 2:12; 2 Peter 1:10-11).
- The warning against falling into unbelief echoes the cautionary example of the Israelites in the wilderness, highlighting the

consequences of unbelief and the importance of faith in entering into God's rest (Hebrews 3:16-19; Hebrews 4:3).

This verse challenges believers to strive earnestly to enter into God's rest through faith and obedience, warning against the dangers of unbelief and disobedience. It emphasizes the need for diligence and perseverance in the Christian life, encouraging believers to learn from the mistakes of the Israelites and to remain steadfast in their faith.

Verse 12 (King James Version):
> For the word of God is quick, and powerful, and sharper than any twoedged sword, piercing even to the dividing asunder of soul and spirit, and of the joints and marrow, and is a discerner of the thoughts and intents of the heart.

Interpretation:
This verse describes the Word of God as living, powerful, and able to penetrate deeply into the innermost thoughts and intentions of a person.

Commentary:
- "For the word of God is quick, and powerful": This phrase emphasizes the living and active nature of the Word of God, suggesting that it has the power to bring about change and transformation in those who hear and believe it.
- "and sharper than any twoedged sword": This phrase compares the Word of God to a sharp sword, indicating its ability to penetrate deeply and to discern the truth.
- "piercing even to the dividing asunder of soul and spirit, and of the joints and marrow": This phrase further emphasizes the penetrating power of the Word of God, suggesting that it can discern the deepest parts of a person's being.

- "and is a discerner of the thoughts and intents of the heart": This phrase indicates that the Word of God has the ability to reveal and expose the thoughts and intentions of a person's heart.

Concordance:
- The description of the Word of God as living and powerful reflects its transformative and life-giving nature (Isaiah 55:11; 1 Peter 1:23).
- The comparison of the Word of God to a sharp sword underscores its ability to discern truth and to expose the innermost thoughts and intentions of the heart (Ephesians 6:17; Psalm 139:23-24).

This verse highlights the power and effectiveness of the Word of God in bringing about change and transformation in the lives of believers. It emphasizes the importance of allowing the Word of God to penetrate deeply into our hearts and minds, exposing any areas of sin or unbelief.

Verse 13 (King James Version):
> Neither is there any creature that is not manifest in his sight: but all things are naked and opened unto the eyes of him with whom we have to do.

Interpretation:
This verse emphasizes the omniscience of God, stating that nothing is hidden from His sight. It underscores the accountability believers have before God, who sees and knows all things.

Commentary:

- "Neither is there any creature that is not manifest in his sight": This phrase indicates that nothing is hidden from God's sight; He sees and knows all things, including the innermost thoughts and intentions of every creature.

- "but all things are naked and opened unto the eyes of him with whom we have to do": This phrase further emphasizes the idea that everything is exposed and laid bare before God, who is the ultimate judge and with whom believers have to give an account.

Concordance:
- The statement "all things are naked and opened unto the eyes of him" reflects the biblical theme of God's omniscience and His ability to see and know all things (Psalm 139:1-4; Proverbs 15:3).

- The phrase "with whom we have to do" underscores the accountability believers have before God, highlighting the importance of living in a manner that is pleasing to Him (2 Corinthians 5:10; Romans 14:12).

This verse reminds believers of the omniscience of God and the accountability they have before Him. It encourages believers to live in a manner that is transparent and honest before God, knowing that He sees and knows all things.

Verse 14 (King James Version):
> Seeing then that we have a great high priest, that is passed into the heavens, Jesus the Son of God, let us hold fast our profession.

Interpretation:
This verse highlights the role of Jesus as the great High Priest who has ascended into heaven, and it encourages believers to hold firmly to their confession of faith in Him.

Commentary:

- "Seeing then that we have a great high priest": This phrase emphasizes the unique role of Jesus as the High Priest who intercedes for believers before God.

- "that is passed into the heavens": This phrase indicates that Jesus has ascended into heaven, where He continues to intercede for believers.

- "Jesus the Son of God": This phrase emphasizes the divinity of Jesus, highlighting His unique position as the Son of God.

- "let us hold fast our profession": This phrase encourages believers to hold firmly to their confession of faith in Jesus, despite any challenges or difficulties they may face.

Concordance:

- The reference to Jesus as the great High Priest underscores His role as the mediator between God and humanity (Hebrews 2:17; Hebrews 7:25).

- The exhortation to "hold fast our profession" emphasizes the importance of remaining steadfast in faith and not wavering in our confession of Jesus as Lord (Hebrews 3:6; Hebrews 10:23).

This verse emphasizes the unique role of Jesus as the great High Priest who intercedes for believers and encourages believers to remain steadfast in their faith in Him. It reminds believers of the importance of holding firm to their confession of faith, knowing that Jesus is able to sympathize with their weaknesses and to help them in their time of need.

Verse 16 (King James Version):
> Let us therefore come boldly unto the throne of grace, that we may obtain mercy, and find grace to help in time of need.

Interpretation:

This verse encourages believers to approach God's throne of grace with confidence, knowing that they will receive mercy and find grace to help them in times of need.

Commentary:

- "Let us therefore come boldly unto the throne of grace": This phrase emphasizes the invitation for believers to approach God's throne with confidence, knowing that He welcomes them with grace and mercy.

- "that we may obtain mercy, and find grace to help in time of need": This phrase highlights the purpose of coming to God's throne—to receive mercy for our sins and to find grace to help us in times of trouble and need.

Concordance:

- The exhortation to "come boldly unto the throne of grace" reflects the biblical theme of approaching God with confidence and assurance, knowing that He is gracious and merciful (Hebrews 10:19-22; Ephesians 3:12).

- The mention of obtaining mercy and finding grace echoes the theme of God's abundant grace and mercy towards those who seek Him (Psalm 86:5; Ephesians 2:4-5).

This verse encourages believers to approach God's throne with confidence, knowing that He will provide them with the grace and mercy they need. It reminds believers of the privilege they have to come to God in prayer and to receive His help and support in times of trouble.

CHAPTER 5
Christ the Way to God

Verse 1 (King James Version):
> For every high priest taken from among men is ordained for men in things pertaining to God, that he may offer both gifts and sacrifices for sins:

Interpretation:
This verse explains the role of a high priest, who is chosen from among men to represent them before God and to offer gifts and sacrifices for sins on their behalf.

Commentary:
- "For every high priest taken from among men": This phrase emphasizes that high priests are chosen from among human beings, indicating their role as mediators between God and humanity.

- "is ordained for men in things pertaining to God": This phrase indicates that high priests are appointed to represent people in matters related to God, serving as intermediaries between God and humanity.

- "that he may offer both gifts and sacrifices for sins": This phrase describes one of the primary duties of a high priest, which is to offer gifts and sacrifices to atone for the sins of the people.

Concordance:

- The description of the high priest's role reflects the Old Testament concept of the high priest as a mediator between God and the people, offering sacrifices for sins (Leviticus 16:6; Hebrews 8:3).

- The mention of offering gifts and sacrifices for sins highlights the central role of the high priest in the sacrificial system, where sacrifices were offered to atone for sins (Hebrews 9:7; Leviticus 4:26).

This verse lays the foundation for understanding the role of a high priest in the Old Testament, highlighting their role as mediators between God and humanity and their responsibility to offer sacrifices for sins. It sets the stage for the comparison between the high priesthood in the Old Testament and the priesthood of Jesus Christ, which is explored further in the following verses.

Verse 2 (King James Version):
> Who can have compassion on the ignorant, and on them that are out of the way; for that he himself also is compassed with infirmity.

Interpretation:
This verse describes the qualities of a high priest, highlighting their ability to empathize with those who are ignorant or have gone astray, because the high priest themselves is subject to weakness.

Commentary:

- "Who can have compassion on the ignorant, and on them that are out of the way": This phrase describes the high priest's ability to empathize with those who are ignorant of God's ways or who have strayed from the right path, showing understanding and sympathy towards them.

- "for that he himself also is compassed with infirmity": This phrase explains the basis for the high priest's empathy, which is their own experience of weakness and frailty, recognizing their own limitations and shortcomings.

Concordance:
- The description of the high priest's ability to have compassion reflects the character of God as compassionate and merciful, who understands human frailty and forgives sins (Psalm 103:13-14; James 5:11).

- The mention of the high priest's own weaknesses emphasizes the humanity of the high priest, highlighting their need for empathy and understanding towards others (Hebrews 2:17-18; Hebrews 4:15).

This verse portrays the high priest as a compassionate and understanding mediator, who is able to empathize with the weaknesses and struggles of others because of their own experience of frailty. It emphasizes the importance of empathy and compassion in the role of a high priest, pointing to Jesus Christ as the ultimate high priest who embodies these qualities perfectly.

Verse 3 (King James Version):
> And by reason hereof he ought, as for the people, so also for himself, to offer for sins.

Interpretation:

This verse explains that a high priest is obligated to offer sacrifices for his own sins as well as for the sins of the people.

Commentary:
- "And by reason hereof he ought, as for the people, so also for himself, to offer for sins": This phrase emphasizes the dual role of the high priest in offering sacrifices for both his own sins and the sins of the people. It highlights the need for the high priest to first seek atonement for his own sins before interceding for others.

Concordance:
- The requirement for the high priest to offer sacrifices for his own sins reflects the principle of atonement and the need for purification before approaching God on behalf of the people (Leviticus 16:6; Hebrews 7:27).
- The emphasis on offering sacrifices for sins underscores the central role of sacrifices in the Old Testament sacrificial system, which pointed to the need for atonement and forgiveness of sins (Leviticus 4:3; Hebrews 9:22).

This verse highlights the need for the high priest to offer sacrifices for his own sins before interceding for the sins of the people. It underscores the importance of purity and atonement in the role of the high priest, pointing to the ultimate atonement provided by Jesus Christ as the perfect high priest who offered Himself as a sacrifice for the sins of all humanity.

Verse 4 (King James Version):
> And no man taketh this honour unto himself, but he that is called of God, as was Aaron.

Interpretation:

This verse states that no one can assume the role of high priest on their own initiative; rather, the high priest must be called by God, similar to how Aaron was chosen by God in the Old Testament.

Commentary:

- "And no man taketh this honour unto himself": This phrase emphasizes that the role of high priest is not something that someone can appoint themselves to; it is a position of honor that must be given by God.

- "but he that is called of God, as was Aaron": This phrase indicates that the high priest must be chosen and appointed by God, just as Aaron was chosen to be the first high priest in the Old Testament.

Concordance:

- The statement "he that is called of God" highlights the importance of divine calling and appointment in the role of the high priest, emphasizing that the high priest serves at God's appointment (Exodus 28:1; Numbers 16:5).

- The reference to Aaron as an example of someone called by God underscores the biblical precedent for God choosing and appointing individuals to serve in specific roles of leadership and ministry (Exodus 28:1; Numbers 17:5).

This verse emphasizes the divine calling and appointment that is required for someone to serve as a high priest. It points to the importance of God's sovereignty in choosing and appointing leaders, highlighting the need for humility and obedience in accepting and fulfilling the roles and responsibilities that God has assigned.

Verse 5 (King James Version):

> So also Christ glorified not himself to be made an high priest; but he that said unto him, Thou art my Son, to day have I begotten thee.

Interpretation:

This verse asserts that Jesus did not appoint Himself as High Priest, but rather was appointed by God, who declared Him to be His Son.

Commentary:

- "So also Christ glorified not himself to be made an high priest": This phrase emphasizes that Jesus did not take upon Himself the role of High Priest, but was appointed to this position by God the Father.

- "but he that said unto him, Thou art my Son, to day have I begotten thee": This phrase refers to God the Father, who declared Jesus to be His Son and appointed Him as High Priest.

Concordance:

- The statement "Christ glorified not himself" highlights Jesus' humility and obedience to the will of God, demonstrating His submission to the Father's authority (Philippians 2:6-8; John 5:30).

- The reference to God declaring Jesus to be His Son echoes similar declarations in the Gospels and emphasizes Jesus' unique relationship with the Father (Matthew 3:17; Mark 1:11; Luke 3:22).

This verse emphasizes Jesus' appointment as High Priest by God the Father, highlighting His obedience and submission to the Father's will. It underscores the unique role of Jesus as the Son of God, who was appointed to the office of High Priest in a manner consistent with the Old Testament pattern of divine appointment.

Verse 6 (King James Version):

> As he saith also in another place, Thou art a priest for ever after the order of Melchisedec.

Interpretation:

This verse refers to a prophecy in the Psalms (specifically, Psalm 110:4) where God declares that the Messiah will be a priest forever in the order of Melchizedek.

Commentary:

- "As he saith also in another place": This phrase indicates that the author is referring to another passage of Scripture, specifically Psalm 110:4.

- "Thou art a priest for ever after the order of Melchisedec": This phrase is a quotation from Psalm 110:4, which is a Messianic prophecy about the eternal priesthood of the coming Messiah in the order of Melchizedek.

Concordance:

- The reference to the order of Melchizedek highlights the superiority of Jesus' priesthood over the Levitical priesthood, which was based on the order of Aaron (Hebrews 7:11-19).

- The prophecy in Psalm 110:4 emphasizes the eternal nature of Jesus' priesthood, contrasting with the temporary and imperfect nature of the Levitical priesthood (Hebrews 7:23-25).

This verse is significant because it connects Jesus' priesthood to the order of Melchizedek, which is portrayed in the Bible as a superior and more ancient priesthood than that of the Levites. This connection is important for the author of Hebrews, who argues that Jesus' priesthood is superior to that of the Levites and is based on a more ancient and enduring order.

Verse 7 (King James Version):

> Who in the days of his flesh, when he had offered up prayers and supplications with strong crying and tears unto him that was able to save him from death, and was heard in that he feared;

Interpretation:

This verse describes Jesus' prayers and supplications during His earthly life, particularly in the Garden of Gethsemane, where He prayed fervently to God, who could save Him from death. Despite His agony, Jesus submitted to God's will with reverence and was heard.

Commentary:

- "Who in the days of his flesh": This phrase refers to Jesus during His earthly life, emphasizing His humanity.

- "when he had offered up prayers and supplications with strong crying and tears": This phrase describes Jesus' intense and heartfelt prayers, especially in Gethsemane before His crucifixion, where He prayed fervently to God.

- "unto him that was able to save him from death": This phrase refers to God the Father, whom Jesus prayed to, acknowledging His power to save Him from the imminent death on the cross.

- "and was heard in that he feared": This phrase indicates that Jesus' prayers were heard by God, not in the sense of being spared from death, but in the sense of being strengthened to endure it in obedience to God's will (Matthew 26:39; Luke 22:42-44).

Concordance:

- The description of Jesus' prayers with strong crying and tears highlights His humanity and the depth of His emotions and struggles (Isaiah 53:3-4; Matthew 26:36-46).

- The reference to Jesus being heard in His prayers emphasizes His perfect obedience and submission to God's will, even in the face of great suffering (Philippians 2:8; Hebrews 10:7-9).

This verse portrays Jesus' humanity and His willingness to endure suffering and death in obedience to God's will. It emphasizes the depth of His prayers and His submission to God, even unto death, as a model for believers to follow in times of trial and difficulty.

Verse 8 (King James Version):
> Though he were a Son, yet learned he obedience by the things which he suffered;

Interpretation:
This verse explains that despite being the Son of God, Jesus learned obedience through the experiences of suffering that He endured.

Commentary:
- "Though he were a Son": This phrase acknowledges Jesus' divine nature as the Son of God.
- "yet learned he obedience by the things which he suffered": This phrase emphasizes that Jesus, despite His divine status, learned the full extent of obedience through the suffering He endured during His earthly life, particularly leading up to His crucifixion.

Concordance:
- The statement "learned he obedience by the things which he suffered" highlights the depth of Jesus' obedience and the role that suffering played in His development of obedience (Philippians 2:8; Romans 5:19).

- The reference to Jesus as the Son of God underscores His divine nature and emphasizes the significance of His obedience as a model for believers (Matthew 3:17; John 5:19-20).

This verse teaches that even Jesus, as the Son of God, learned obedience through His experiences of suffering. It emphasizes the importance of obedience in the life of a believer and points to Jesus as the ultimate example of obedience, even in the face of suffering.

Verse 9 (King James Version):
> And being made perfect, he became the author of eternal salvation unto all them that obey him;

Interpretation:
This verse states that Jesus, through His suffering and obedience, was perfected and became the source of eternal salvation for all who obey Him.

Commentary:
- "And being made perfect": This phrase does not imply moral imperfection in Jesus, but rather completeness or fullness of His mission and role as the Savior, achieved through His suffering and obedience (Hebrews 2:10; Hebrews 7:28).
- "he became the author of eternal salvation": This phrase signifies that Jesus is the source or originator of eternal salvation, offering it to all who believe in Him (Hebrews 9:12; Acts 4:12).
- "unto all them that obey him": This phrase highlights the condition for receiving eternal salvation, which is obedience to Jesus' teachings and commands (John 14:15; Romans 6:17-18).

Concordance:

- The statement "he became the author of eternal salvation" emphasizes Jesus' unique role as the source and giver of salvation, contrasting with the temporary and imperfect salvation offered by the Old Testament sacrificial system (Hebrews 7:22-25; Hebrews 9:11-15).

- The reference to obedience underscores the importance of faith and obedience in receiving the benefits of Jesus' sacrifice and salvation (Hebrews 11:6; James 2:17-26).

This verse proclaims Jesus as the author and source of eternal salvation for all who believe and obey Him. It highlights the significance of Jesus' suffering and obedience in accomplishing salvation and emphasizes the importance of obedience to His teachings in receiving the benefits of salvation.

Verse 10 (King James Version):
> Called of God an high priest after the order of Melchisedec.

Interpretation:
This verse affirms that Jesus was appointed by God to be a high priest in the order of Melchizedek, as prophesied in Psalm 110:4.

Commentary:
- "Called of God": This phrase emphasizes that Jesus' appointment as a high priest was a divine calling, not something He assumed on His own authority (Hebrews 5:4).

- "an high priest after the order of Melchisedec": This phrase refers to Jesus' unique priesthood, which is likened to that of Melchizedek, a priest-king who lived in the time of Abraham and was considered a type of Christ (Hebrews 7:1-3).

Concordance:

- The reference to Jesus as a high priest after the order of Melchizedek underscores the superiority of His priesthood over the Levitical priesthood, which was based on the order of Aaron (Hebrews 7:11-19).

- The mention of Melchizedek as a type of Christ highlights the foreshadowing of Jesus' priesthood in the Old Testament and the fulfillment of that typology in Jesus (Hebrews 7:15-17).

This verse reinforces the idea that Jesus' priesthood is superior to that of the Levitical priesthood because it is based on the order of Melchizedek. It underscores the divine calling and appointment of Jesus as a high priest and highlights His unique role in fulfilling the prophetic promises of the Old Testament.

Verse 11 (King James Version):
> Of whom we have many things to say, and hard to be uttered, seeing ye are dull of hearing.

Interpretation:
This verse indicates that there are many profound truths to discuss regarding Jesus as the high priest in the order of Melchizedek, but the audience is finding it difficult to understand because they are slow to comprehend.

Commentary:
- "Of whom we have many things to say": This phrase suggests that the author has much more to teach about Jesus as the high priest in the order of Melchizedek, indicating that there are deeper spiritual truths to explore.

- "and hard to be uttered": This phrase suggests that the truths about Jesus' priesthood are profound and complex, making them challenging to explain or articulate.

- "seeing ye are dull of hearing": This phrase implies that the audience is spiritually sluggish or slow to understand, hindering their ability to grasp the deeper truths being presented.

Concordance:
- The reference to the audience as "dull of hearing" reflects the author's frustration with their spiritual immaturity and lack of receptivity to deeper truths (Hebrews 5:12-14; Hebrews 6:1-3).
- The statement "hard to be uttered" emphasizes the depth and complexity of the theological concepts being discussed, which require careful explanation and understanding (2 Peter 3:16; Romans 16:25-26).

This verse highlights the challenge of teaching deeper spiritual truths to an audience that is spiritually immature and slow to comprehend. It underscores the need for spiritual growth and maturity in order to fully grasp the profound truths of Jesus' priesthood in the order of Melchizedek.

Verse 12 (King James Version):
> For when for the time ye ought to be teachers, ye have need that one teach you again which be the first principles of the oracles of God; and are become such as have need of milk, and not of strong meat.

Interpretation:
This verse rebukes the audience for their spiritual immaturity, indicating that instead of being able to teach others, they still need to be taught the basic principles of God's Word, like infants who require milk instead of solid food.

Commentary:

- "For when for the time ye ought to be teachers": This phrase suggests that by now, the audience should have matured enough in their faith to be able to teach others.

- "ye have need that one teach you again which be the first principles of the oracles of God": This phrase indicates that instead of being able to teach others, the audience still needs to be taught the foundational truths of God's Word, indicating their spiritual immaturity.

- "and are become such as have need of milk, and not of strong meat": This phrase compares the audience to infants who require milk for nourishment, indicating that they are not yet ready for deeper, more complex teachings (1 Corinthians 3:1-2; 1 Peter 2:2).

Concordance:

- The metaphor of milk and solid food is used elsewhere in the New Testament to describe spiritual maturity and the ability to grasp deeper truths (1 Corinthians 3:1-2; 1 Peter 2:2).

- The concept of needing to be taught again the first principles of God's Word reflects the ongoing process of spiritual growth and learning that believers experience (Hebrews 6:1-3; 2 Peter 1:12-15).

This verse highlights the importance of spiritual maturity and growth in the Christian life. It emphasizes the need for believers to progress from basic teachings to deeper truths and to be able to teach others as they mature in their faith.

Verse 13 (King James Version):

> For every one that useth milk is unskilful in the word of righteousness: for he is a babe.

Interpretation:

This verse continues the metaphor of spiritual maturity, stating that those who rely on milk (basic teachings) are inexperienced in understanding and applying the deeper truths of God's Word, likening them to infants.

Commentary:
- "For every one that useth milk is unskilful in the word of righteousness": This phrase indicates that those who continue to rely on basic teachings (milk) are lacking in skill or experience in understanding and applying the deeper truths of God's Word.
- "for he is a babe": This phrase compares such individuals to infants, emphasizing their spiritual immaturity and need for growth (1 Corinthians 3:1-2; Ephesians 4:14).

Concordance:
- The metaphor of milk and solid food is used to illustrate the difference between spiritual immaturity and maturity (1 Corinthians 3:1-2; 1 Peter 2:2).
- The concept of being unskilful in the word of righteousness underscores the need for ongoing study, growth, and application of God's Word to mature in the faith (2 Timothy 2:15; James 1:22-25).

This verse emphasizes the importance of progressing from basic teachings to deeper truths in order to grow in spiritual maturity. It encourages believers to continually study and apply God's Word in order to become skilled in understanding and living according to His righteousness.

Verse 14 (King James Version):

> But strong meat belongeth to them that are of full age, even those who by reason of use have their senses exercised to discern both good and evil.

Interpretation:

This verse contrasts with the previous one, stating that those who are mature (of full age) in their faith are able to digest and benefit from deeper truths (strong meat), having trained themselves through practice to discern between good and evil.

Commentary:

- "But strong meat belongeth to them that are of full age": This phrase indicates that deeper, more complex truths of God's Word (strong meat) are appropriate for those who are spiritually mature and have grown in their faith.

- "even those who by reason of use have their senses exercised": This phrase suggests that through regular practice and application of God's Word, mature believers have trained themselves to discern between good and evil, developing spiritual discernment.

- "to discern both good and evil": This phrase highlights the ability of mature believers to distinguish between right and wrong, indicating their spiritual maturity and growth (Philippians 1:9-10; 1 Thessalonians 5:21-22).

Concordance:

- The concept of strong meat and milk is used to illustrate the difference between spiritual immaturity and maturity (1 Corinthians 3:1-2; 1 Peter 2:2).

- The idea of exercising the senses to discern good and evil emphasizes the importance of spiritual discernment in the Christian life (1 John 4:1; Philippians 1:9-10).

This verse encourages believers to strive for spiritual maturity and growth, moving beyond the basics of the faith to deeper truths. It emphasizes the importance of regular study and application of God's Word in developing spiritual discernment and maturity.

CHAPTER 6
God's Oath Unchanging

Verse 1 (King James Version):
> Therefore leaving the principles of the doctrine of Christ, let us go on unto perfection; not laying again the foundation of repentance from dead works, and of faith toward God,

Interpretation:
This verse encourages believers to move beyond the basic teachings of the doctrine of Christ and strive for perfection or maturity in their faith. It emphasizes the need to build on the foundational truths of repentance and faith without continually re-laying that foundation.

Commentary:
- "Therefore leaving the principles of the doctrine of Christ": This phrase suggests that while the foundational teachings of Christ are

important, believers should not remain stagnant but should progress to deeper understanding and maturity in their faith.

- "let us go on unto perfection": This phrase urges believers to strive for spiritual perfection or maturity, which involves a deeper understanding and application of God's Word in their lives.

- "not laying again the foundation of repentance from dead works, and of faith toward God": This phrase emphasizes that while repentance and faith are foundational to the Christian life, believers should not need to constantly revisit these basic principles but should instead build upon them (Hebrews 11:6; 2 Peter 1:5-8).

Concordance:
- The concept of moving on to perfection or maturity is echoed in other New Testament passages that emphasize spiritual growth and maturity (Ephesians 4:13-15; Philippians 3:12-14).
- The idea of not laying again the foundation of repentance and faith emphasizes the need for believers to continually grow and progress in their faith (2 Peter 1:5-9; Hebrews 10:22-23).

This verse challenges believers to move beyond the basics of their faith and strive for deeper understanding and maturity. It emphasizes the need for continual growth and progression in the Christian life, building upon the foundational truths of repentance and faith.

Verse 2 (King James Version):
> Of the doctrine of baptisms, and of laying on of hands, and of resurrection of the dead, and of eternal judgment.

Interpretation:

This verse lists several foundational teachings of Christianity that believers should understand and build upon: baptisms (which likely refers to both water baptism and the baptism of the Holy Spirit), the laying on of hands (for various purposes such as imparting blessings or ordaining leaders), the resurrection of the dead, and eternal judgment.

Commentary:

- "Of the doctrine of baptisms": This phrase likely refers to the various baptisms taught in the New Testament, including water baptism as a symbol of cleansing and identification with Christ, and the baptism of the Holy Spirit as an empowering for ministry (Matthew 3:11; Acts 2:38-39).

- "and of laying on of hands": This phrase refers to the practice of laying hands on believers for various purposes, such as imparting blessings, ordaining leaders, or imparting spiritual gifts (Acts 6:6; Acts 13:3; 1 Timothy 4:14).

- "and of resurrection of the dead": This phrase refers to the foundational Christian belief in the resurrection of believers to eternal life, as taught by Jesus and affirmed throughout the New Testament (John 11:25-26; 1 Corinthians 15:20-23).

- "and of eternal judgment": This phrase refers to the belief in a final judgment where all people will be judged according to their deeds, resulting in either eternal life or eternal punishment (Matthew 25:31-46; Revelation 20:11-15).

Concordance:

- The doctrine of baptisms and the laying on of hands reflects the early practices of the church and the teachings of the apostles (Acts 2:38; Acts 8:17; Acts 19:6).

- The resurrection of the dead and eternal judgment are foundational beliefs of Christianity, affirming the future hope and accountability of believers (1 Thessalonians 4:16-17; Revelation 20:11-15).

This verse emphasizes the importance of understanding and building upon foundational teachings of Christianity, including baptism, the laying on of hands, the resurrection of the dead, and eternal judgment. It encourages believers to deepen their understanding of these doctrines as they mature in their faith.

Verse 3 (King James Version):
> And this will we do, if God permit.

Interpretation:
This verse expresses the author's intention to move on from the foundational teachings listed in the previous verse to deeper spiritual truths, with the understanding that they will do so if it is in accordance with God's will.

Commentary:
- "And this will we do": This phrase indicates the author's determination to progress in their understanding and teaching of the faith, moving beyond the basics to deeper truths.
- "if God permit": This phrase acknowledges that the ability to progress in understanding and teaching deeper truths is ultimately dependent on God's permission and guidance (James 4:15).

Concordance:
- The phrase "if God permit" reflects the biblical teaching that all plans and actions are subject to God's sovereign will (Proverbs 19:21; James 4:13-15).

- The author's intention to move on to deeper truths aligns with the biblical exhortation for believers to continually grow and mature in their faith (2 Peter 3:18; Ephesians 4:15).

This verse demonstrates the author's desire to move beyond the foundational teachings of the faith to deeper spiritual truths, recognizing that such progression is dependent on God's guidance and permission. It underscores the importance of seeking God's will in all aspects of spiritual growth and understanding.

Verse 4 (King James Version):
> For it is impossible for those who were once enlightened, and have tasted of the heavenly gift, and were made partakers of the Holy Ghost,

Interpretation:
This verse presents a challenging statement about the severity of apostasy, suggesting that for those who have experienced certain aspects of the Christian faith and then fall away, it is impossible for them to be renewed to repentance.

Commentary:
- "For it is impossible": This phrase emphasizes the severity of the situation being described, indicating that a certain condition has been reached where restoration is no longer possible.
- "for those who were once enlightened": This phrase likely refers to those who have received some measure of spiritual understanding or illumination, possibly through the preaching of the gospel or the work of the Holy Spirit (John 1:9; Ephesians 1:18).
- "and have tasted of the heavenly gift": This phrase suggests that these individuals have experienced the blessings and benefits of

salvation, at least to some extent, indicating that they have had a personal encounter with Christ (Hebrews 2:9; 1 Peter 2:3).

- "and were made partakers of the Holy Ghost": This phrase indicates that these individuals have experienced the presence and work of the Holy Spirit in their lives, suggesting that they have been born again or regenerated (John 3:5-8; Titus 3:5).

Concordance:
- The concept of falling away or apostasy is addressed in other New Testament passages, warning believers of the dangers of abandoning their faith (Matthew 24:10-13; 1 Timothy 4:1; 2 Peter 2:20-22).

- The idea that it is impossible to renew certain individuals to repentance highlights the seriousness of apostasy and underscores the need for believers to persevere in their faith (Hebrews 10:26-31; 2 Peter 2:20-22).

This verse presents a sobering warning about the dangers of apostasy, emphasizing the importance of perseverance and faithfulness in the Christian life. It serves as a cautionary reminder to believers to take their spiritual walk seriously and to guard against falling away from the faith.

Verse 5 (King James Version):
> And have tasted the good word of God, and the powers of the world to come,

Interpretation:
This verse continues the description of those who have fallen away, stating that they have also experienced the benefits of hearing and

understanding God's Word, as well as witnessing the miraculous works of the Holy Spirit that give a foretaste of the future kingdom of God.

Commentary:
- "And have tasted the good word of God": This phrase indicates that these individuals have experienced the goodness and truth of God's Word, suggesting that they have understood and appreciated its teachings (Psalm 34:8; 1 Peter 2:2).
- "and the powers of the world to come": This phrase refers to the miraculous works of the Holy Spirit that are a foretaste of the future kingdom of God, demonstrating God's power and authority (Matthew 12:28; Acts 1:8).

Concordance:
- The idea of tasting the good word of God is related to the concept of spiritual growth and maturity, where believers grow in their understanding and appreciation of God's Word (1 Peter 2:2-3).
- The powers of the world to come refer to the miraculous works of the Holy Spirit that point to the future kingdom of God, demonstrating the reality and power of God's kingdom (Acts 2:22; Romans 15:18-19).

This verse adds to the description of those who have fallen away, indicating that they have not only experienced the benefits of hearing and understanding God's Word but have also witnessed the miraculous works of the Holy Spirit. This underscores the seriousness of apostasy and the need for believers to persevere in their faith.

Verse 6 (King James Version):
> If they shall fall away, to renew them again unto repentance; seeing they crucify to themselves the Son of God afresh, and put him to an open shame.

Interpretation:

This verse continues the discussion of those who have fallen away, stating that if they do fall away, it is impossible to renew them to repentance. This is because by turning away from the faith, they are essentially rejecting Christ anew and subjecting Him to public disgrace.

Commentary:

- "If they shall fall away": This phrase indicates the possibility of falling away from the faith, suggesting a deliberate turning away from Christ and His teachings (Matthew 24:10; 1 Timothy 4:1).

- "to renew them again unto repentance": This phrase suggests that for those who have fallen away, it is impossible to restore them to a state of repentance and faith. This does not mean that God is unwilling to forgive, but rather that those who persist in unbelief and rejection of Christ will not repent (Hebrews 10:26-27).

- "seeing they crucify to themselves the Son of God afresh, and put him to an open shame": This phrase explains why it is impossible to renew those who have fallen away. By rejecting Christ and His sacrifice, they are essentially crucifying Him again and subjecting Him to public disgrace, which is an affront to the work of Christ on the cross (Hebrews 10:29; 1 Peter 2:24).

Concordance:

- The idea of falling away and rejecting Christ is a serious warning found throughout the New Testament, emphasizing the need for believers to persevere in their faith (Matthew 10:22; 1 Corinthians 10:12; 1 Timothy 1:19-20).

- The concept of crucifying Christ afresh underscores the seriousness of apostasy and the need for believers to remain steadfast in their commitment to Christ (Hebrews 10:29; 1 Peter 4:14-16).

This verse serves as a sobering warning about the consequences of falling away from the faith. It emphasizes the need for believers to remain steadfast in their commitment to Christ and to avoid turning away from Him.

Verse 7 (King James Version):
> For the earth which drinketh in the rain that cometh oft upon it, and bringeth forth herbs meet for them by whom it is dressed, receiveth blessing from God:

Interpretation:
This verse uses an agricultural metaphor to illustrate the contrast between those who persevere in the faith and those who fall away. Just as the earth that receives rain produces a fruitful harvest, those who remain faithful to God receive His blessings.

Commentary:
- "For the earth which drinketh in the rain that cometh oft upon it": This phrase describes the earth that regularly receives rain, which is necessary for the growth of crops.
- "and bringeth forth herbs meet for them by whom it is dressed": This phrase explains that the earth produces a harvest suitable for those who cultivate it and care for it.
- "receiveth blessing from God": This phrase indicates that the earth that produces a fruitful harvest receives a blessing from God for its productivity.

Concordance:
- The metaphor of rain representing God's blessings is used in various places in the Bible to signify God's provision and favor (Isaiah 55:10-11; Joel 2:23-24).

- The idea of the earth producing a harvest as a result of receiving rain is used to illustrate spiritual growth and fruitfulness in the Christian life (Galatians 5:22-23; Colossians 1:10).

This verse encourages believers to remain faithful and steadfast in their commitment to God, knowing that their perseverance will result in blessings from Him. It serves as a reminder that just as the earth produces a harvest when it receives rain, so believers will bear fruit in their lives when they remain faithful to God.

Verse 8 (King James Version):
> But that which beareth thorns and briers is rejected, and is nigh unto cursing; whose end is to be burned.

Interpretation:
This verse continues the agricultural metaphor, contrasting the fate of land that produces a fruitful harvest with that which produces thorns and briers. The land that produces thorns and briers is rejected, cursed, and ultimately destroyed by fire.

Commentary:
- "But that which beareth thorns and briers is rejected": This phrase describes the land that produces useless or harmful vegetation instead of a fruitful harvest. Such land is rejected because it does not fulfill its intended purpose.
- "and is nigh unto cursing": This phrase indicates that the land that produces thorns and briers is close to being cursed or condemned. It is not receiving the blessing that comes from producing a fruitful harvest.

- "whose end is to be burned": This phrase describes the ultimate fate of the land that produces thorns and briers. It will be destroyed by fire, indicating a final judgment.

Concordance:
- The metaphor of land producing thorns and briers is used elsewhere in the Bible to symbolize unfruitfulness and judgment (Isaiah 5:1-7; Matthew 13:7, 22).
- The idea of land being rejected and destroyed by fire is used to illustrate the consequences of unfaithfulness and disobedience (Matthew 7:19; 2 Peter 3:7).

This verse serves as a warning to believers about the consequences of falling away from the faith and failing to produce spiritual fruit in their lives. It emphasizes the importance of remaining faithful to God and bearing fruit that is pleasing to Him.

Verse 9 (King James Version):
> But, beloved, we are persuaded better things of you, and things that accompany salvation, though we thus speak.

Interpretation:
This verse contrasts the previous warning about apostasy by expressing confidence in the readers' faith and salvation. The author believes that the readers will continue to persevere in their faith and produce the fruit of salvation.

Commentary:
- "But, beloved, we are persuaded better things of you": This phrase expresses the author's confidence in the readers, believing that they will not fall away but will continue to grow in their faith and produce spiritual fruit.

- "and things that accompany salvation": This phrase refers to the evidence of salvation in the readers' lives, such as faith, love, obedience, and perseverance (1 Thessalonians 1:3; 2 Peter 1:10-11).

- "though we thus speak": This phrase acknowledges the seriousness of the warning about apostasy given in the previous verses but assures the readers that the author's confidence in them remains strong.

Concordance:
- The idea of being persuaded of better things is a reminder that God is faithful to complete the work He has begun in believers (Philippians 1:6; 1 Thessalonians 5:24).

- The concept of producing the fruit of salvation is a recurring theme in the New Testament, emphasizing the evidence of genuine faith in the lives of believers (Galatians 5:22-23; James 2:14-26).

This verse provides encouragement to believers, assuring them of the author's confidence in their faith and salvation. It serves as a reminder that while the warning about apostasy is serious, God's grace is sufficient to keep believers and enable them to persevere in their faith.

Verse 10 (King James Version):
> For God is not unrighteous to forget your work and labour of love, which ye have shewed toward his name, in that ye have ministered to the saints, and do minister.

Interpretation:
This verse reassures believers that God is just and will not overlook their efforts and acts of love done in His name. It acknowledges their past and ongoing service to fellow believers.

Commentary:

- "For God is not unrighteous to forget your work and labour of love": This phrase emphasizes God's justice and faithfulness. He remembers and rewards the work and sacrifices made by believers out of love for Him and others (Hebrews 11:6; 1 Corinthians 15:58).

- "which ye have showed toward his name, in that ye have ministered to the saints, and do minister": This phrase specifies the nature of their work and love, which is directed toward God's name and expressed through their service to fellow believers. It highlights the importance of practical expressions of love and service in the Christian life (Matthew 25:34-40; James 2:14-17).

Concordance:

- The idea that God remembers and rewards the work of believers is a consistent theme in Scripture, emphasizing the importance of faithfulness and perseverance in serving God (Hebrews 10:35-36; Revelation 22:12).

- The concept of ministering to the saints and showing love through service is a central teaching in the New Testament, reflecting the selfless example of Christ and the early church (John 13:34-35; Acts 20:35).

This verse provides assurance to believers that God recognizes and values their service and acts of love done in His name. It encourages believers to continue serving and loving others, knowing that their efforts are not in vain and will be rewarded by a just and faithful God.

Verse 11 (King James Version):

> And we desire that every one of you do shew the same diligence to the full assurance of hope unto the end:

Interpretation:

This verse expresses the author's desire for believers to continue diligently in their faith, maintaining a full assurance of hope until the end of their lives.

Commentary:
- "And we desire that every one of you do show the same diligence": This phrase indicates the author's desire for all believers to exhibit the same level of diligence and commitment in their faith.
- "to the full assurance of hope unto the end": This phrase describes the goal of their diligence—maintaining a full and unwavering assurance of hope in their salvation and future inheritance until the end of their lives (Hebrews 10:22; 1 Peter 1:3-5).

Concordance:
- The call to show diligence and perseverance in the faith is a common theme in the New Testament, emphasizing the importance of enduring faithfulness (Hebrews 10:36; Revelation 2:10).
- The concept of full assurance of hope is related to the believer's confident expectation of eternal life and the fulfillment of God's promises (Romans 8:24-25; Colossians 1:27).

This verse encourages believers to continue steadfastly in their faith, maintaining a full assurance of hope in God's promises. It emphasizes the importance of perseverance and diligence in the Christian life, reminding believers of the eternal significance of their faith and commitment to Christ.

Verse 12 (King James Version):
> That ye be not slothful, but followers of them who through faith and patience inherit the promises.

Interpretation:

This verse urges believers not to be lazy or negligent in their faith but to imitate those who, through faith and patience, have received the fulfillment of God's promises.

Commentary:

- "That ye be not slothful": This phrase warns against laziness or sluggishness in the Christian life, emphasizing the need for active and diligent faith (Romans 12:11; 2 Thessalonians 3:11-12).

- "but followers of them who through faith and patience inherit the promises": This phrase encourages believers to imitate the example of those in the Bible who, through their unwavering faith and patient endurance, received the fulfillment of God's promises (Hebrews 11:8-12, 17-19).

Concordance:

- The exhortation to be followers or imitators of those who have gone before us in the faith is a common theme in the New Testament, emphasizing the importance of learning from the examples of faithful believers (1 Corinthians 11:1; Philippians 3:17; 1 Thessalonians 1:6).

- The idea of inheriting the promises through faith and patience underscores the biblical teaching that God's promises are fulfilled in the lives of those who trust in Him and patiently await His timing (Hebrews 10:36; James 1:12).

This verse challenges believers to be diligent and active in their faith, following the example of those who have gone before them and received the fulfillment of God's promises. It emphasizes the importance of faith and patience in inheriting the promises of God and encourages believers to persevere in their walk with Christ.

Verse 13 (King James Version):

> For when God made promise to Abraham, because he could swear by no greater, he sware by himself,

Interpretation:
This verse refers to God's promise to Abraham and emphasizes the certainty and importance of God's promise by highlighting that He swore by Himself, as there was no greater authority by which He could swear.

Commentary:
- "For when God made promise to Abraham": This phrase refers to God's covenant with Abraham, in which He promised to bless him and make him a great nation (Genesis 12:1-3; 15:1-6).
- "because he could swear by no greater, he swore by himself": This phrase explains why God swore by Himself when making the promise to Abraham. Since there is no higher authority than God, He confirmed the certainty of His promise by appealing to His own nature and character (Genesis 22:16; Psalm 89:35; Hebrews 7:21).

Concordance:
- The concept of God swearing by Himself emphasizes the absolute certainty and unchangeable nature of His promises (Isaiah 45:23; Jeremiah 22:5; Hebrews 6:17-18).
- The promise to Abraham is significant in the Bible because it foreshadows God's plan of salvation through faith and serves as a foundation for understanding the relationship between faith and God's promises (Galatians 3:6-9; Romans 4:13-25).

This verse highlights the certainty and significance of God's promises, using the example of His promise to Abraham. It underscores the trustworthiness of God's word and His faithfulness in fulfilling His promises, encouraging believers to trust in Him and His promises.

Verse 14 (King James Version):
> Saying, Surely blessing I will bless thee, and multiplying I will multiply thee.

Interpretation:
This verse quotes part of God's promise to Abraham, emphasizing the certainty and abundance of the blessings God would bestow upon him.

Commentary:
- "Saying, Surely blessing I will bless thee, and multiplying I will multiply thee": This phrase quotes God's promise to Abraham recorded in Genesis 22:17. God assures Abraham of His abundant blessings and the multiplication of his descendants.

Concordance:
- This promise to Abraham is significant because it is cited as an example of God's faithfulness in fulfilling His promises and underscores the principle of faith as the basis for receiving God's blessings (Romans 4:16-22; Galatians 3:6-9).
- The promise to bless and multiply Abraham is also connected to the broader theme of God's redemptive plan, as the fulfillment of this promise ultimately leads to the birth of Jesus Christ, who brings blessing to all nations (Galatians 3:14-16).

This verse highlights God's faithfulness in fulfilling His promises and serves as a reminder to believers of His abundant blessings. It encourages believers to trust in God's promises and to have faith in His provision and goodness.

Verse 15 (King James Version):

> And so, after he had patiently endured, he obtained the promise.

Interpretation:

This verse describes how Abraham, through patient endurance, ultimately received the fulfillment of God's promise to him.

Commentary:

- "And so, after he had patiently endured": This phrase emphasizes Abraham's patient endurance and faithfulness to God's promise over a long period of time. Despite various challenges and obstacles, Abraham remained steadfast in his faith.

- "he obtained the promise": This phrase indicates that Abraham finally received the fulfillment of God's promise to bless him and multiply his descendants (Genesis 21:1-7).

Concordance:

- The concept of patiently enduring to receive God's promises is a recurring theme in the Bible, highlighting the importance of faith and perseverance in the Christian life (James 5:11; Hebrews 10:36).

- Abraham's example of faith and patient endurance is cited in the New Testament as a model for believers to follow, illustrating the nature of true faith and its outcome (Romans 4:20-21; Galatians 3:6-9).

This verse uses Abraham as an example of faith and perseverance, encouraging believers to remain steadfast in their faith and trust in God's promises. It demonstrates that God is faithful to fulfill His promises to those who patiently endure in faith.

Verse 16 (King James Version):

> For men verily swear by the greater: and an oath for confirmation is to them an end of all strife.

Interpretation:

This verse explains the cultural practice of swearing oaths for confirmation and how it relates to the certainty of God's promises.

Commentary:

- "For men verily swear by the greater": This phrase acknowledges the common practice among humans to swear oaths by invoking something greater than themselves, such as God or a sacred object, to affirm the truth of their statements.

- "and an oath for confirmation is to them an end of all strife": This phrase indicates that when people swear an oath, it is considered a final confirmation of their commitment or statement, resolving any doubts or disputes that may exist.

Concordance:

- This verse reflects the cultural practice of oath-taking in biblical times, which was often used to solemnize agreements and affirm the truthfulness of statements (Genesis 21:23-24; Matthew 26:63-64).

- The concept of swearing oaths is also discussed elsewhere in the New Testament, with Jesus cautioning against taking oaths lightly and emphasizing the importance of speaking truthfully (Matthew 5:33-37; James 5:12).

This verse is used to illustrate the certainty and finality of God's promises, contrasting human oath-taking with God's unchanging nature and faithfulness. It underscores the reliability of God's promises and serves as a reminder of His trustworthiness in fulfilling them.

Verse 17 (King James Version):
> Wherein God, willing more abundantly to shew unto the heirs of promise the immutability of his counsel, confirmed it by an oath:

Interpretation:
This verse explains that God, desiring to demonstrate more convincingly to those who would inherit His promises the unchangeable nature of His purpose, confirmed His promise with an oath.

Commentary:
- "Wherein God, willing more abundantly to shew unto the heirs of promise the immutability of his counsel": This phrase indicates that God, in His desire to make the unchangeable nature of His purpose abundantly clear to those who would receive His promises, chose to confirm His promise with an oath.
- "confirmed it by an oath": This phrase emphasizes that God, to underscore the certainty of His promise, went beyond mere words and swore an oath by Himself, as there is no higher authority by which He could swear (Hebrews 6:13).

Concordance:
- The idea of God confirming His promises with an oath underscores the reliability and trustworthiness of His word, highlighting His faithfulness in fulfilling His promises (Hebrews 6:18; Psalm 89:35).

- The concept of God's unchangeable purpose and counsel is a recurring theme in Scripture, emphasizing the sovereignty and steadfastness of God's plan (Isaiah 46:10; Romans 11:29).

This verse emphasizes the certainty and unchangeable nature of God's promises by highlighting His decision to confirm His promise with an oath. It underscores the reliability of God's word and His faithfulness in fulfilling His promises, encouraging believers to trust in His promises with confidence.

Verse 18 (King James Version):
> That by two immutable things, in which it was impossible for God to lie, we might have a strong consolation, who have fled for refuge to lay hold upon the hope set before us:

Interpretation:
This verse highlights the reliability of God's promises, emphasizing that He cannot lie. Believers can find strong consolation and hope in God's unchanging nature and His promises.

Commentary:
- "That by two immutable things": This phrase refers to God's promise and His oath, which are unchangeable and serve as a double guarantee of the certainty of His promises.
- "in which it was impossible for God to lie": This phrase underscores the absolute trustworthiness of God's word. Because of His nature, God cannot lie or deceive (Numbers 23:19; Titus 1:2).
- "we might have a strong consolation": This phrase indicates that believers can find strong comfort and assurance in the unchanging nature of God's promises.
- "who have fled for refuge to lay hold upon the hope set before us": This phrase describes believers who have placed their trust in God's

promises as a source of refuge and hope in times of trouble (Psalm 46:1; Hebrews 10:23).

Concordance:
- The idea that it is impossible for God to lie is a foundational truth in Scripture, highlighting His trustworthiness and faithfulness (Hebrews 6:18; Numbers 23:19; Titus 1:2).
- The concept of finding refuge and hope in God's promises is a recurring theme in the Bible, emphasizing the comfort and strength that believers can find in trusting God (Psalm 62:8; Isaiah 40:31).

This verse reassures believers of the certainty of God's promises and encourages them to find strong consolation and hope in His unchanging nature. It emphasizes the trustworthiness of God's word and His faithfulness in fulfilling His promises, providing comfort and encouragement to those who trust in Him.

Verse 19 (King James Version):
> Which hope we have as an anchor of the soul, both sure and stedfast, and which entereth into that within the veil;

Interpretation:
This verse describes the hope that believers have in God's promises as an anchor for the soul. This hope is described as sure, steadfast, and entering into the inner sanctuary, symbolizing the believer's access to God's presence and the certainty of His promises.

Commentary:
- "Which hope we have as an anchor of the soul": This phrase compares the believer's hope in God's promises to an anchor for a ship. Just as an anchor provides stability and security for a ship in turbulent

waters, so too does our hope in God provide stability and security for our souls in the midst of life's trials and challenges.

- "both sure and stedfast": This phrase emphasizes the certainty and steadfastness of our hope in God. It is not based on shifting circumstances or emotions but on the unchanging nature of God and His promises (Romans 5:5; 1 Thessalonians 5:8).

- "and which entereth into that within the veil": This phrase likely refers to the inner sanctuary of the tabernacle or temple, which symbolizes the presence of God. Our hope in God's promises gives us access to His presence and assures us of the fulfillment of His promises (Hebrews 9:3, 12, 24).

Concordance:
- The image of hope as an anchor is a powerful metaphor used elsewhere in the New Testament to describe the steadfastness and security of our faith in God's promises (Colossians 1:27; 1 Timothy 1:1; Titus 2:13).

- The idea of our hope entering into the inner sanctuary symbolizes our access to God's presence and the fulfillment of His promises through Christ (Hebrews 10:19-22; Ephesians 2:18).

This verse portrays the believer's hope in God's promises as an anchor for the soul, providing stability, security, and access to God's presence. It emphasizes the certainty and steadfastness of our hope, encouraging believers to trust in God's promises with confidence.

Verse 20 (King James Version):
> Whither the forerunner is for us entered, even Jesus, made an high priest for ever after the order of Melchisedec.

Interpretation:

This verse explains that Jesus, as the forerunner, has entered into the inner sanctuary on our behalf. He has become our eternal high priest in the order of Melchizedek.

Commentary:

- "Whither the forerunner is for us entered, even Jesus": This phrase refers to Jesus entering into the inner sanctuary of God's presence, symbolizing His role as our representative and mediator before God (Hebrews 9:11-12; 10:19-20).

- "made an high priest for ever after the order of Melchisedec": This phrase highlights Jesus' eternal priesthood in the order of Melchizedek, which is contrasted with the temporary and imperfect priesthood of the Levitical system (Hebrews 5:6; 7:17).

Concordance:

- The concept of Jesus as our forerunner and high priest is central to the book of Hebrews, emphasizing His role in securing our salvation and mediating between us and God (Hebrews 2:17-18; 4:14-16).

- The reference to Melchizedek highlights Jesus' superior priesthood, which is based on His eternal nature and His ability to bring about a perfect salvation (Hebrews 7:11-28).

This verse underscores the unique and essential role of Jesus as our forerunner and high priest. It highlights His ability to enter into God's presence on our behalf, securing our access to God and guaranteeing our salvation. It also emphasizes the superiority of His priesthood over the Levitical priesthood, pointing to His eternal priesthood in the order of Melchizedek.

CHAPTER 7

The Priesthood of Melchisedec

Verse 1 (King James Version):
> For this Melchisedec, king of Salem, priest of the most high God, who met Abraham returning from the slaughter of the kings, and blessed him;

Interpretation:
This verse introduces Melchizedek, the king of Salem and priest of the most high God, who blessed Abraham after his victory over the kings.

Commentary:
- "For this Melchisedec, king of Salem, priest of the most high God": This phrase describes Melchizedek as both a king and a priest, a

unique combination that sets him apart from the Levitical priesthood. "Salem" is believed to be an early name for Jerusalem.

- "who met Abraham returning from the slaughter of the kings": This phrase refers to the meeting between Melchizedek and Abraham after Abraham's victory over the kings who had captured his nephew Lot (Genesis 14:17-20).

- "and blessed him": This phrase highlights Melchizedek's blessing of Abraham, which is significant because it establishes Melchizedek's superiority over Abraham, as the one who blesses is greater than the one who receives the blessing (Hebrews 7:7).

Concordance:

- Melchizedek is a mysterious figure in the Old Testament, mentioned briefly in Genesis 14:18-20. He is presented as a priest of the most high God who blesses Abraham.

- The author of Hebrews uses Melchizedek as a type or foreshadowing of Jesus Christ, emphasizing His eternal priesthood and superiority over the Levitical priesthood (Hebrews 7:3, 15-17).

This verse sets the stage for the author's discussion of Melchizedek in the following verses, highlighting his unique role as a king and priest and his interaction with Abraham. It sets the foundation for the comparison between Melchizedek and Jesus Christ as superior priests.

Verse 2 (King James Version):
> To whom also Abraham gave a tenth part of all; first being by interpretation King of righteousness, and after that also King of Salem, which is, King of peace;

Interpretation:

This verse describes how Abraham gave a tithe (a tenth) of all his spoils to Melchizedek. It also explains the meaning of Melchizedek's name, which signifies "King of righteousness" and "King of Salem" (which means "King of peace").

Commentary:
- "To whom also Abraham gave a tenth part of all": This phrase refers to Abraham's act of giving a tithe of his spoils to Melchizedek, acknowledging Melchizedek's superiority and authority (Genesis 14:20).
- "first being by interpretation King of righteousness": This phrase explains the meaning of the name "Melchizedek," which can be interpreted as "King of righteousness," highlighting Melchizedek's role as a righteous and just king.
- "and after that also King of Salem, which is, King of peace": This phrase further explains the significance of Melchizedek's name, indicating that he was not only a king of righteousness but also a king of peace, symbolizing his role in bringing peace and reconciliation.

Concordance:
- The act of tithing to Melchizedek is seen as significant because it predates the establishment of the Levitical priesthood and demonstrates Melchizedek's superiority over Abraham (Hebrews 7:4-10).
- The names "King of righteousness" and "King of peace" attributed to Melchizedek are seen as pointing to Jesus Christ, who is described as the ultimate fulfillment of these titles (Isaiah 9:6; Romans 5:1; 2 Corinthians 5:21).

This verse emphasizes the unique and honorable status of Melchizedek, as demonstrated by Abraham's tithing to him and the meanings of his name. It sets the stage for the author's comparison between Melchizedek and Jesus Christ, highlighting their similarities and the superiority of Christ's priesthood.

Verse 3 (King James Version):
> Without father, without mother, without descent, having neither beginning of days, nor end of life; but made like unto the Son of God; abideth a priest continually.

Interpretation:
This verse describes Melchizedek as a priest who appears in the biblical narrative without any recorded genealogy or lineage, suggesting a unique and eternal nature. He is likened to the Son of God and is said to continue as a priest forever.

Commentary:
- "Without father, without mother, without descent": This phrase emphasizes the absence of any recorded genealogy for Melchizedek in the biblical narrative, highlighting his unique status. This lack of genealogy is contrasted with the Levitical priests, whose genealogies were meticulously recorded and who were limited by their lineage (Hebrews 7:5-6).
- "having neither beginning of days, nor end of life": This phrase further underscores the mysterious and eternal nature of Melchizedek, suggesting that he appears in the biblical narrative without any recorded birth or death, symbolizing his perpetual priesthood.
- "but made like unto the Son of God": This phrase compares Melchizedek to the Son of God, Jesus Christ, highlighting the similarity in their eternal and unchangeable priesthoods. Melchizedek serves as a type or foreshadowing of Christ, whose priesthood is eternal and superior to the Levitical priesthood (Hebrews 7:15-17).

- "abideth a priest continually": This phrase emphasizes that Melchizedek continues as a priest forever, symbolizing the eternal nature of his priesthood and its superiority over the temporary priesthood of the Levitical system (Hebrews 7:24-25).

Concordance:
- The description of Melchizedek as a priest without recorded genealogy or lineage is unique in the Old Testament and sets him apart as a mysterious and significant figure (Hebrews 7:3; Genesis 14:18-20).
- The comparison between Melchizedek and the Son of God underscores the typological relationship between Melchizedek and Jesus Christ, highlighting Christ's superior and eternal priesthood (Hebrews 7:15-17).

This verse emphasizes the unique and mysterious nature of Melchizedek's priesthood, highlighting his eternal and unchangeable status. It sets the stage for the author's comparison between Melchizedek and Jesus Christ, illustrating Christ's superior priesthood and the fulfillment of the Melchizedekian priesthood in Him.

Verse 4 (King James Version):
> Now consider how great this man was, unto whom even the patriarch Abraham gave the tenth of the spoils.

Interpretation:
This verse calls attention to the greatness of Melchizedek, highlighting Abraham's acknowledgment of his greatness by giving him a tenth of the spoils.

Commentary:
- "Now consider how great this man was": This phrase invites the reader to reflect on the greatness of Melchizedek, particularly in

comparison to Abraham. The author is emphasizing Melchizedek's superiority and significance.

- "unto whom even the patriarch Abraham gave the tenth of the spoils": This phrase refers back to the event recorded in Genesis 14:20, where Abraham gave a tithe of the spoils of war to Melchizedek. This act demonstrated Abraham's recognition of Melchizedek's authority and greatness, as well as the superiority of Melchizedek's priesthood over his own.

Concordance:
- The act of Abraham giving a tithe to Melchizedek is seen as significant because it establishes Melchizedek's superiority over Abraham and the Levitical priesthood, which descended from Abraham (Hebrews 7:5-10).
- The greatness of Melchizedek is further emphasized by his role as a king and priest, as well as by his lack of recorded genealogy, which sets him apart as a mysterious and significant figure (Hebrews 7:1-3).

This verse highlights the greatness of Melchizedek, particularly in comparison to Abraham. It underscores the significance of Melchizedek's priesthood and sets the stage for the author's argument regarding the superiority of the Melchizedekian priesthood over the Levitical priesthood.

Verse 5 (King James Version):
> And verily they that are of the sons of Levi, who receive the office of the priesthood, have a commandment to take tithes of the people according to the law, that is, of their brethren, though they come out of the loins of Abraham:

Interpretation:

This verse contrasts the Levitical priesthood with the priesthood of Melchizedek. It explains that the Levites, who receive the priesthood according to the law, are commanded to take tithes from the Israelites, who are their brethren and descendants of Abraham.

Commentary:

- "And verily they that are of the sons of Levi, who receive the office of the priesthood": This phrase refers to the Levites, who were descendants of Levi and were appointed to the priesthood under the Mosaic law (Numbers 3:5-10).

- "have a commandment to take tithes of the people according to the law": This phrase explains that the Levites were commanded by the Mosaic law to collect tithes from the people of Israel. This tithe was a tenth of the produce of the land and the increase of the flocks, which was given to support the Levites and the priesthood (Numbers 18:21-24).

- "that is, of their brethren, though they come out of the loins of Abraham": This phrase highlights that the Levites, who received tithes from the Israelites, were themselves descendants of Abraham, specifically through his great-grandson Levi. This emphasizes the close familial relationship between the Levites and the rest of the Israelites.

Concordance:

- The Levitical priesthood was established under the Mosaic law and was based on genealogical descent from Levi (Exodus 28:1; Numbers 3:5-10).

- The Levites were supported by the tithes of the people because they did not receive a land inheritance like the other tribes of Israel (Numbers 18:20-24; Deuteronomy 10:9).

This verse contrasts the priesthood of Melchizedek, which was not based on genealogy or the Mosaic law, with the Levitical priesthood, which was. It emphasizes the unique and superior nature of Melchizedek's priesthood, setting the stage for the author's argument regarding the superiority of Christ's priesthood over the Levitical priesthood.

Verse 6 (King James Version):
> But he whose descent is not counted from them received tithes of Abraham, and blessed him that had the promises.

Interpretation:
This verse continues to contrast the priesthood of Melchizedek with the Levitical priesthood. It explains that Melchizedek, whose genealogy is not recorded, received tithes from Abraham and blessed him, even though the promises were given to Abraham.

Commentary:
- "But he whose descent is not counted from them": This phrase refers to Melchizedek, whose genealogy is not recorded in the biblical narrative, unlike the Levites, whose descent is traced back to Levi.
- "received tithes of Abraham": This phrase refers to the event recorded in Genesis 14:20, where Abraham gave a tithe of his spoils to Melchizedek. This act is significant because it demonstrates Melchizedek's superiority over Abraham, as the one who receives tithes is considered greater (Hebrews 7:7).
- "and blessed him that had the promises": This phrase refers to Melchizedek's blessing of Abraham, which is mentioned in Genesis 14:19. This blessing is significant because it acknowledges Melchizedek's spiritual authority and superiority over Abraham, the recipient of God's promises.

Concordance:

- Melchizedek's receipt of tithes from Abraham and his blessing of Abraham are seen as significant because they demonstrate Melchizedek's superiority over Abraham and the Levitical priesthood (Hebrews 7:7-10).

- The promises mentioned in this verse likely refer to the covenant promises that God made to Abraham, including the promise of a great nation and blessings for all nations through his descendants (Genesis 12:1-3).

This verse reinforces the superiority of Melchizedek's priesthood over the Levitical priesthood by highlighting Melchizedek's receipt of tithes from Abraham and his blessing of Abraham. It emphasizes Melchizedek's unique and superior status, setting the stage for the author's argument regarding the superiority of Christ's priesthood over the Levitical priesthood.

Verse 8 (King James Version):
> And here men that die receive tithes; but there he receiveth them, of whom it is witnessed that he liveth.

Interpretation:
This verse contrasts the Levitical priests, who receive tithes but eventually die, with Melchizedek, who is described as receiving tithes and is witnessed to continue living.

Commentary:
- "And here men that die receive tithes": This phrase refers to the Levitical priests, who were mortal and eventually died. Despite their mortality, they received tithes from the people of Israel according to the Mosaic law.
- "but there he receiveth them, of whom it is witnessed that he liveth": This phrase contrasts the Levitical priests with Melchizedek.

While the Levitical priests died and were succeeded by others in the priesthood, Melchizedek is described as receiving tithes and as one of whom it is witnessed that he lives. This emphasizes the eternal and unchangeable nature of Melchizedek's priesthood, in contrast to the temporary and mortal nature of the Levitical priesthood.

Concordance:
- The contrast between the mortality of the Levitical priests and the eternal nature of Melchizedek's priesthood emphasizes the superiority of Melchizedek's priesthood and prefigures the eternal priesthood of Jesus Christ (Hebrews 7:23-25).
- The description of Melchizedek as one of whom it is witnessed that he lives suggests a type of foreshadowing of Christ's resurrection and eternal priesthood, which is a central theme in the book of Hebrews (Hebrews 7:24-25).

This verse emphasizes the temporary and mortal nature of the Levitical priesthood, highlighting the superiority of Melchizedek's priesthood, which is described as eternal and unchangeable. It sets the stage for the author's argument regarding the superiority of Christ's priesthood over the Levitical priesthood, emphasizing Christ's eternal and unchangeable priesthood.

Verse 9 (King James Version):
> And as I may so say, Levi also, who receiveth tithes, payed tithes in Abraham.

Interpretation:
This verse points out that even though Levi, the ancestor of the Levites who received tithes under the Mosaic law, was not yet born

when Abraham paid tithes to Melchizedek, Levi is considered to have paid tithes through Abraham.

Commentary:

- "And as I may so say": This phrase is used by the author to introduce a statement that might seem unusual or unexpected but is nevertheless true.

- "Levi also, who receiveth tithes, payed tithes in Abraham": This statement highlights the fact that Levi, who was a descendant of Abraham and the ancestor of the Levitical priests, is considered to have paid tithes to Melchizedek through Abraham's act of paying tithes. This demonstrates the superiority of Melchizedek's priesthood over the Levitical priesthood, as even the ancestor of the Levites acknowledged Melchizedek's authority and greatness.

Concordance:

- The idea that Levi paid tithes to Melchizedek through Abraham is based on the principle of representation or solidarity, where the actions of a forefather are considered to represent the actions of his descendants (Hebrews 7:10).

- This concept highlights the superiority of Melchizedek's priesthood, as it predates and encompasses the Levitical priesthood, indicating a higher order of priesthood that transcends genealogy and the Mosaic law (Hebrews 7:11-12).

This verse underscores the superiority of Melchizedek's priesthood over the Levitical priesthood by showing that even the ancestor of the Levites, Levi, acknowledged Melchizedek's authority. It emphasizes the continuity and significance of Melchizedek's priesthood, setting the stage for the author's argument regarding the superiority of Christ's priesthood over the Levitical priesthood.

Verse 10 (King James Version):
> For he was yet in the loins of his father, when Melchisedec met him.

Interpretation:
This verse explains further the concept introduced in the previous verse, stating that Levi, the ancestor of the Levitical priests, was still in the loins of his forefather Abraham when Abraham met Melchizedek and paid tithes to him.

Commentary:
- "For he was yet in the loins of his father": This phrase emphasizes the idea of representation or solidarity, suggesting that Levi, as Abraham's descendant, was included in Abraham's actions and therefore also participated in paying tithes to Melchizedek.
- "when Melchisedec met him": This phrase refers to the meeting between Abraham and Melchizedek, as recorded in Genesis 14:17-20, where Abraham paid tithes to Melchizedek. This meeting took place before Levi was born, indicating that Levi's participation in paying tithes to Melchizedek was through his forefather Abraham.

Concordance:
- The concept of Levi paying tithes to Melchizedek through Abraham is based on the idea of federal headship, where the actions of a representative ancestor are attributed to his descendants (Romans 5:12-21; 1 Corinthians 15:22).
- This verse further emphasizes the superiority of Melchizedek's priesthood, as it predates and encompasses the Levitical priesthood, indicating a higher order of priesthood that transcends genealogy and the Mosaic law (Hebrews 7:11-12).

This verse strengthens the argument for the superiority of Melchizedek's priesthood over the Levitical priesthood by highlighting the concept of representation, showing that Levi participated in paying tithes to Melchizedek through his forefather Abraham. It underscores the continuity and significance of Melchizedek's priesthood, setting the stage for the author's argument regarding the superiority of Christ's priesthood over the Levitical priesthood.

Verse 11 (King James Version):

> If therefore perfection were by the Levitical priesthood, (for under it the people received the law,) what further need was there that another priest should rise after the order of Melchisedec, and not be called after the order of Aaron?

Interpretation:

This verse poses a rhetorical question, suggesting that if the Levitical priesthood could bring about perfection (i.e., full reconciliation between humanity and God), there would have been no need for another priest to arise after the order of Melchizedek, rather than the order of Aaron.

Commentary:

- "If therefore perfection were by the Levitical priesthood": This phrase introduces the hypothetical scenario that if the Levitical priesthood could achieve perfection or complete reconciliation between humanity and God, there would be no need for another priesthood.

- "(for under it the people received the law,)": This parenthetical statement emphasizes that the Levitical priesthood was closely associated with the giving of the Mosaic law at Mount Sinai. The law was given to regulate the priesthood and the worship practices of the Israelites.

- "what further need was there that another priest should rise after the order of Melchisedec": This question highlights the insufficiency of the Levitical priesthood to bring about perfection. If the Levitical priesthood was sufficient, there would have been no need for another priest to arise after the order of Melchizedek, as typified by Jesus Christ.

- "and not be called after the order of Aaron?": This phrase contrasts the priesthood of Jesus Christ, which is after the order of Melchizedek, with the Levitical priesthood, which is after the order of Aaron. This indicates a change in the priesthood, suggesting that the priesthood of Jesus Christ is superior to the Levitical priesthood.

Concordance:
- The Levitical priesthood, associated with the Mosaic law, was unable to bring about perfection or complete reconciliation between humanity and God (Hebrews 7:18-19; 9:9-10).
- The priesthood of Jesus Christ, after the order of Melchizedek, is presented as superior to the Levitical priesthood, offering a more perfect way of reconciliation with God (Hebrews 7:15-17; 8:6).

This verse challenges the idea that the Levitical priesthood could bring about perfection and argues for the necessity of a new priesthood after the order of Melchizedek, fulfilled in Jesus Christ. It sets the stage for the author's argument regarding the superiority of Christ's priesthood over the Levitical priesthood.

Verse 12 (King James Version):
> For the priesthood being changed, there is made of necessity a change also of the law.

Interpretation:

This verse asserts that with the change of the priesthood from the Levitical priesthood to the priesthood of Jesus Christ after the order of Melchizedek, there is also a necessary change in the law.

Commentary:

- "For the priesthood being changed": This phrase refers to the change from the Levitical priesthood to the priesthood of Jesus Christ. The author argues that this change in priesthood necessitates a change in the law.

- "there is made of necessity a change also of the law": This statement indicates that a change in the priesthood requires a corresponding change in the law. The Mosaic law, which regulated the Levitical priesthood, is now superseded by a new law or covenant associated with the priesthood of Jesus Christ.

Concordance:

- The change in the priesthood from the Levitical priesthood to the priesthood of Jesus Christ is associated with a change in the law, indicating a transition from the old covenant to the new covenant (Hebrews 7:18-19; 8:6-13).

- The new covenant, established through the priesthood of Jesus Christ, is characterized by better promises and a more perfect way of approaching God (Hebrews 8:6; 9:15; 10:19-22).

This verse emphasizes the inseparable connection between the priesthood and the law in the biblical narrative. It asserts that the change in the priesthood necessitates a corresponding change in the law, highlighting the superiority of the priesthood of Jesus Christ and the new covenant over the Levitical priesthood and the old covenant.

Verse 13 (King James Version):

> For he of whom these things are spoken pertaineth to another tribe, of which no man gave attendance at the altar.

Interpretation:
This verse explains that Jesus, of whom these things are spoken regarding his priesthood after the order of Melchizedek, belongs to a different tribe (Judah) than the Levites, who served at the altar under the Levitical priesthood.

Commentary:
- "For he of whom these things are spoken": This refers to Jesus Christ, of whom the author has been speaking regarding his priesthood after the order of Melchizedek.
- "pertaineth to another tribe": Jesus belongs to the tribe of Judah, not the tribe of Levi, from which the Levitical priests were chosen. This is significant because according to the Mosaic law, only those from the tribe of Levi could serve as priests (Numbers 3:6-10).
- "of which no man gave attendance at the altar": This phrase emphasizes that Jesus, being from the tribe of Judah, did not serve at the altar according to the Levitical priesthood regulations. This highlights the unique and different nature of his priesthood compared to the Levitical priesthood.

Concordance:
- Jesus' priesthood after the order of Melchizedek, being from the tribe of Judah, is distinct from the Levitical priesthood, which was limited to those from the tribe of Levi (Hebrews 7:14-15).
- The priesthood of Jesus, being after the order of Melchizedek, is described as an eternal priesthood, surpassing the limitations of the Levitical priesthood (Hebrews 7:16-17).

This verse underscores the uniqueness and superiority of Jesus' priesthood over the Levitical priesthood. Jesus, as a member of the tribe of Judah, is a priest of a different order, not based on genealogy or the Mosaic law, but on the eternal and unchangeable priesthood of Melchizedek.

Verse 14 (King James Version):

> For it is evident that our Lord sprang out of Juda; of which tribe Moses spake nothing concerning priesthood.

Interpretation:

This verse reiterates the point that Jesus, our Lord, came from the tribe of Judah, and Moses did not mention this tribe concerning priesthood in the context of the Levitical priesthood.

Commentary:

- "For it is evident that our Lord sprang out of Juda": This statement emphasizes the genealogical lineage of Jesus, tracing his ancestry to the tribe of Judah, as prophesied in the Old Testament (Genesis 49:10; Isaiah 11:1, 10).

- "of which tribe Moses spake nothing concerning priesthood": This indicates that according to the Mosaic law, the priesthood was designated for the tribe of Levi, and Moses did not mention Judah in this context. This highlights the unique nature of Jesus' priesthood, which is not based on the Levitical priesthood regulations.

Concordance:

- The genealogical lineage of Jesus from the tribe of Judah is significant, as it fulfills Old Testament prophecies regarding the Messiah (Genesis 49:10; Isaiah 11:1, 10; Micah 5:2).

- Jesus' priesthood, being after the order of Melchizedek and not based on the Levitical priesthood regulations, is described as an eternal priesthood (Hebrews 7:15-17).

This verse emphasizes the fulfillment of Old Testament prophecies in Jesus and highlights the unique nature of his priesthood, which is not based on the Mosaic law or genealogical descent from Levi but on the eternal priesthood of Melchizedek.

Verse 15 (King James Version):
> And it is yet far more evident: for that after the similitude of Melchisedec there ariseth another priest,

Interpretation:
This verse emphasizes the clarity and significance of the priesthood of Jesus Christ, stating that another priest arises after the likeness or pattern of Melchizedek.

Commentary:
- "And it is yet far more evident": This phrase indicates that the superiority of Jesus' priesthood over the Levitical priesthood is even more evident or clear.
- "for that after the similitude of Melchisedec there ariseth another priest": This statement reaffirms that Jesus' priesthood is according to the pattern or likeness of Melchizedek, as described in Psalm 110:4. This priesthood is different from the Levitical priesthood, indicating a new and superior order of priesthood.

Concordance:

- The priesthood of Jesus Christ is described as being after the order of Melchizedek, emphasizing its superiority over the Levitical priesthood (Hebrews 7:17).

- The priesthood of Jesus is eternal and unchangeable, unlike the Levitical priesthood, which was temporary and based on genealogy (Hebrews 7:23-24).

This verse underscores the unique and superior nature of Jesus' priesthood, which is based on the eternal and unchangeable priesthood of Melchizedek, in contrast to the temporary and changeable nature of the Levitical priesthood.

Verse 16 (King James Version):
> Who is made, not after the law of a carnal commandment, but after the power of an endless life.

Interpretation:
This verse explains that Jesus' priesthood is not based on the law of a physical or earthly commandment (referring to the Levitical priesthood) but on the power of an indestructible life.

Commentary:
- "Who is made, not after the law of a carnal commandment": This phrase contrasts Jesus' priesthood with the Levitical priesthood, which was established according to the law given through Moses and was focused on physical rituals and regulations.

- "but after the power of an endless life": This highlights the unique nature of Jesus' priesthood, which is based on his resurrection and eternal life. His priesthood is not limited by death but is eternal, providing believers with access to God's presence forever.

Concordance:

- Jesus' priesthood, being based on the power of an endless life, is described as eternal and unchangeable (Hebrews 7:24).
- The priesthood of Jesus provides believers with a better hope and access to God, surpassing the limitations of the Levitical priesthood (Hebrews 7:19, 22; 10:19-22).

This verse emphasizes the superiority of Jesus' priesthood over the Levitical priesthood. Jesus' priesthood is not limited by physical constraints or earthly regulations but is based on his eternal life and resurrection, providing believers with access to God's presence forever.

Verse 17 (King James Version):
> For he testifieth, Thou art a priest for ever after the order of Melchisedec.

Interpretation:
This verse quotes Psalm 110:4, where God declares that the Messiah will be a priest forever according to the order of Melchizedek.

Commentary:
- "For he testifieth": This indicates that God bears witness or testifies to the eternal priesthood of Jesus Christ.
- "Thou art a priest for ever after the order of Melchisedec": This quote from Psalm 110:4 is used by the author of Hebrews to demonstrate the eternal nature of Jesus' priesthood. The order of Melchizedek is characterized by its eternal and unchanging nature, in contrast to the temporary and changeable nature of the Levitical priesthood.

Concordance:

- The eternal nature of Jesus' priesthood after the order of Melchizedek is emphasized throughout the book of Hebrews (Hebrews 5:6, 10; 6:20; 7:21).

- Jesus' priesthood, being eternal, provides believers with a secure and unchanging hope, unlike the temporary priesthood of the Levites (Hebrews 7:19, 23-24).

This verse reinforces the eternal nature of Jesus' priesthood and its superiority over the Levitical priesthood. It highlights the unchanging and secure hope that believers have in Jesus Christ as their eternal High Priest.

Verse 18 (King James Version):
> For there is verily a disannulling of the commandment going before for the weakness and unprofitableness thereof.

Interpretation:
This verse explains that the former commandment (referring to the Mosaic law and the Levitical priesthood) is annulled or set aside because of its weakness and inability to bring about true profit or perfection.

Commentary:
- "For there is verily a disannulling of the commandment going before": This indicates that the Mosaic law and the Levitical priesthood are set aside or annulled in light of the new covenant established through Jesus Christ.
- "for the weakness and unprofitableness thereof": The weakness and unprofitableness of the former commandment refer to its inability to bring about true forgiveness of sins and spiritual transformation. The Levitical sacrifices were insufficient to

permanently cleanse sin and bring people into a right relationship with God.

Concordance:
- The new covenant, established through Jesus Christ, is described as providing a better hope and access to God, surpassing the limitations of the old covenant (Hebrews 7:19, 22; 8:6-7, 13).
- The priesthood of Jesus Christ, being after the order of Melchizedek, is eternal and unchangeable, in contrast to the temporary and changeable nature of the Levitical priesthood (Hebrews 7:21, 24).

This verse emphasizes the superiority of the new covenant and the priesthood of Jesus Christ over the old covenant and the Levitical priesthood. It highlights the inadequacy of the former commandment and the need for a new and better covenant that can truly bring about forgiveness of sins and spiritual transformation.

Verse 19 (King James Version):
> For the law made nothing perfect, but the bringing in of a better hope did; by the which we draw nigh unto God.

Interpretation:
This verse explains that the Mosaic law could not bring about perfection or complete forgiveness of sins, but the introduction of a better hope through Jesus Christ accomplishes this. Through Jesus, believers are able to draw near to God.

Commentary:
- "For the law made nothing perfect": This statement emphasizes the limitations of the Mosaic law in providing complete forgiveness of sins and spiritual transformation.

- "but the bringing in of a better hope did": The better hope refers to the new covenant established through Jesus Christ, which provides complete forgiveness of sins and access to God.

- "by the which we draw nigh unto God": Through Jesus Christ, believers are able to draw near to God in a way that was not possible under the old covenant.

Concordance:

- The new covenant, established through Jesus Christ, is described as providing a better hope and access to God, surpassing the limitations of the old covenant (Hebrews 7:18, 22; 8:6-7, 13).

- Believers are encouraged to draw near to God with full assurance of faith, knowing that Jesus Christ has provided access to God through his sacrifice (Hebrews 10:19-22).

This verse highlights the inadequacy of the Mosaic law in providing complete forgiveness of sins and the need for the new covenant established through Jesus Christ. Through Jesus, believers are able to draw near to God and experience the fullness of forgiveness and relationship with Him.

Verse 20 (King James Version):
> And inasmuch as not without an oath he was made priest:

Interpretation:
This verse emphasizes that Jesus was made a priest with an oath, highlighting the special nature and significance of his priesthood.

Commentary:
- "And inasmuch as not without an oath he was made priest": This phrase underscores the unique and special nature of Jesus' priesthood. Unlike the Levitical priests who were appointed without an

oath, Jesus was appointed as a priest with an oath, emphasizing the certainty and permanence of his priesthood.

Concordance:
- The priesthood of Jesus Christ, being established with an oath, is described as unchangeable and eternal, in contrast to the changeable and temporary nature of the Levitical priesthood (Hebrews 7:21).
- The oath sworn by God regarding the priesthood of Jesus Christ underscores the certainty and reliability of his priesthood (Hebrews 7:21).

This verse highlights the special nature of Jesus' priesthood, which was established with an oath by God, indicating its certainty, permanence, and superiority over the Levitical priesthood.

Verse 21 (King James Version):
> (For those priests were made without an oath; but this with an oath by him that said unto him, The Lord sware and will not repent, Thou art a priest for ever after the order of Melchisedec:)

Interpretation:
This verse contrasts the appointment of the Levitical priests, who were appointed without an oath, with the appointment of Jesus as a priest, which was done with an oath by God.

Commentary:
- "(For those priests were made without an oath)": This refers to the Levitical priests, who were appointed by God to serve in the tabernacle and later the temple but were not appointed with an oath.
- "but this with an oath by him that said unto him": This refers to Jesus, who was appointed as a priest with an oath by God.

- "The Lord sware and will not repent, Thou art a priest for ever after the order of Melchisedec": This is a quotation from Psalm 110:4, where God declares that the Messiah will be a priest forever according to the order of Melchizedek. This oath emphasizes the eternal nature of Jesus' priesthood and its superiority over the Levitical priesthood.

Concordance:

- The priesthood of Jesus Christ, being established with an oath, is described as unchangeable and eternal, in contrast to the changeable and temporary nature of the Levitical priesthood (Hebrews 7:20-21).

- The oath sworn by God regarding the priesthood of Jesus Christ underscores the certainty and reliability of his priesthood (Hebrews 7:21).

This verse reinforces the superiority of Jesus' priesthood over the Levitical priesthood by highlighting the fact that Jesus was appointed as a priest with an oath by God, indicating the certainty and permanence of his priesthood.

Verse 22 (King James Version):
> By so much was Jesus made a surety of a better testament.

Interpretation:
This verse explains that Jesus became the guarantor or surety of a better covenant or testament.

Commentary:
- "By so much was Jesus made a surety": This phrase indicates that Jesus became the guarantor or surety of the new covenant established through his blood.
- "of a better testament": The new covenant established through Jesus Christ is described as better than the old covenant because it

provides complete forgiveness of sins and access to God (Hebrews 7:22; 8:6).

Concordance:
- Jesus is described as the mediator of the new covenant, which is established on better promises than the old covenant (Hebrews 8:6).
- The new covenant provides believers with a better hope and access to God, surpassing the limitations of the old covenant (Hebrews 7:18, 22; 8:6-7, 13).

This verse emphasizes that Jesus, through his sacrifice and priesthood, became the guarantor or surety of the new covenant, which is superior to the old covenant because it provides complete forgiveness of sins and access to God.

Verse 23 (King James Version):
> And they truly were many priests, because they were not suffered to continue by reason of death:

Interpretation:
This verse explains that there were many Levitical priests because they were not able to continue serving as priests due to death.

Commentary:
- "And they truly were many priests": This refers to the Levitical priesthood, which consisted of many priests serving in the tabernacle and later the temple.
- "because they were not suffered to continue by reason of death": This explains why there were many priests. The Levitical priests served for a limited time because they were mortal and subject to death. As a result, there was a constant need for new priests to take their place.

Concordance:

- The Levitical priests served in the tabernacle and later the temple, offering sacrifices for the forgiveness of sins, but their priesthood was limited by death (Hebrews 7:23).

- In contrast, Jesus, as a priest after the order of Melchizedek, has an unchangeable priesthood because he lives forever (Hebrews 7:24).

This verse contrasts the Levitical priesthood, which consisted of many priests who served for a limited time due to death, with the priesthood of Jesus Christ, which is unchangeable and eternal because he lives forever.

Verse 24 (King James Version):

> But this man, because he continueth ever, hath an unchangeable priesthood.

Interpretation:

This verse contrasts the priesthood of Jesus Christ with the Levitical priesthood, highlighting the eternal nature of Jesus' priesthood.

Commentary:

- "But this man, because he continueth ever": This refers to Jesus Christ, whose priesthood is characterized by his eternal existence. Unlike the Levitical priests, who were mortal and subject to death, Jesus continues forever.

- "hath an unchangeable priesthood": Because Jesus continues forever, his priesthood is unchangeable and permanent. He does not need to be replaced by another priest, as was the case with the Levitical priesthood.

Concordance:

- Jesus, as a priest after the order of Melchizedek, has an unchangeable priesthood because he lives forever, unlike the Levitical priests who served for a limited time due to death (Hebrews 7:24).

- The unchangeable priesthood of Jesus Christ is contrasted with the changeable and temporary nature of the Levitical priesthood, highlighting the superiority of Jesus' priesthood (Hebrews 7:23-24).

This verse emphasizes the eternal nature of Jesus' priesthood, which is unchangeable and permanent because he continues forever. This contrasts with the Levitical priesthood, which was temporary and subject to change due to the mortality of the priests.

Verse 25 (King James Version):

> Wherefore he is able also to save them to the uttermost that come unto God by him, seeing he ever liveth to make intercession for them.

Interpretation:

This verse emphasizes that Jesus is able to save completely those who come to God through him because he lives forever to intercede for them.

Commentary:

- "Wherefore he is able also to save them to the uttermost": This indicates that Jesus is able to save completely and perfectly those who come to God through him. His sacrifice is sufficient to cleanse believers from all sin and to secure their eternal salvation.

- "that come unto God by him": Salvation is only possible through Jesus Christ. Those who come to God must do so through faith in Jesus as their mediator and Savior.

- "seeing he ever liveth to make intercession for them": Jesus' eternal priesthood enables him to continually intercede for believers. He is always alive, ensuring that his intercession on behalf of believers is continuous and effective.

Concordance:

- Jesus is the mediator of the new covenant, which provides believers with a better hope and access to God, enabling him to save them completely (Hebrews 7:22; 8:6; 10:19-22).

- The intercession of Jesus Christ on behalf of believers is a central aspect of his priestly ministry, ensuring their salvation and security in him (Hebrews 7:25; 9:24).

This verse highlights the sufficiency of Jesus' sacrifice and the effectiveness of his intercession for believers. Because he lives forever, Jesus is able to save completely those who come to God through him, providing them with access to God and securing their eternal salvation.

Verse 26 (King James Version):
> For such an high priest became us, who is holy, harmless, undefiled, separate from sinners, and made higher than the heavens;

Interpretation:
This verse describes the qualifications of Jesus as a high priest who is suitable for humanity, being holy, innocent, undefiled, separate from sinners, and exalted above the heavens.

Commentary:
- "For such an high priest became us": This phrase suggests that Jesus is the high priest who is fitting and suitable for us as human beings. He meets all the necessary qualifications to represent us before God.

- "who is holy, harmless, undefiled": These characteristics describe the moral purity and perfection of Jesus. He is completely free from sin and moral blemish.

- "separate from sinners": This indicates that Jesus, although he lived among sinners during his earthly ministry, was distinct from them in that he himself was sinless.

- "and made higher than the heavens": This phrase emphasizes the exalted status of Jesus. He has been exalted to the highest place, far above all other created beings and even the heavens themselves.

Concordance:

- Jesus, as a high priest, is described as holy, blameless, pure, set apart from sinners, and exalted above the heavens, making him the perfect mediator between God and humanity (Hebrews 7:26).

- The high priesthood of Jesus Christ is superior to the Levitical priesthood because he is sinless and exalted above all created things (Hebrews 7:26-28).

This verse highlights the unique and perfect qualifications of Jesus as a high priest. He is holy, blameless, pure, separate from sinners, and exalted above the heavens, making him the ideal mediator between God and humanity.

Verse 27 (King James Version):

> Who needeth not daily, as those high priests, to offer up sacrifice, first for his own sins, and then for the people's: for this he did once, when he offered up himself.

Interpretation:

This verse contrasts the Levitical high priests, who had to offer sacrifices daily for their own sins and then for the sins of the people, with Jesus, who offered himself as a sacrifice once for all.

Commentary:

- "Who needeth not daily, as those high priests, to offer up sacrifice": Unlike the Levitical high priests, who had to offer sacrifices daily, Jesus does not need to offer sacrifices repeatedly.

- "first for his own sins, and then for the people's": The Levitical high priests had to first offer sacrifices for their own sins before offering sacrifices for the sins of the people. This highlighted their own sinfulness and the need for ongoing sacrifices.

- "for this he did once, when he offered up himself": Jesus offered himself as a sacrifice once for all, fulfilling the need for sacrifice completely and permanently. His sacrifice was sufficient to atone for all sin for all time.

Concordance:

- Jesus, as a high priest, offered himself as a sacrifice once for all, unlike the Levitical priests who had to offer sacrifices daily for their own sins and then for the sins of the people (Hebrews 7:27; 9:12, 26).

- The sacrifice of Jesus Christ is superior to the sacrifices of the Levitical system because it is able to cleanse believers from all sin and provide eternal redemption (Hebrews 9:12, 14, 26-28).

This verse emphasizes the once-for-all nature of Jesus' sacrifice, contrasting it with the repeated sacrifices of the Levitical system. Jesus, as the perfect high priest, offered himself as a sacrifice once for all, fulfilling the need for sacrifice completely and permanently.

Verse 28 (King James Version):

> For the law maketh men high priests which have infirmity; but the word of the oath, which was since the law, maketh the Son, who is consecrated for evermore.

Interpretation:

This verse contrasts the appointment of high priests under the law, who were imperfect and subject to weakness, with the appointment of Jesus as high priest by the word of God's oath, which establishes him as the eternal and perfect high priest.

Commentary:

- "For the law maketh men high priests which have infirmity": The Levitical priesthood, established by the law, appointed men as high priests who were subject to weaknesses and imperfections. They were sinners who needed to offer sacrifices for their own sins.

- "but the word of the oath, which was since the law": In contrast to the Levitical priesthood, the appointment of Jesus as high priest was not based on the law but on God's oath. This oath, which came after the law, established Jesus as the eternal high priest.

- "maketh the Son, who is consecrated for evermore": The oath of God establishes Jesus, the Son, as the eternal high priest. He is consecrated forever, ensuring his permanent and perfect role as high priest.

Concordance:

- The Levitical priesthood, established by the law, appointed men who were subject to weaknesses and imperfections as high priests. They needed to offer sacrifices for their own sins as well as for the sins of the people (Hebrews 7:28; 5:1-3).

- In contrast, Jesus was appointed as high priest by the word of God's oath, establishing him as the eternal high priest who is sinless and able to save completely those who come to God through him (Hebrews 7:28; 5:5-10).

This verse emphasizes the superiority of Jesus as high priest compared to the Levitical priests. While the Levitical priests were subject to weaknesses and imperfections, Jesus, appointed by the word of God's oath, is the eternal high priest who is sinless and able to save completely.

C H A P T E R   8
The superiority of the New Covenant

Verse 1 (King James Version):
> Now of the things which we have spoken this is the sum: We have such an high priest, who is set on the right hand of the throne of the Majesty in the heavens;

Interpretation:
This verse summarizes the previous discussion, highlighting that believers have a high priest, Jesus Christ, who is seated at the right hand of God's throne in heaven.

Commentary:
- "Now of the things which we have spoken this is the sum": The author is summarizing the main points of the previous discussion, particularly regarding the high priesthood of Jesus Christ.

- "We have such an high priest": Believers have Jesus Christ as their high priest. This emphasizes the personal and accessible nature of Jesus' role as high priest.

- "who is set on the right hand of the throne of the Majesty in the heavens": Jesus is currently seated at the right hand of God's throne in heaven. This position signifies his exaltation and authority.

Concordance:

- Jesus is described as the high priest who is seated at the right hand of God's throne, indicating his exalted position and authority (Hebrews 8:1; 1:3, 13; 10:12; 12:2).

- The high priesthood of Jesus Christ is superior to the Levitical priesthood because it is based on a better covenant and provides believers with better promises (Hebrews 8:6).

This verse emphasizes the exalted position of Jesus Christ as high priest. He is seated at the right hand of God's throne in heaven, indicating his authority and the completion of his redemptive work on behalf of believers.

Verse 2 (King James Version):

> A minister of the sanctuary, and of the true tabernacle, which the Lord pitched, and not man.

Interpretation:

This verse describes Jesus as a minister of the sanctuary and the true tabernacle, which God Himself established, contrasting it with the earthly tabernacle built by human hands.

Commentary:

- "A minister of the sanctuary": Jesus serves as a minister in the sanctuary, fulfilling the role of high priest in the heavenly sanctuary. This highlights his active and ongoing ministry on behalf of believers.

- "and of the true tabernacle": Jesus ministers in the true tabernacle, which is the heavenly counterpart to the earthly tabernacle. The true tabernacle represents the presence of God and the reality of His dwelling among His people.

- "which the Lord pitched, and not man": Unlike the earthly tabernacle, which was constructed by human hands, the true tabernacle was established by the Lord Himself. This emphasizes the heavenly origin and divine nature of the true tabernacle.

Concordance:

- Jesus is described as a minister in the true tabernacle, which is the heavenly sanctuary established by the Lord, contrasting it with the earthly tabernacle constructed by human hands (Hebrews 8:2; 9:11).

- The earthly tabernacle was a copy and shadow of the true tabernacle in heaven, where Jesus now serves as high priest (Hebrews 8:5; 9:24).

This verse highlights the superior nature of Jesus' ministry compared to the Levitical priesthood. Jesus serves as a minister in the true tabernacle, which is the heavenly sanctuary established by God Himself, in contrast to the earthly tabernacle.

Verse 3 (King James Version):

> For every high priest is ordained to offer gifts and sacrifices: wherefore it is of necessity that this man have somewhat also to offer.

Interpretation:

This verse explains the role of a high priest, highlighting the necessity for Jesus, as the high priest, to have something to offer. Unlike the Levitical priests who offered gifts and sacrifices according to the law, Jesus also had to offer something.

Commentary:

- "For every high priest is ordained to offer gifts and sacrifices": The primary function of a high priest is to offer gifts and sacrifices, as prescribed by the law of Moses. This emphasizes the role of the high priest as a mediator between God and the people, making atonement for sin.

- "wherefore it is of necessity that this man have somewhat also to offer": Since Jesus is the high priest, it is necessary for him to have something to offer. This indicates that Jesus, as the high priest, also offered a sacrifice, but unlike the Levitical priests who offered animal sacrifices, Jesus offered himself as the perfect and final sacrifice for sin.

Concordance:

- The high priests under the law were ordained to offer gifts and sacrifices for sins, highlighting their role as mediators between God and the people (Hebrews 8:3; 5:1; 9:9-14).

- Jesus, as the high priest, offered himself as the perfect and final sacrifice for sins, fulfilling the role of the high priest in a superior way (Hebrews 8:3; 9:26-28; 10:10-14).

This verse underscores the unique and superior nature of Jesus' sacrifice compared to the offerings of the Levitical priests. While the Levitical priests offered animal sacrifices repeatedly, Jesus offered himself once for all, providing eternal redemption for believers.

Verse 4 (King James Version):

> For if he were on earth, he should not be a priest, seeing that there are priests that offer gifts according to the law:

Interpretation:
This verse contrasts the priesthood of Jesus with the earthly priesthood under the law of Moses. It explains that if Jesus were on earth, he would not be a priest because there are already priests who offer gifts according to the law.

Commentary:
- "For if he were on earth, he should not be a priest": This statement reflects the limitations of the Levitical priesthood. If Jesus were on earth, he would not be able to serve as a priest according to the Levitical order because the priesthood was restricted to the tribe of Levi and the family of Aaron.
- "seeing that there are priests that offer gifts according to the law": The Levitical priests were responsible for offering gifts and sacrifices according to the requirements of the Mosaic law. Their role was to mediate between God and the people through these offerings.

Concordance:
- The Levitical priesthood was limited to those who were descendants of Aaron and served in the earthly tabernacle, offering gifts according to the law (Hebrews 8:4; 7:11; 9:6-9).
- Jesus, as the high priest, serves in the true tabernacle in heaven, offering himself as the perfect sacrifice for sins (Hebrews 8:1-2; 9:11-14).

This verse emphasizes the unique and superior nature of Jesus' priesthood. Unlike the Levitical priests who served on earth and offered gifts according to the law, Jesus serves as a high priest in the heavenly tabernacle, offering himself as the perfect and final sacrifice for sins.

Verse 5 (King James Version):
> Who serve unto the example and shadow of heavenly things, as Moses was admonished of God when he was about to make the tabernacle: for, See, saith he, that thou make all things according to the pattern shewed to thee in the mount.

Interpretation:
This verse explains that the earthly tabernacle and the Levitical priesthood served as a copy and shadow of heavenly realities. When Moses was instructed by God to build the tabernacle, he was told to make everything according to the pattern shown to him on Mount Sinai.

Commentary:
- "Who serve unto the example and shadow of heavenly things": The earthly tabernacle and the Levitical priesthood were a representation and shadow of heavenly realities. They served as a visual and symbolic representation of spiritual truths, pointing forward to the ministry of Christ.
- "as Moses was admonished of God when he was about to make the tabernacle": This refers to God's instructions to Moses regarding the construction of the tabernacle. Moses was specifically instructed to make everything according to the pattern that was revealed to him on Mount Sinai.
- "for, See, saith he, that thou make all things according to the pattern shewed to thee in the mount": God instructed Moses to ensure that everything in the tabernacle was made according to the pattern that was revealed to him. This emphasizes the divine origin and significance of the tabernacle as a representation of heavenly realities.

Concordance:

- The earthly tabernacle and the Levitical priesthood were a shadow and copy of the heavenly realities, serving as a foreshadowing of the ministry of Christ (Hebrews 8:5; 9:23-24; 10:1).

- God instructed Moses to make the tabernacle and its furnishings according to the pattern that was shown to him on Mount Sinai, highlighting the divine origin and design of the tabernacle (Hebrews 8:5; Exodus 25:40).

This verse underscores the symbolic nature of the tabernacle and the Levitical priesthood, which foreshadowed the ministry of Christ. Just as the earthly tabernacle was a copy and shadow of heavenly realities, so too is the ministry of Christ the fulfillment and reality of what was prefigured in the Old Testament.

Verse 6 (King James Version):

> But now hath he obtained a more excellent ministry, by how much also he is the mediator of a better covenant, which was established upon better promises.

Interpretation:

This verse contrasts the ministry of Jesus with that of the Levitical priests. It highlights that Jesus has obtained a more excellent ministry because he is the mediator of a better covenant, which is established on better promises.

Commentary:

- "But now hath he obtained a more excellent ministry": This phrase emphasizes the superiority of Jesus' ministry compared to the ministry of the Levitical priests. Jesus' ministry is more excellent because it is based on his role as the mediator of a better covenant.

- "by how much also he is the mediator of a better covenant": Jesus serves as the mediator of a better covenant, which refers to the new covenant that he established through his death and resurrection. This new covenant is superior to the old covenant because it is based on better promises and is founded on the perfect sacrifice of Christ.

- "which was established upon better promises": The new covenant is established on better promises than the old covenant. These promises include forgiveness of sins, the indwelling of the Holy Spirit, and eternal life, all of which are made possible through the work of Christ.

Concordance:

- Jesus has obtained a more excellent ministry as the mediator of a better covenant, which is established on better promises (Hebrews 8:6; 9:15; 12:24).

- The new covenant, established by the blood of Christ, provides better promises than the old covenant, including forgiveness of sins and the gift of the Holy Spirit (Hebrews 8:6; 9:11-15).

This verse highlights the superiority of Jesus' ministry and the new covenant he established. Unlike the ministry of the Levitical priests, which was based on the old covenant and the offering of animal sacrifices, Jesus' ministry is based on the new covenant and his perfect sacrifice, which provides believers with better promises and a closer relationship with God.

Verse 7 (King James Version):

> For if that first covenant had been faultless, then should no place have been sought for the second.

Interpretation:

This verse suggests that if the first covenant (referring to the Mosaic covenant) had been faultless, there would have been no need or reason to seek a second covenant (referring to the new covenant established by Jesus).

Commentary:

- "For if that first covenant had been faultless": This statement does not imply that the Mosaic covenant was inherently flawed or imperfect, but rather that it was limited in its ability to bring about complete forgiveness of sins and transformation of the heart. The Mosaic covenant served as a preparation and foreshadowing of the new covenant in Christ.

- "then should no place have been sought for the second": This phrase indicates that the establishment of a new covenant implies a recognition of the limitations of the old covenant. The new covenant, established by Jesus, provides what the old covenant could not— complete forgiveness of sins and a new heart through the indwelling of the Holy Spirit.

Concordance:

- The new covenant, established by Jesus, is superior to the old covenant because it provides complete forgiveness of sins and a new heart through the indwelling of the Holy Spirit (Hebrews 8:7-13; 9:15).

- The old covenant, though holy and just, was unable to provide complete forgiveness of sins and transformation of the heart, leading to the establishment of a new and better covenant in Christ (Hebrews 8:7-13; 10:1-18).

This verse underscores the need for a new covenant that is based on better promises and provides what the old covenant could not. The new covenant, established by Jesus, is faultless and complete, offering believers forgiveness of sins and a new heart through the work of Christ.

Verse 8 (King James Version):
> For finding fault with them, he saith, Behold, the days come, saith the Lord, when I will make a new covenant with the house of Israel and with the house of Judah:

Interpretation:
This verse explains that God found fault with the people under the old covenant, not with the covenant itself. As a result, God prophesied through the prophet Jeremiah about the coming of a new covenant with the house of Israel and the house of Judah.

Commentary:
- "For finding fault with them": This phrase indicates that the fault lay with the people of Israel, who were unable to keep the requirements of the old covenant due to their sinfulness (Hebrews 8:7). The old covenant exposed their need for a new and better covenant.
- "he saith, Behold, the days come, saith the Lord, when I will make a new covenant with the house of Israel and with the house of Judah": This quotation is from Jeremiah 31:31-34, where the prophet Jeremiah prophesied about the coming of a new covenant that would replace the old covenant. This new covenant would not be like the old covenant, which the people broke, but would be one in which God would write His laws on their hearts, forgive their sins, and remember them no more.

Concordance:
- God prophesied through Jeremiah about the coming of a new covenant that would replace the old covenant and be based on better promises (Hebrews 8:8-13; Jeremiah 31:31-34).

- The new covenant, established by Jesus, is based on better promises than the old covenant, including forgiveness of sins and a new heart through the indwelling of the Holy Spirit (Hebrews 8:8-13; 9:15).

This verse emphasizes the need for a new covenant because of the failure of the people to keep the old covenant. The new covenant, prophesied by Jeremiah and fulfilled in Christ, addresses the shortcomings of the old covenant by providing forgiveness of sins and a new heart through the work of Christ.

Verse 9 (King James Version):
> Not according to the covenant that I made with their fathers in the day when I took them by the hand to lead them out of the land of Egypt; because they continued not in my covenant, and I regarded them not, saith the Lord.

Interpretation:
In this verse, the author of Hebrews quotes from Jeremiah 31:32, emphasizing that the new covenant would not be like the old covenant made at Sinai, which the people of Israel broke by not continuing in it. God's promise for a new covenant is based on His grace and the need for a deeper relationship with His people.

Commentary:
- "Not according to the covenant that I made with their fathers": This refers to the Mosaic covenant, the covenant made with the people of Israel at Mount Sinai, which the author contrasts with the new covenant promised by God through Jeremiah.
- "because they continued not in my covenant, and I regarded them not": The failure of the people to continue in the covenant made at Sinai resulted in God withdrawing His favor from them. This

highlights the need for a new covenant that would enable a more intimate and lasting relationship between God and His people.

Concordance:
- The new covenant is not like the old covenant made at Sinai, which the people of Israel broke, but is based on better promises (Hebrews 8:9-13; Jeremiah 31:31-34).
- The old covenant, though holy and just, was unable to provide complete forgiveness of sins and transformation of the heart, leading to the establishment of a new and better covenant in Christ (Hebrews 8:7-13; 10:1-18).

This verse emphasizes the need for a new covenant because of the failure of the people to keep the old covenant. The new covenant, promised by God and fulfilled in Christ, provides forgiveness of sins and a deeper, more intimate relationship with God.

Verse 10 (King James Version):
> For this is the covenant that I will make with the house of Israel after those days, saith the Lord; I will put my laws into their mind, and write them in their hearts: and I will be to them a God, and they shall be to me a people.

Interpretation:
In this verse, the author quotes from Jeremiah 31:33 to describe the nature of the new covenant. God promises to write His laws on the minds and hearts of His people, indicating a deep, personal relationship where His laws are internalized and followed willingly.

Commentary:
- "For this is the covenant that I will make with the house of Israel after those days": This indicates that the new covenant is distinct

from the old covenant and will be established in the future, emphasizing its prophetic nature.

- "I will put my laws into their mind, and write them in their hearts": This metaphorical language signifies that under the new covenant, God's laws will be internalized and obeyed from the heart, indicating a transformation of character and a genuine desire to follow God.

- "and I will be to them a God, and they shall be to me a people": This reaffirms the covenantal relationship between God and His people, indicating a close, intimate bond where God is their God and they are His people.

Concordance:
- The new covenant, promised by God and fulfilled in Christ, involves God writing His laws on the minds and hearts of His people, indicating a deep, personal relationship (Hebrews 8:10-13; Jeremiah 31:31-34).

- The new covenant is based on better promises than the old covenant, including forgiveness of sins and a new heart through the work of Christ (Hebrews 8:8-13; 9:15).

This verse highlights the relational aspect of the new covenant, where God's laws are not merely external rules but are written on the hearts of His people. It emphasizes the transformational nature of the new covenant, where God's people are characterized by an internalized obedience born out of a genuine relationship with Him.

Verse 11 (King James Version):
> And they shall not teach every man his neighbour, and every man his brother, saying, Know the Lord: for all shall know me, from the least to the greatest.

166

Interpretation:

This verse, also from Jeremiah 31:34, speaks of a future state under the new covenant where there will be a universal knowledge of God among His people. This knowledge will be personal and direct, removing the need for intermediaries to teach others about God.

Commentary:

- "And they shall not teach every man his neighbour... Know the Lord": This does not mean that teaching and learning about God will cease, but rather that there will be a direct and personal knowledge of God that transcends mere instruction. This knowledge will be so profound that it will not require external teaching to deepen or reinforce it.

- "for all shall know me, from the least to the greatest": This knowledge of God will be universal among God's people, from the least to the greatest, indicating that it will be comprehensive and inclusive of all.

Concordance:

- Under the new covenant, there will be a universal knowledge of God among His people, removing the need for external teaching to know Him (Hebrews 8:11-13; Jeremiah 31:31-34).

- The new covenant is characterized by a direct and personal knowledge of God, available to all believers, which is a fulfillment of prophecy (Hebrews 8:11-13; Jeremiah 31:31-34).

This verse underscores the intimacy and accessibility of the new covenant, where all believers will have a personal and direct knowledge of God. It points to a future reality where the relationship between God and His people will be so profound that external teaching about God will no longer be necessary.

Verse 12 (King James Version):

> For I will be merciful to their unrighteousness, and their sins and their iniquities will I remember no more.

Interpretation:

This verse emphasizes the aspect of forgiveness and mercy in the new covenant. God promises to forgive the sins and unrighteousness of His people and to remember their sins no more. This highlights the complete and final nature of God's forgiveness under the new covenant.

Commentary:

- "For I will be merciful to their unrighteousness": This indicates God's gracious attitude towards the sins and failures of His people. His mercy extends to their unrighteousness, offering forgiveness and reconciliation.

- "and their sins and their iniquities will I remember no more": This statement emphasizes the complete forgiveness and forgetfulness of sins under the new covenant. God chooses not to hold their sins against them, demonstrating His mercy and grace.

Concordance:

- The new covenant is characterized by God's forgiveness and mercy towards His people, with their sins and iniquities being remembered no more (Hebrews 8:12; Jeremiah 31:31-34).

- The forgiveness of sins under the new covenant is based on the sacrifice of Christ, who offered Himself once for all to secure eternal redemption (Hebrews 9:11-14, 26-28; 10:10-18).

This verse highlights the central theme of forgiveness in the new covenant, showing God's gracious disposition towards His people's sins. It emphasizes the completeness and finality of God's forgiveness, offering hope and assurance to believers.

Verse 13 (King James Version):
> In that he saith, A new covenant, he hath made the first old. Now that which decayeth and waxeth old is ready to vanish away.

Interpretation:
This verse reflects on the transition from the old covenant to the new covenant. It signifies that with the establishment of the new covenant, the old covenant has become obsolete. The old covenant, characterized by its temporary and fading nature, is now ready to vanish away, giving way to the permanence and efficacy of the new covenant.

Commentary:
- "A new covenant, he hath made the first old": This statement indicates that the establishment of the new covenant renders the old covenant obsolete. The new covenant inaugurated by Christ supersedes and replaces the old covenant, which was given through Moses.

- "Now that which decayeth and waxeth old is ready to vanish away": This refers to the temporary and fading nature of the old covenant. It is likened to something that is decaying and growing old, implying that its time is coming to an end. The phrase "ready to vanish away" suggests that the old covenant is in the process of disappearing, being replaced by the new covenant.

Concordance:

- The establishment of the new covenant signifies the obsolescence of the old covenant, which is characterized by its temporary and fading nature (Hebrews 8:13; Jeremiah 31:31-34).

- The new covenant is described as superior to the old covenant, offering better promises and based on better sacrifices (Hebrews 8:6-7; 9:11-15; 10:1-18).

This verse underscores the superiority and permanence of the new covenant established through Christ. It highlights the transition from the old covenant, which was temporary and imperfect, to the new covenant, which is permanent and complete in Christ.

C H A P T E R 9

Temporary sacrifices by Levites

Verse 1 (King James Version):
> Then verily the first covenant had also ordinances of divine service, and a worldly sanctuary.

Interpretation:
This verse introduces the discussion of the old covenant's system of worship, which included regulations for divine service and a physical sanctuary on earth.

Commentary:
- "Then verily the first covenant had also ordinances of divine service": This refers to the regulations and practices associated with the

worship under the old covenant. It included rituals, sacrifices, and ceremonies that were part of the religious service prescribed by God.

- "and a worldly sanctuary": The old covenant worship was centered around a physical sanctuary, namely the tabernacle (later replaced by the temple in Jerusalem). This sanctuary was considered worldly or earthly in contrast to the heavenly reality it symbolized.

Concordance:
- The old covenant included regulations for divine service and a physical sanctuary (Hebrews 9:1; Exodus 25-40; Leviticus).
- The earthly sanctuary and its services were a shadow of the heavenly realities revealed in Christ under the new covenant (Hebrews 8:5; 9:11-12, 23-24; 10:1).

This verse sets the stage for the comparison between the old and new covenants, highlighting the external and earthly nature of the old covenant worship as opposed to the spiritual and heavenly realities of the new covenant.

Verse 2 (King James Version):
> For there was a tabernacle made; the first, wherein was the candlestick, and the table, and the shewbread; which is called the sanctuary.

Interpretation:
This verse describes the layout and contents of the first part of the tabernacle, known as the Holy Place, which contained the candlestick (or lampstand), the table for the showbread, and other items used in the worship rituals.

Commentary:

- "For there was a tabernacle made": This refers to the portable tent-like structure constructed by the Israelites in the wilderness according to God's instructions (Exodus 25-27). It served as a place of worship and a symbol of God's presence among His people.

- "the first, wherein was the candlestick, and the table, and the shewbread": This describes the contents of the Holy Place, the first section of the tabernacle. The candlestick (or lampstand) provided light, the table held the showbread (or bread of the Presence), which was replaced weekly and symbolized God's provision and the fellowship of His people with Him.

- "which is called the sanctuary": The Holy Place is referred to as the sanctuary, emphasizing its sacredness and the presence of God among His people.

Concordance:
- The tabernacle consisted of two main parts: the Holy Place and the Most Holy Place (Hebrews 9:2-5; Exodus 26-27).
- The tabernacle and its furnishings were symbolic of heavenly realities and served as a foreshadowing of Christ's redemptive work (Hebrews 8:5; 9:8-12, 23-24).

This verse highlights the physical aspects of the tabernacle and its furnishings, which served as symbols and types pointing to spiritual truths and the redemptive work of Christ under the new covenant.

Verse 3 (King James Version):
> And after the second veil, the tabernacle which is called the Holiest of all;

Interpretation:

This verse describes the innermost part of the tabernacle, called the Most Holy Place or the Holy of Holies, which was separated from the Holy Place by a veil.

Commentary:
- "And after the second veil": This refers to the veil that separated the Holy Place from the Most Holy Place (Exodus 26:31-33). The presence of a second veil indicates the significance and sacredness of the Most Holy Place.
- "the tabernacle which is called the Holiest of all": This is a reference to the Most Holy Place, which housed the ark of the covenant and the mercy seat. It was considered the most sacred part of the tabernacle, representing the presence of God among His people.

Concordance:
- The Most Holy Place was accessed only once a year by the high priest on the Day of Atonement (Hebrews 9:3; Leviticus 16).
- The veil separating the Holy Place from the Most Holy Place was torn in two at the moment of Jesus' death, symbolizing the opening of access to God through Christ's sacrifice (Matthew 27:51; Hebrews 10:19-20).

This verse emphasizes the sacredness and separation of the Most Holy Place within the tabernacle, highlighting the need for mediation and atonement for sin, which would ultimately be fulfilled in Christ under the new covenant.

Verse 4 (King James Version):
> Which had the golden censer, and the ark of the covenant overlaid round about with gold, wherein was the golden pot that had manna, and Aaron's rod that budded, and the tables of the covenant;

Interpretation:

This verse describes the contents of the Most Holy Place, including the golden censer, the ark of the covenant, and the items contained within the ark.

Commentary:

- "Which had the golden censer": The golden censer was used by the high priest to offer incense before the mercy seat in the Most Holy Place (Leviticus 16:12-13). It symbolized the prayers of the people ascending to God.

- "and the ark of the covenant overlaid round about with gold": The ark of the covenant was a sacred chest made of acacia wood and overlaid with gold, containing the tablets of the Ten Commandments (Exodus 25:10-22). It symbolized God's presence and covenant with His people.

- "wherein was the golden pot that had manna": The golden pot containing manna, the bread-like substance provided by God to the Israelites in the wilderness, was placed inside the ark as a reminder of God's provision (Exodus 16:32-34).

- "and Aaron's rod that budded": Aaron's rod, which miraculously budded as a sign of his God-given authority as high priest (Numbers 17:8), was also kept inside the ark.

- "and the tables of the covenant": The tablets of the covenant, containing the Ten Commandments given to Moses on Mount Sinai, were placed inside the ark as a symbol of God's law and covenant with His people.

Concordance:

- The items inside the ark symbolized God's provision (manna), His authority (Aaron's rod), and His law (tables of the covenant).

- The ark of the covenant and its contents were considered the most sacred objects in Israelite worship, representing God's presence among His people (Hebrews 9:4; Exodus 25:22).

This verse highlights the significance of the items within the Most Holy Place, emphasizing their symbolic importance in Israelite worship and their foreshadowing of Christ's redemptive work under the new covenant.

Verse 5 (King James Version):
> And over it the cherubims of glory shadowing the mercyseat; of which we cannot now speak particularly.

Interpretation:
This verse mentions the cherubim that overshadowed the mercy seat on the ark of the covenant in the Most Holy Place.

Commentary:
- "And over it the cherubims of glory shadowing the mercyseat": The mercy seat was the lid of the ark of the covenant, and it symbolized the place where God's presence dwelt among His people. The cherubim, angelic beings, were placed on either side of the mercy seat, their wings overshadowing it. This imagery symbolizes the heavenly realm and God's throne.
- "of which we cannot now speak particularly": The author of Hebrews indicates that there are more details about these things that could be discussed, but he chooses not to elaborate at this moment, likely due to the focus of his message.

Concordance:

- The cherubim and the mercy seat were considered the earthly throne of God, representing His presence and authority among His people (Hebrews 9:5; Exodus 25:17-22).

- The mercy seat was where the high priest would sprinkle blood on the Day of Atonement, symbolizing the covering of sins and reconciliation with God (Leviticus 16:14-15; Hebrews 9:7).

This verse underscores the sacredness of the Most Holy Place and the symbolism of the mercy seat and the cherubim, highlighting their role in Israelite worship and their significance in pointing to the redemptive work of Christ under the new covenant.

Verse 6 (King James Version):
> Now when these things were thus ordained, the priests went always into the first tabernacle, accomplishing the service of God.

Interpretation:
This verse describes the regular duties of the priests in the first tabernacle (the Holy Place) in contrast to the Most Holy Place.

Commentary:
- "Now when these things were thus ordained": Refers to the arrangements and regulations concerning the tabernacle and its services as prescribed by God (Exodus 25-31).

- "the priests went always into the first tabernacle": The priests regularly entered the first tabernacle, or the Holy Place, to perform their duties. This area contained the lampstand, the table of showbread, and the altar of incense (Exodus 30:1-10).

- "accomplishing the service of God": The priests' duties included tending to the lampstand, replacing the showbread, burning incense on the altar, and offering daily sacrifices (Exodus 30:7-8; Leviticus 24:5-9).

Concordance:

- The regular service of the priests in the Holy Place symbolized the ongoing need for atonement and the imperfect nature of the Old Covenant sacrifices (Hebrews 9:6; Hebrews 10:1-4).

- The duties of the priests in the Holy Place prefigured Christ's priestly ministry in the heavenly tabernacle, offering Himself as the perfect sacrifice for sin (Hebrews 9:11-14; Hebrews 10:11-14).

This verse highlights the continuous nature of the priestly service in the tabernacle, underscoring the temporal and provisional nature of the Old Covenant system, which required repeated sacrifices and offerings for sins.

Verse 7 (King James Version):

> But into the second went the high priest alone once every year, not without blood, which he offered for himself, and for the errors of the people:

Interpretation:

This verse describes the high priest's annual entry into the Most Holy Place (the second part of the tabernacle) on the Day of Atonement to offer sacrifices for his sins and the sins of the people.

Commentary:

- "But into the second went the high priest alone once every year": The high priest entered the Most Holy Place alone, symbolizing his role as the mediator between God and the people, and he did this once a year on the Day of Atonement (Leviticus 16:1-34).

- "not without blood": The high priest entered with blood from the sacrificial animals, symbolizing the need for atonement for sins.

This blood was sprinkled on the mercy seat to make atonement for himself and for the sins of the people (Leviticus 16:14-15).

- "which he offered for himself, and for the errors of the people": The high priest offered sacrifices first for his own sins and then for the sins of the people, acknowledging the need for purification and forgiveness.

Concordance:
- The high priest's entry into the Most Holy Place and his offering of blood for atonement foreshadowed Christ's once-for-all sacrifice for sin (Hebrews 9:7; Hebrews 9:11-14; Hebrews 10:10-14).
- The Day of Atonement ritual highlighted the need for cleansing from sin and the temporary nature of the Old Covenant sacrifices, pointing forward to the perfect sacrifice of Christ (Hebrews 9:9-10; Hebrews 9:24-28).

This verse underscores the limitations of the Old Covenant system, which required repeated sacrifices and offerings for sin, and it points to the superior and ultimate sacrifice of Christ under the new covenant.

Verse 8 (King James Version):
> The Holy Ghost this signifying, that the way into the holiest of all was not yet made manifest, while as the first tabernacle was yet standing:

Interpretation:
This verse explains that the Holy Spirit was indicating that the way into the Most Holy Place (the holiest of all) was not yet revealed while the tabernacle system was still in place.

Commentary:

- "The Holy Ghost this signifying": The author is indicating that the Holy Spirit was teaching or revealing something significant through the tabernacle system and its rituals.

- "that the way into the holiest of all was not yet made manifest": The way into the Most Holy Place, symbolizing access to God's presence, was not yet fully revealed or accessible under the Old Covenant system. Access was limited to the high priest, and even then, it was only once a year on the Day of Atonement.

- "while as the first tabernacle was yet standing": This limitation persisted as long as the tabernacle (or temple) system was in place, emphasizing its temporary and incomplete nature.

Concordance:
- The tabernacle system, with its restricted access to the Most Holy Place, symbolized the incomplete and temporary nature of the Old Covenant (Hebrews 9:8).

- Christ's sacrificial death and resurrection opened the way for believers to enter boldly into God's presence through Him (Hebrews 10:19-22).

This verse underscores the limitations of the Old Covenant system in providing full access to God's presence and highlights the need for a new and better covenant, which Christ inaugurated through His sacrificial death.

Verse 9 (King James Version):
> Which was a figure for the time then present, in which were offered both gifts and sacrifices, that could not make him that did the service perfect, as pertaining to the conscience;

Interpretation:

This verse explains that the tabernacle and its rituals were symbolic of the present time and were insufficient to cleanse the worshipers' consciences from sin.

Commentary:

- "Which was a figure for the time then present": The tabernacle system, with its gifts and sacrifices, served as a symbol or a representation of the present time under the Old Covenant.

- "in which were offered both gifts and sacrifices": The tabernacle rituals included various offerings and sacrifices prescribed by the Mosaic law, such as burnt offerings, sin offerings, and peace offerings.

- "that could not make him that did the service perfect": These offerings and sacrifices could not fully cleanse or perfect the worshipers. They provided temporary purification but did not address the root issue of sin or bring about complete reconciliation with God.

- "as pertaining to the conscience": The inability of these offerings to perfect the worshipers was particularly evident in their inability to cleanse the conscience from the guilt and defilement of sin.

Concordance:

- The sacrifices and offerings of the Old Covenant were temporary and symbolic, unable to cleanse the worshipers' consciences or provide lasting forgiveness (Hebrews 9:9).

- Christ's sacrifice, on the other hand, is described as offering eternal redemption and cleansing the conscience from dead works to serve the living God (Hebrews 9:14).

This verse emphasizes the inadequacy of the Old Covenant sacrifices to fully cleanse the worshipers' consciences and points to the need for a more effective sacrifice, which Christ accomplished through His death on the cross.

Verse 10 (King James Version):
> Which stood only in meats and drinks, and divers washings, and carnal ordinances, imposed on them until the time of reformation.

Interpretation:
This verse explains that the rituals of the tabernacle, including dietary restrictions, drink offerings, various washings, and other physical regulations, were imposed on the Israelites until the time of a new order or reformation.

Commentary:
- "Which stood only in meats and drinks, and divers washings, and carnal ordinances": The rituals of the tabernacle were centered around physical regulations related to food, drink, washings, and other external observances. These practices were symbolic and did not provide ultimate spiritual purification.
- "imposed on them until the time of reformation": These regulations were temporary and were imposed on the Israelites until a time of reformation or change. This "time of reformation" refers to the coming of Christ and the establishment of the New Covenant, which would bring about a change in the way people would relate to God.

Concordance:
- The Old Covenant rituals, including dietary laws and various washings, were temporary and symbolic, pointing forward to the time of Christ's redemptive work (Hebrews 9:10).
- Christ's sacrifice inaugurated a new covenant, replacing the temporary and symbolic practices of the Old Covenant with a more perfect and eternal redemption (Hebrews 9:11-12).

This verse highlights the temporary nature of the Old Covenant rituals and their role as symbolic foreshadowing of the greater redemption and spiritual transformation brought about by Christ under the New Covenant.

Verse 11 (King James Version):
> But Christ being come an high priest of good things to come, by a greater and more perfect tabernacle, not made with hands, that is to say, not of this building;

Interpretation:
This verse introduces Christ as the High Priest of the good things that were to come. He ministers in a greater and more perfect tabernacle, not made with human hands, which signifies a spiritual, heavenly realm rather than a physical structure.

Commentary:
- "But Christ being come an high priest of good things to come": Jesus is portrayed as the High Priest who has already come, contrasting with the temporary priests of the Old Covenant. He brings the good things that were promised and fulfilled in Him.
- "by a greater and more perfect tabernacle, not made with hands": This refers to the heavenly tabernacle or sanctuary where Christ now serves as High Priest. It is superior to the earthly tabernacle because it is not a man-made structure but one that is eternal and spiritual in nature.
- "that is to say, not of this building": The earthly tabernacle was a physical building, but the tabernacle in which Christ serves is not of this world. It is a heavenly realm, indicating the superior nature of Christ's priesthood and ministry.

Concordance:

- Christ is the High Priest of the good things to come, serving in a greater and more perfect tabernacle, not made with hands (Hebrews 9:11).

- Through His own blood, Christ entered the heavenly sanctuary once for all, obtaining eternal redemption (Hebrews 9:12).

This verse emphasizes the superiority of Christ's priesthood and ministry over the Old Covenant system, highlighting His role as the mediator of the New Covenant and the bringer of eternal redemption.

Verse 12 (King James Version):
> Neither by the blood of goats and calves, but by his own blood he entered in once into the holy place, having obtained eternal redemption for us.

Interpretation:
This verse contrasts the Old Testament sacrificial system, which used the blood of goats and calves for atonement, with the sacrifice of Jesus Christ. Jesus entered the heavenly sanctuary, not with the blood of animals, but with His own blood, securing eternal redemption for humanity.

Commentary:
- "Neither by the blood of goats and calves": The Old Testament sacrificial system required the blood of animals, particularly goats and calves, for the atonement of sins. However, these sacrifices were temporary and could not provide ultimate redemption.
- "but by his own blood he entered in once into the holy place": Jesus, as the High Priest, offered His own blood as a once-for-all sacrifice for sin. He entered the heavenly sanctuary, not a physical one like the earthly tabernacle, to make atonement for humanity's sins.

- "having obtained eternal redemption for us": Through His sacrifice, Jesus obtained eternal redemption for all who believe in Him. This redemption is not temporary or partial but complete and everlasting, securing salvation for believers.

Concordance:
- Christ entered the holy place once for all, not with the blood of goats and calves, but with His own blood, obtaining eternal redemption for us (Hebrews 9:12).
- The blood of Christ, who through the eternal Spirit offered Himself without spot to God, cleanses our conscience from dead works to serve the living God (Hebrews 9:14).

This verse underscores the uniqueness and efficacy of Christ's sacrifice, which provides eternal redemption and cleanses believers from sin. His sacrifice is contrasted with the temporary and inadequate sacrifices of the Old Covenant, highlighting the superiority of the New Covenant in Christ.

Verse 13 (King James Version):
> For if the blood of bulls and of goats, and the ashes of an heifer sprinkling the unclean, sanctifieth to the purifying of the flesh:

Interpretation:
This verse refers to the ritual purification practices of the Old Testament, where the blood of animals, such as bulls and goats, and the ashes of a heifer were used to cleanse the people ceremonially. However, these rituals only purified the flesh and were insufficient for true spiritual cleansing.

Commentary:

- "For if the blood of bulls and of goats": The author is drawing a comparison between the Old Testament sacrificial system, which used the blood of animals, and the sacrifice of Christ. The blood of animals could not provide true forgiveness of sins but served as a temporary covering.

- "and the ashes of an heifer sprinkling the unclean": This refers to the purification ritual described in Numbers 19, where the ashes of a red heifer were mixed with water and used to cleanse those who had become ceremonially unclean.

- "sanctifieth to the purifying of the flesh": These rituals were effective in purifying the flesh ceremonially, making people outwardly clean in a ritualistic sense. However, they did not address the deeper issue of sin and the need for true spiritual cleansing.

Concordance:

- The blood of bulls and goats, and the ashes of a heifer sprinkling the unclean, sanctified for the purifying of the flesh (Hebrews 9:13).

- How much more shall the blood of Christ, who through the eternal Spirit offered Himself without spot to God, cleanse your conscience from dead works to serve the living God (Hebrews 9:14).

This verse emphasizes the limitations of the Old Testament sacrificial system in providing true spiritual purification. It sets the stage for the superiority of Christ's sacrifice, which cleanses believers not just outwardly but inwardly, purifying their conscience and enabling them to serve the living God.

Verse 14 (King James Version):

> How much more shall the blood of Christ, who through the eternal Spirit offered himself without spot to God, purge your conscience from dead works to serve the living God?

Interpretation:

This verse contrasts the efficacy of the blood of Christ with the limitations of the Old Testament sacrificial system. It emphasizes that Christ's sacrifice is far superior, as it cleanses not just the outward appearance but also the conscience of believers, enabling them to serve God in a new way.

Commentary:

- "How much more shall the blood of Christ": This phrase highlights the superiority of Christ's sacrifice over the blood of animals. If the blood of animals could sanctify for the purifying of the flesh (verse 13), then the blood of Christ, being infinitely more precious, can cleanse even more effectively.

- "who through the eternal Spirit offered himself without spot to God": This refers to the fact that Jesus, by the power of the eternal Spirit, offered Himself as a sacrifice without any blemish or sin. This perfect sacrifice is what makes His blood so efficacious.

- "purge your conscience from dead works": The blood of Christ is not only effective in purifying outwardly but also in cleansing the conscience of believers from dead works. This means that through Christ's sacrifice, believers are freed from the guilt and condemnation of their sins, enabling them to serve God with a clear conscience.

- "to serve the living God": The ultimate purpose of this purification is to enable believers to serve the living God. Unlike the dead works of the Old Testament rituals, which could not bring life, the sacrifice of Christ brings spiritual life and empowers believers to serve God in a new and living way.

Concordance:

- How much more shall the blood of Christ, who through the eternal Spirit offered Himself without spot to God, cleanse your conscience from dead works to serve the living God (Hebrews 9:14).

- And for this reason He is the Mediator of the new covenant, by means of death, for the redemption of the transgressions under the first covenant, that those who are called may receive the promise of the eternal inheritance (Hebrews 9:15).

This verse underscores the transformative power of Christ's sacrifice, which not only cleanses believers from sin but also empowers them to serve God in a way that was not possible under the old covenant. It highlights the central role of Christ as the Mediator of the new covenant, through whom believers receive the promise of eternal inheritance.

Verse 15 (King James Version):

> And for this cause he is the mediator of the new testament, that by means of death, for the redemption of the transgressions that were under the first testament, they which are called might receive the promise of eternal inheritance.

Interpretation:

This verse explains the purpose of Jesus Christ as the mediator of the new covenant. He died to redeem people from the sins committed under the old covenant and to enable those who are called to receive the promise of eternal inheritance.

Commentary:

- "And for this cause he is the mediator of the new testament": Jesus Christ serves as the mediator of the new covenant between God and humanity. His role is to reconcile sinners to God and to bring about a new relationship between God and His people.

- "that by means of death": The means by which Jesus accomplished this mediation was through His death on the cross. His sacrificial death was necessary to atone for the sins of humanity and to fulfill the requirements of the law.

- "for the redemption of the transgressions that were under the first testament": Jesus' death not only covers the sins committed under the new covenant but also those committed under the old covenant. It is through His sacrifice that people are redeemed from the guilt and penalty of their sins.

- "they which are called might receive the promise of eternal inheritance": The ultimate goal of Jesus' mediation is that those who respond to God's call might receive the promise of eternal inheritance. This inheritance includes salvation, eternal life, and the blessings of God's kingdom.

Concordance:

- And for this reason He is the Mediator of the new covenant, by means of death, for the redemption of the transgressions under the first covenant, that those who are called may receive the promise of the eternal inheritance (Hebrews 9:15).

- And for this cause he is the mediator of the new testament, that by means of death, for the redemption of the transgressions that were under the first testament, they which are called might receive the promise of eternal inheritance (Hebrews 9:15).

This verse highlights the unique role of Jesus Christ as the mediator of the new covenant and emphasizes the universality of His atonement, which covers sins committed under both the old and new covenants. It also underscores the hope and assurance of eternal inheritance for those who respond to God's call.

Verse 16 (King James Version):
> For where a testament is, there must also of necessity be the death of the testator.

Interpretation:
This verse explains the concept of a testament or will, stating that it only goes into effect after the death of the one who made it.

Commentary:
- "For where a testament is": This refers to a will or covenant, indicating a legal arrangement or agreement.
- "there must also of necessity be the death of the testator": The effectiveness of a testament or covenant is dependent on the death of the one who made it. In the case of the new covenant, Jesus Christ is the testator, and His death is necessary for the covenant to come into effect.

Concordance:
- For where a testament is, there must also of necessity be the death of the testator (Hebrews 9:16).

This verse illustrates the principle that a testament or covenant is not valid until the death of the one who made it. In the context of the new covenant, it underscores the importance of Jesus Christ's sacrificial death as the basis for the new covenant between God and humanity.

Verse 17 (King James Version):
> For a testament is of force after men are dead: otherwise it is of no strength at all while the testator liveth.

Interpretation:
This verse further emphasizes that a testament or will only becomes legally binding after the death of the one who made it. While the testator is alive, the testament has no legal effect.

Commentary:
- "For a testament is of force after men are dead": This reiterates the principle that a will or covenant is legally valid only after the death of the one who made it.
- "otherwise it is of no strength at all while the testator liveth": While the one who made the testament is alive, the testament has no legal power or effect.

Concordance:
- For a testament is of force after men are dead: otherwise it is of no strength at all while the testator liveth (Hebrews 9:17).

This verse underscores the legal principle that a testament or covenant is only valid after the death of the one who made it. In the context of the new covenant, it emphasizes the significance of Jesus Christ's death as the basis for the new covenant between God and humanity.

Verse 18 (King James Version):
> Whereupon neither the first testament was dedicated without blood.

Interpretation:
This verse suggests that even the first covenant, established with Israel through Moses, was not inaugurated without the shedding of blood.

Commentary:

- "Whereupon neither the first testament was dedicated without blood": This indicates that the old covenant, inaugurated with the people of Israel through Moses, was also established with a blood sacrifice. This likely refers to the sacrificial system established in the Mosaic Law, where blood was used in various rituals and ceremonies to atone for sin and consecrate the covenant.

Concordance:

- Whereupon neither the first testament was dedicated without blood (Hebrews 9:18).

This verse underscores the idea that both the old and new covenants were established through blood, highlighting the importance of sacrifice in God's redemptive plan and pointing to the ultimate sacrifice of Jesus Christ.

Verse 19 (King James Version):

> For when Moses had spoken every precept to all the people according to the law, he took the blood of calves and of goats, with water, and scarlet wool, and hyssop, and sprinkled both the book, and all the people,

Interpretation:

This verse describes the ritual that Moses performed to inaugurate the old covenant with the people of Israel. After delivering all the commandments of the law to the people, Moses used the blood of calves and goats, along with water, scarlet wool, and hyssop, to sprinkle both the book of the law and all the people.

Commentary:

- "For when Moses had spoken every precept to all the people according to the law": This refers to the giving of the law at Mount Sinai, where Moses delivered all the commandments and instructions to the people of Israel as recorded in the Old Testament.

- "He took the blood of calves and of goats, with water, and scarlet wool, and hyssop, and sprinkled both the book, and all the people": This describes the ritual of sprinkling blood to inaugurate the covenant. The use of blood symbolized the seriousness of the covenant and the need for atonement for sin. The sprinkling of the blood on the book of the law symbolized the binding of the people to the covenant, and the sprinkling on the people symbolized their purification and consecration to God.

Concordance:

- For when Moses had spoken every precept to all the people according to the law, he took the blood of calves and of goats, with water, and scarlet wool, and hyssop, and sprinkled both the book, and all the people (Hebrews 9:19).

This verse highlights the significance of blood in the establishment of the old covenant and foreshadows the ultimate sacrifice of Jesus Christ, whose blood would ratify the new covenant.

Verse 20 (King James Version):

> Saying, This is the blood of the testament which God hath enjoined unto you.

Interpretation:

In this verse, the writer of Hebrews describes how Moses declared to the people that the blood he used in the covenant ceremony was the blood of the covenant that God had commanded them to follow.

Commentary:

- "Saying, This is the blood of the testament which God hath enjoined unto you": This statement by Moses affirmed that the blood used in the covenant ceremony was the blood of the covenant that God had commanded them to observe. This blood symbolized the binding agreement between God and the people of Israel, where they promised to obey God's commandments, and God promised to bless and protect them as His chosen people.

Concordance:

- Saying, This is the blood of the testament which God hath enjoined unto you (Hebrews 9:20).

This verse emphasizes the solemnity and divine origin of the covenant, reinforcing the importance of obedience to God's commandments in the Old Testament.

Verse 21 (King James Version):
> Moreover he sprinkled with blood both the tabernacle, and all the vessels of the ministry.

Interpretation:
This verse describes how Moses sprinkled blood not only on the people but also on the tabernacle and all its articles used in worship.

Commentary:

- "Moreover he sprinkled with blood both the tabernacle, and all the vessels of the ministry": This act of sprinkling blood on the tabernacle and its furnishings was a symbolic way of purifying them and dedicating them to God's service. The blood represented the atonement for sin and the sanctification of the place of worship and its instruments.

Concordance:
- Moreover he sprinkled with blood both the tabernacle, and all the vessels of the ministry (Hebrews 9:21).

This verse underscores the sacredness and holiness of the tabernacle, which was the place where God dwelt among His people, and emphasizes the importance of atonement and purification for approaching God in worship.

Verse 22 (King James Version):
> And almost all things are by the law purged with blood; and without shedding of blood is no remission.

Interpretation:
This verse explains the necessity of bloodshed for the forgiveness of sins according to the law. It emphasizes that forgiveness or remission of sins under the Old Covenant required the shedding of blood.

Commentary:
- "And almost all things are by the law purged with blood": This statement highlights the central role of blood sacrifices in the Old Testament system of worship. Various offerings prescribed by the Mosaic law involved the shedding of blood to purify people and objects from sin.

- "Without shedding of blood is no remission": This phrase underscores the principle that forgiveness of sins required the offering of a blood sacrifice as a substitute for the sinner. The shedding of blood symbolized the seriousness of sin and the need for atonement to satisfy divine justice.

Concordance:
- And almost all things are by the law purged with blood; and without shedding of blood is no remission (Hebrews 9:22).

This verse emphasizes the importance of blood sacrifices in the Old Testament as a means of atonement for sin. It also points to the ultimate sacrifice of Jesus Christ, whose shed blood provides complete and eternal remission of sins for those who believe in Him.

Verse 23 (King James Version):
> It was therefore necessary that the patterns of things in the heavens should be purified with these; but the heavenly things themselves with better sacrifices than these.

Interpretation:
This verse discusses the necessity of purifying the earthly tabernacle, which was a copy of the heavenly sanctuary, with the blood of animal sacrifices. However, the heavenly sanctuary required a better sacrifice than those offered on earth.

Commentary:
- "It was therefore necessary that the patterns of things in the heavens should be purified with these": This statement refers to the earthly tabernacle and its furnishings, which were replicas or patterns of the heavenly realities. These earthly symbols needed to be purified through sacrifices prescribed by the law to maintain their symbolic purity and reflect the holiness of God's dwelling place in heaven.

- "But the heavenly things themselves with better sacrifices than these": This part of the verse contrasts the purification of earthly things with the purification of heavenly things. While the earthly tabernacle required repeated sacrifices, the heavenly sanctuary required a superior and more effective sacrifice to cleanse it from sin once and for all.

Concordance:

- It was therefore necessary that the patterns of things in the heavens should be purified with these; but the heavenly things themselves with better sacrifices than these (Hebrews 9:23).

This verse underscores the inadequacy of animal sacrifices to fully cleanse sin and points to the need for a superior sacrifice, which is found in Jesus Christ, who offered Himself as the perfect and eternal sacrifice for sin.

Verse 24 (King James Version):

> For Christ is not entered into the holy places made with hands, which are the figures of the true; but into heaven itself, now to appear in the presence of God for us:

Interpretation:

This verse highlights the contrast between the earthly tabernacle, which was a representation of the true heavenly sanctuary, and Christ's entry into the actual heavenly sanctuary. Christ entered into heaven itself, not into a man-made sanctuary, and now stands in the presence of God on behalf of believers.

Commentary:

- "For Christ is not entered into the holy places made with hands, which are the figures of the true": This statement emphasizes that Christ did not enter into the earthly tabernacle or temple, which were mere representations or shadows of the true heavenly sanctuary. The earthly holy places were made by human hands and served as symbols or patterns of the heavenly realities.

- "But into heaven itself, now to appear in the presence of God for us": In contrast to the earthly tabernacle, Christ entered into the actual heavenly sanctuary, where He now stands in the presence of God. His presence in heaven signifies His completed work of redemption and His ongoing intercession on behalf of believers. Christ's presence in heaven assures believers of His continual advocacy and mediation for them before God.

Concordance:
- For Christ is not entered into the holy places made with hands, which are the figures of the true; but into heaven itself, now to appear in the presence of God for us (Hebrews 9:24).

This verse underscores the superiority of Christ's ministry over the Old Testament sacrificial system. While the high priest entered the earthly tabernacle once a year with the blood of animal sacrifices, Christ entered heaven itself with His own blood, offering a perfect and eternal sacrifice for sin.

Verse 25 (King James Version):
> Nor yet that he should offer himself often, as the high priest entereth into the holy place every year with blood of others;

Interpretation:
This verse contrasts Christ's sacrifice with the repeated offerings of the high priest in the Old Testament. Unlike the high priest who had to offer sacrifices year after year, Christ offered Himself once for all, eliminating the need for further sacrifices.

Commentary:

- "Nor yet that he should offer himself often": This phrase emphasizes the uniqueness of Christ's sacrifice. Unlike the high priest who offered sacrifices repeatedly, Christ offered Himself once for all, accomplishing redemption completely and permanently.

- "As the high priest entereth into the holy place every year with blood of others": This refers to the annual Day of Atonement when the high priest entered the Most Holy Place with the blood of animal sacrifices to atone for the sins of the people. The repetition of this ritual highlighted the inadequacy of animal sacrifices to fully remove sin.

Concordance:

- Nor yet that he should offer himself often, as the high priest entereth into the holy place every year with blood of others (Hebrews 9:25).

This verse emphasizes the superiority of Christ's sacrifice over the Old Testament sacrificial system. Christ's sacrifice was offered once for all, providing eternal redemption for believers, while the sacrifices offered by the high priest were temporary and needed to be repeated annually.

Verse 26 (King James Version):

> For then must he often have suffered since the foundation of the world: but now once in the end of the world hath he appeared to put away sin by the sacrifice of himself.

Interpretation:

This verse highlights the contrast between the repeated sacrifices required by the Levitical priesthood and the singular, effective sacrifice of Jesus Christ. It emphasizes that Christ's sacrifice was offered once, at the culmination of the ages, to remove sin.

Commentary:
- "For then must he often have suffered since the foundation of the world": This phrase suggests that if Christ's sacrifice had been like the offerings under the Levitical system, He would have had to suffer repeatedly throughout history. However, the efficacy of Christ's sacrifice lies in its singularity and completeness.
- "But now once in the end of the world hath he appeared to put away sin by the sacrifice of himself": This clause emphasizes the unique nature of Christ's sacrifice. He appeared at the appointed time, fulfilling the purpose of the sacrificial system by offering Himself as the ultimate sacrifice for sin, accomplishing what the blood of animals could never do.

Concordance:
- For then must he often have suffered since the foundation of the world: but now once in the end of the world hath he appeared to put away sin by the sacrifice of himself (Hebrews 9:26).

This verse underscores the uniqueness and sufficiency of Christ's sacrifice as the means by which sin is eradicated. His sacrifice is effective for all time, putting an end to the need for repeated sacrifices.

Verse 27 (King James Version):
> And as it is appointed unto men once to die, but after this the judgment:

Interpretation:

This verse speaks to the inevitability of death and judgment for all people. It suggests that each person will experience physical death once, followed by a judgment of their deeds.

Commentary:
- "And as it is appointed unto men once to die": This phrase reflects the universal experience of death among human beings. It emphasizes the certainty of death as a part of the human condition.
- "But after this the judgment": Following death, according to this verse, comes judgment. This implies a belief in an afterlife where individuals will be held accountable for their actions.

Concordance:
- And as it is appointed unto men once to die, but after this the judgment (Hebrews 9:27).

This verse underscores the importance of living a life that is mindful of the eventual judgment. It serves as a reminder of the importance of spiritual preparedness for the afterlife.

Verse 28 (King James Version):
> So Christ was once offered to bear the sins of many; and unto them that look for him shall he appear the second time without sin unto salvation.

Interpretation:
This verse highlights the sacrificial role of Jesus Christ in bearing the sins of many. It also speaks of His second coming, which will be for the salvation of those who eagerly await Him.

Commentary:

- "So Christ was once offered to bear the sins of many": This part of the verse emphasizes the unique and sufficient sacrifice of Christ on the cross, which was offered once for all to bear the sins of many. This sacrifice is seen as fulfilling the Old Testament sacrificial system.

- "And unto them that look for him shall he appear the second time": Here, the verse speaks of the future return of Christ. This return is eagerly anticipated by believers who are looking forward to His coming.

- "Without sin unto salvation": This phrase suggests that when Christ returns, He will not bear the sins of others as He did in His first coming but will come to bring salvation to those who have believed in Him.

Concordance:

- So Christ was once offered to bear the sins of many; and unto them that look for him shall he appear the second time without sin unto salvation (Hebrews 9:28).

This verse encapsulates the central themes of the Christian faith: the sacrificial death of Christ for the forgiveness of sins and the hope of His second coming for the salvation of believers.

CHAPTER 10
The appeal to hold fast

Verse 1 (King James Version):
> For the law having a shadow of good things to come, and not the very image of the things, can never with those sacrifices which they offered year by year continually make the comers thereunto perfect.

Interpretation:
This verse contrasts the limitations of the Old Testament sacrificial system with the perfect and complete salvation brought by Jesus Christ. The Old Testament law and its sacrificial system were a foreshadowing of the better things to come through Christ, but they were unable to provide complete forgiveness or perfection.

Commentary:

- "For the law having a shadow of good things to come": The Old Testament law and its sacrifices were symbolic representations, or shadows, of the future work of Christ. They pointed forward to the ultimate sacrifice and salvation found in Him.

- "And not the very image of the things": While the law foreshadowed the coming reality in Christ, it was not the actual substance or image of that reality. The law could not provide the complete fulfillment that Christ would bring.

- "Can never with those sacrifices which they offered year by year continually make the comers thereunto perfect": This part of the verse emphasizes the limitations of the Old Testament sacrifices. The repeated sacrifices offered under the law could not fully cleanse or perfect those who offered them. They were a temporary measure until the perfect sacrifice of Christ.

Concordance:
- For the law having a shadow of good things to come, and not the very image of the things, can never with those sacrifices which they offered year by year continually make the comers thereunto perfect (Hebrews 10:1).

This verse sets the stage for the superiority of Christ's sacrifice over the Old Testament sacrifices, highlighting the inability of the law to provide complete redemption and perfection compared to the once-for-all sacrifice of Christ.

Verse 2 (King James Version):
> For then would they not have ceased to be offered? because that the worshippers once purged should have had no more conscience of sins.

Interpretation:

This verse emphasizes the inefficacy of the Old Testament sacrifices in truly purging sins. If those sacrifices had been effective, there would have been no need for them to be offered repeatedly, and the worshippers would have been cleansed of sin once and for all.

Commentary:

- "For then would they not have ceased to be offered?": This rhetorical question highlights the fact that the repeated offering of sacrifices in the Old Testament demonstrates their ineffectiveness in permanently dealing with sin. If they had truly purified the worshippers, there would have been no need for further sacrifices.

- "Because that the worshippers once purged should have had no more conscience of sins": This statement emphasizes the desired outcome of purification – that those who have been cleansed of sin should no longer be burdened by a guilty conscience regarding their sins. However, the fact that the sacrifices had to be offered repeatedly indicates that they were not able to achieve this ultimate goal.

Concordance:

- For then would they not have ceased to be offered? because that the worshippers once purged should have had no more conscience of sins (Hebrews 10:2).

This verse further underscores the insufficiency of the Old Testament sacrifices to fully cleanse sins, pointing to the need for a better sacrifice that can provide complete purification and freedom from guilt.

Verse 3 (King James Version):
> But in those sacrifices there is a remembrance again made of sins every year.

Interpretation:

This verse highlights the limitation of the Old Testament sacrifices, which, instead of permanently removing sins, served as a reminder of sins, needing to be offered year after year.

Commentary:

- "But in those sacrifices there is a remembrance again made of sins every year": The sacrifices prescribed by the Mosaic Law were insufficient to permanently remove sins. Instead, they served as a reminder of sins, requiring annual repetition. This repetition highlighted the ongoing nature of sin and the need for a more effective sacrifice.

Concordance:

- But in those sacrifices there is a remembrance again made of sins every year (Hebrews 10:3).

This verse contrasts the temporary nature of the Old Testament sacrifices with the permanent efficacy of the sacrifice of Jesus Christ, which is the central theme of the book of Hebrews.

Verse 4 (King James Version):

> For it is not possible that the blood of bulls and of goats should take away sins.

Interpretation:

This verse emphasizes the inadequacy of animal sacrifices to truly remove sins. The blood of animals could not accomplish what was needed; it required a greater sacrifice.

Commentary:

- "For it is not possible that the blood of bulls and of goats should take away sins": This statement underscores the insufficiency of animal sacrifices to fully atone for sins. The repetition of these sacrifices in the Old Testament pointed to the need for a perfect and lasting sacrifice, which Jesus Christ fulfilled through His death on the cross.

Strong's Concordance:

- Possible (Strong's #1415, Greek: δυνατός, dunatos): capable, able, powerful; it denotes "possible" when applied to persons or things that can or could do something; it signifies "possible" when used of things that could happen or might be done.

- Take away (Strong's #851, Greek: αἴρω, airo): to lift up, raise up, take away, remove; it is used in a variety of applications, such as to take up or away, to remove, to carry off, to raise up or elevate.

- Sins (Strong's #266, Greek: ἁμαρτία, hamartia): sin, offence, sinfulness, guilt; it refers to both the sin itself and the condition of sinfulness.

This verse emphasizes the inability of animal sacrifices to permanently remove sins, contrasting with the efficacious sacrifice of Jesus Christ, which provides true forgiveness and cleansing.

Verse 6 (King James Version):
> In burnt offerings and sacrifices for sin thou hast had no pleasure.

Interpretation:

This verse suggests that God did not take pleasure in the repeated burnt offerings and sacrifices for sin prescribed by the Mosaic Law. These sacrifices were insufficient to fully atone for sin.

Commentary:

- "In burnt offerings and sacrifices for sin thou hast had no pleasure": This echoes sentiments found in the Old Testament (e.g., Psalm 40:6) that emphasize the importance of obedience and a contrite heart over ritualistic sacrifices. God desires genuine repentance and obedience rather than mere ritual observance.

Strong's Concordance:

- Burnt offerings (Strong's #3646, Greek: ὁλοκαυτώματα, holokautōmata): a whole burnt offering, a burnt sacrifice; it refers to offerings in which the entire animal was burned on the altar as an act of worship or atonement.

- Sacrifices (Strong's #2378, Greek: θυσία, thysia): a sacrifice, offering; it refers to any offering made to God as an act of worship or propitiation.

- Pleasure (Strong's #2106, Greek: εὐδοκέω, eudokeo): to think well of, that is, approve (an act); it indicates a positive regard or approval. Here, it suggests that God did not find satisfaction or pleasure in the mere ritual of sacrifices but desired a deeper, more meaningful relationship with His people.

This verse highlights the importance of genuine repentance and obedience to God's will over external religious practices. God desires heartfelt devotion rather than empty rituals.

Verse 7 (King James Version):

> Then said I, Lo, I come (in the volume of the book it is written of me,) to do thy will, O God.

Interpretation:

This verse reflects the willingness of Christ to fulfill God's will, as expressed in the Scriptures. It emphasizes Christ's obedience and his readiness to come to earth and fulfill the purpose for which he was sent.

Commentary:

- "Then said I, Lo, I come": This is a reference to Christ's declaration of his readiness to come to earth in obedience to God's will. This willingness is seen as a contrast to the insufficiency of the Old Testament sacrifices, which could not fully atone for sin.

- "(in the volume of the book it is written of me,)": This phrase suggests that the entirety of the Old Testament, particularly the prophecies and types, pointed to the coming of Christ and his redemptive work. Christ is the fulfillment of these Scriptures.

- "to do thy will, O God": Christ's mission on earth was to fulfill the will of God, which included his sacrificial death for the forgiveness of sins (Hebrews 10:10). His obedience contrasts with the disobedience of Israel and the insufficiency of the Old Testament sacrifices.

Concordance:

- Volume (Strong's #976, Greek: βιβλίον, biblion): a book, scroll, writing; it refers to a written document or record. In this context, it likely refers to the Old Testament Scriptures, which contained prophecies and types pointing to Christ.

- Written (Strong's #1125, Greek: γράφω, grapho): to write; it indicates that Christ's coming and mission were foretold and recorded in the Scriptures.

- Will (Strong's #2307, Greek: θέλημα, thelema): will, choice, inclination, desire; it refers to God's sovereign will and purpose, which Christ came to fulfill.

This verse highlights the centrality of Christ in God's plan of redemption and emphasizes his obedience and willingness to fulfill the Father's will.

Verse 8 (King James Version):
> Above when he said, Sacrifice and offering and burnt offerings and offering for sin thou wouldest not, neither hadst pleasure therein; which are offered by the law;

Interpretation:
This verse refers to God's rejection of the Old Testament sacrificial system as a sufficient means of atonement for sin. Despite the offering of sacrifices according to the law, God did not find pleasure in them because they were insufficient to truly remove sin.

Commentary:
- "Above when he said": This refers to the previous verse (verse 7) where Christ declares his willingness to come and fulfill God's will.

- "Sacrifice and offering and burnt offerings and offering for sin thou wouldest not": This phrase emphasizes that God did not desire or take pleasure in the animal sacrifices offered under the Old Covenant.

These sacrifices, though prescribed by the law, were unable to remove sin or satisfy God's justice.

- "which are offered by the law": This clarifies that the sacrifices being referred to are those mandated by the Mosaic law. Despite their regular observance, these sacrifices could not bring about true forgiveness of sins or reconciliation with God.

Concordance:
- Sacrifice (Strong's #2378, Greek: θυσία, thysia): an offering, sacrifice; it refers to the act of presenting an offering to God as an act of worship or atonement.

- Offering (Strong's #4376, Greek: προσφορά, prosphora): an offering, gift; it refers to the offering of sacrifices or gifts to God.

- Burnt offerings (Strong's #3646, Greek: ὁλοκαύτωμα, holokautoma): a whole burnt offering; it refers to an offering that was completely consumed on the altar, symbolizing complete devotion to God.

- Offering for sin (Strong's #1435, Greek: περὶ ἁμαρτίας προσφορά, peri hamartias prosphora): an offering for sin; it refers to sacrifices offered for the forgiveness of sins.

This verse underscores the inadequacy of the Old Testament sacrificial system and prepares the way for the discussion of Christ's superior sacrifice, which is capable of truly atoning for sin.

Verse 9 (King James Version):
> Then said he, Lo, I come to do thy will, O God. He taketh away the first, that he may establish the second.

Interpretation:

This verse emphasizes Christ's obedience to God's will and His purpose to establish a new covenant that supersedes the old covenant. By fulfilling God's will, Christ takes away the first covenant (the Old Testament sacrificial system) to establish the second covenant (the New Testament).

Commentary:

- "Then said he, Lo, I come to do thy will, O God": This phrase echoes the words of Christ, expressing His willingness to come into the world and fulfill God's plan of salvation through His sacrificial death on the cross.

- "He taketh away the first, that he may establish the second": This statement highlights the purpose of Christ's sacrifice. By offering Himself as the ultimate sacrifice for sin, He fulfills and thereby ends the need for the Old Testament sacrificial system, establishing the new covenant based on His sacrifice.

Concordance:

- First (Strong's #4413, Greek: πρῶτος, protos): first, chief, principal; it refers to the Old Covenant or the old way of relating to God through the Mosaic law and sacrificial system.

- Second (Strong's #1208, Greek: δεύτερος, deuteros): second, the second time; it refers to the New Covenant or the new way of relating to God through faith in Christ's sacrifice.

This verse emphasizes the superiority of Christ's sacrifice and the establishment of the new covenant, which provides believers with forgiveness of sins and a new way of approaching God.

Verse 10 (King James Version):
> By the which will we are sanctified through the offering of the body of Jesus Christ once for all.

Interpretation:
This verse explains that believers are sanctified (made holy) through the offering of Jesus Christ's body. This sanctification is achieved once and for all time, emphasizing the completeness and efficacy of Christ's sacrifice.

Commentary:
- "By the which will we are sanctified": This phrase indicates that sanctification is accomplished according to God's will, which is to sanctify believers through Christ's sacrifice.

- "Through the offering of the body of Jesus Christ": Sanctification is achieved through the sacrificial death of Jesus Christ on the cross, where He offered His body as a sacrifice for sin.

- "Once for all": This phrase emphasizes the finality and sufficiency of Christ's sacrifice. Unlike the repeated sacrifices of the Old Testament, Christ's sacrifice was offered once for all time, effectively accomplishing the sanctification of believers.

Concordance:
- Sanctified (Strong's #37, Greek: ἁγιάζω, hagiazo): to make holy, set apart for God's use; it signifies the process or result of being made holy or consecrated to God.

- Offering (Strong's #4376, Greek: προσφορά, prosphora): an offering, sacrifice; it refers to the act of presenting something to God as an offering, particularly in the context of Christ's sacrifice of Himself.

- Once for all (Strong's #2178, Greek: ἐφάπαξ, ephapax): once for all, once and for all time; it emphasizes the finality and completeness of Christ's sacrifice, which does not need to be repeated.

This verse highlights the central role of Christ's sacrifice in the sanctification of believers. Through His offering, believers are made holy and set apart for God's use, with no need for further sacrifice or offering for sin.

Verse 11 (King James Version):
> And every priest standeth daily ministering and offering oftentimes the same sacrifices, which can never take away sins.

Interpretation:
This verse contrasts the continuous sacrifices offered by the priests under the Old Covenant with the once-for-all sacrifice of Jesus Christ under the New Covenant. It highlights the inadequacy of the Old Covenant sacrifices to truly take away sins.

Commentary:
- "Every priest standeth daily ministering": In the Old Testament, priests had to continually offer sacrifices for sin, as their work was never finished. They stood daily, symbolizing the ongoing nature of their ministry.

- "Offering oftentimes the same sacrifices": The priests offered the same sacrifices repeatedly because those sacrifices could never completely remove sin. They were a temporary solution, pointing forward to the ultimate sacrifice of Christ.

- "Which can never take away sins": This phrase emphasizes the insufficiency of the Old Covenant sacrifices. They could cover sin temporarily but could not remove sin permanently. Only the sacrifice of Jesus Christ has the power to truly take away sins.

Concordance:

- Standeth (Strong's #2476, Greek: ἵστημι, histemi): to stand, stand by, stand still; it indicates the posture of the priests as they ministered in the tabernacle or temple.

- Ministering (Strong's #3008, Greek: λειτουργέω, leitourgeo): to serve, minister; it refers to the priestly service of offering sacrifices and performing other duties in the tabernacle or temple.

- Offering (Strong's #4374, Greek: προσφορά, prosphora): an offering, sacrifice; it underscores the nature of the sacrifices offered by the priests, which were a central part of their ministry.

- Never (Strong's #3763, Greek: οὐδέποτε, oudepote): never, at no time; it emphasizes the inability of the Old Covenant sacrifices to permanently remove sin.

This verse highlights the contrast between the Old Covenant sacrifices, which were repeated but could not truly remove sin, and the sacrifice of Jesus Christ, which was offered once for all and has the power to completely take away sin.

Verse 12 (King James Version):

> But this man, after he had offered one sacrifice for sins for ever, sat down on the right hand of God;

Interpretation:

This verse contrasts the continuous standing of the priests with the sitting down of Jesus after offering a single, perfect sacrifice for sins. His sacrifice is effective forever, unlike the repeated sacrifices of the Old Covenant.

Commentary:

- "But this man": Refers to Jesus Christ, contrasting him with the priests of the Old Covenant.

- "After he had offered one sacrifice for sins for ever": Jesus offered himself as a sacrifice once for all time, and this sacrifice is effective forever. It does not need to be repeated, unlike the sacrifices of the Old Covenant.

- "Sat down on the right hand of God": Sitting down symbolizes the completion of Jesus' work of redemption. In Jewish tradition, the high priest never sat down because his work was never finished. Jesus, having completed his sacrifice, sits down at the right hand of God, indicating his exaltation and the completion of his redemptive work.

Concordance:

- Sacrifice (Strong's #2378, Greek: θυσία, thysia): a sacrifice, offering; it refers to the offering of Jesus Christ as a sacrifice for sin, which is effective for all time.

- For ever (Strong's #1519, Greek: εἰς τὸ διηνεκές, eis to dienekes): to the perpetual, continual, or eternal; it emphasizes the permanent effectiveness of Jesus' sacrifice.

- Sat down (Strong's #2523, Greek: καθίζω, kathizo): to sit, be seated; it signifies the completion of Jesus' sacrificial work and his exaltation to the right hand of God.

This verse highlights the superiority of Jesus' sacrifice over the sacrifices of the Old Covenant. His sacrifice is sufficient to atone for sins once and for all, and he now reigns in glory at the right hand of God.

Verse 13 (King James Version):
> From henceforth expecting till his enemies be made his footstool.

Interpretation:
This verse suggests that Jesus is waiting for the time when all his enemies will be subjected to him, symbolized by making them his footstool. This reflects a common ancient Near Eastern practice where victorious kings would put their feet on the necks of their conquered enemies as a symbol of triumph and submission.

Commentary:
- "From henceforth expecting": Jesus is now in a position of waiting or expectation, indicating a future event that will take place according to God's plan.

- "Till his enemies be made his footstool": This imagery is drawn from Psalm 110:1, which is a Messianic prophecy. It symbolizes the complete defeat and subjugation of all opposing powers and authorities under the reign of Christ. This victory is certain, but its timing is according to God's plan.

Concordance:
- Expecting (Strong's #553, Greek: ἐκδέχομαι, ekdechomai): to expect, wait for, look for; it implies a confident anticipation of a future event.

- His enemies (Strong's #2190, Greek: ἐχθρός, echthros): an enemy, a foe; it refers to those who oppose Jesus and his reign.

- Be made his footstool (Strong's #5286, Greek: ὑποπόδιον, hypopodion): a footstool; it signifies the complete subjugation and defeat of Jesus' enemies.

This verse emphasizes the ultimate victory of Christ over all opposing powers. While Jesus has already accomplished redemption through his sacrifice, there is a future aspect to his reign where all opposition will be vanquished, and he will reign supreme.

Verse 14 (King James Version):
> For by one offering he hath perfected for ever them that are sanctified.

Interpretation:
This verse highlights the completeness and permanence of the sanctification achieved by Christ's sacrifice. It emphasizes that through Christ's single sacrifice, believers are perfected and sanctified forever.

Commentary:

- "By one offering": This refers to Christ's sacrifice on the cross, which was a once-for-all offering that accomplished complete redemption.

- "He hath perfected for ever": The word "perfected" here means to complete or make perfect. It indicates that through Christ's sacrifice, believers are made spiritually complete and whole in God's sight.

- "Them that are sanctified": This refers to believers who have been set apart or sanctified for God's purposes. The sanctification process is ongoing in the life of a believer, but it is ultimately completed and perfected by Christ's sacrifice.

Concordance:
- One offering (Strong's #4413, Greek: προσφορά, prosphora): an offering, sacrifice; it refers to Christ's sacrificial death on the cross.

- Hath perfected (Strong's #5048, Greek: τελειόω, teleioo): to complete, make perfect; it indicates the finality and completeness of the sanctification achieved through Christ.

- For ever (Strong's #1519, Greek: εἰς τὸν αἰῶνα, eis ton aiona): unto the age, forever; it emphasizes the eternal nature of the sanctification and perfection accomplished by Christ's sacrifice.

This verse underscores the unique and unparalleled nature of Christ's sacrifice, which brings about a complete and permanent sanctification for believers. It assures believers of their secure and eternal standing before God because of Christ's finished work on the cross.

Verse 15 (King James Version):

> Wherefore the Holy Ghost also is a witness to us: for after that
he had said before,

Interpretation:
This verse refers to the Holy Spirit as a witness to the truth of
the preceding statement. The Holy Spirit confirms the efficacy and
sufficiency of Christ's sacrifice for believers.

Commentary:
- "Whereof the Holy Ghost also is a witness to us": The Holy
Spirit bears witness to the truth and significance of Christ's sacrifice.
The Spirit's role is to testify to believers about the work of Christ and
its implications for their lives.

- "For after that he had said before": This phrase suggests that
the Holy Spirit's witness is based on what was previously stated or
prophesied. It indicates the continuity and fulfillment of God's plan
through Christ.

Concordance:
- Holy Ghost (Strong's #40, Greek: πνεῦμα ἅγιον, pneuma
hagion): the Holy Spirit; the third person of the Trinity who empowers,
guides, and bears witness to believers.

- Is a witness (Strong's #3140, Greek: μαρτυρέω, martureo): to
bear witness, testify; it emphasizes the Spirit's role in confirming the
truth of Christ's sacrifice.

- To us (Strong's #2254, Greek: ἡμῖν, hemin): to us, for us; it
indicates that the witness of the Holy Spirit is directed towards
believers, confirming the truth of Christ's sacrifice in their hearts.

This verse highlights the ongoing work of the Holy Spirit in confirming the truth of Christ's sacrifice in the hearts of believers. The Spirit's witness assures believers of the sufficiency of Christ's sacrifice and strengthens their faith in Him.

Verse 16 (King James Version):
> This is the covenant that I will make with them after those days, saith the Lord, I will put my laws into their hearts, and in their minds will I write them;

Interpretation:
This verse quotes a prophecy from Jeremiah 31:33, emphasizing the new covenant God will establish with His people. In this covenant, God promises to write His laws on the hearts and minds of believers, indicating a deep internalization and understanding of His commands.

Commentary:
- "This is the covenant that I will make with them after those days": This refers to the new covenant promised by God through the prophet Jeremiah (Jeremiah 31:31-34) and fulfilled in Christ. This new covenant replaces the old covenant of the Mosaic Law and is characterized by God's grace, forgiveness, and intimate relationship with His people.

- "Saith the Lord": This phrase emphasizes that the covenant is established by God Himself and carries His authority and faithfulness to fulfill His promises.

- "I will put my laws into their hearts, and in their minds will I write them": This indicates the internalization and personalization of God's laws under the new covenant. Unlike the external tablets of stone in the old covenant, God's laws are written on the hearts and minds of believers, enabling them to live according to His will from within.

Concordance:
- Covenant (Strong's #1242, Greek: διαθήκη, diatheke): a disposition, arrangement, testament, covenant; it refers to a binding agreement or contract between two parties, often used in the Bible to describe God's relationship with His people.

- Laws (Strong's #3551, Greek: νόμος, nomos): law, custom, principle; it refers to God's commands and instructions, especially those given in the Old Testament.

- Hearts (Strong's #2588, Greek: καρδία, kardia): heart; it symbolizes the innermost being, the seat of desires, thoughts, and emotions.

- Minds (Strong's #1271, Greek: διάνοια, dianoia): the mind, understanding, intellect; it represents the faculty of reasoning and comprehension.

This verse underscores the transformative nature of the new covenant, where God's laws are no longer external rules but internal principles guiding believers from within. It reflects God's desire for a personal, intimate relationship with His people, characterized by heartfelt obedience and a renewed mind.

Verse 17 (King James Version):
> And their sins and iniquities will I remember no more.

Interpretation:

In the context of the new covenant, this verse highlights one of its key features: God's forgiveness and forgetfulness of sins. Under the new covenant, God promises to forgive sins and remember them no more, emphasizing His complete and perfect forgiveness through Jesus Christ.

Commentary:

- "And their sins and iniquities will I remember no more": This statement emphasizes the completeness of God's forgiveness under the new covenant. Unlike the temporary forgiveness provided by the sacrificial system of the old covenant, where sins were remembered year after year (Hebrews 10:3), in the new covenant, God chooses to completely forget the sins of His people, granting them full and eternal forgiveness.

Concordance:

- Sins (Strong's #266, Greek: ἁμαρτία, hamartia): sin, wrongdoing, offense; it refers to any action, thought, or attitude that falls short of God's perfect standard.

- Iniquities (Strong's #93, Greek: ἀνομία, anomia): lawlessness, wickedness, iniquity; it denotes actions that violate God's law or are contrary to His will.

- Remember (Strong's #3403, Greek: μνησθήσομαι, mnesthesomai): to remember, recall, be mindful; it indicates the act of keeping something in one's mind or memory.

This verse emphasizes the radical nature of God's forgiveness under the new covenant. Through the sacrifice of Jesus Christ, God not only forgives but also chooses to completely forget the sins of His people, offering them a clean slate and a fresh start. This highlights the depth of God's love, grace, and mercy towards those who trust in Him.

Verse 18 (King James Version):
> Now where remission of these is, there is no more offering for sin.

Interpretation:
This verse underscores the completeness of the forgiveness provided by Christ's sacrifice. It signifies that once sins are forgiven through Christ, there is no longer a need for further sacrifices for sin.

Commentary:
- "Now where remission of these is, there is no more offering for sin": This statement emphasizes the finality and sufficiency of Christ's sacrifice for sin. In the Old Testament, sacrifices were offered repeatedly, indicating their temporary nature and the ongoing need for atonement. However, through Christ's sacrifice, sins are completely remitted, and there is no longer a need for additional offerings.

Concordance:
- Remission (Strong's #859, Greek: ἄφεσις, aphesis): forgiveness, pardon, release; it refers to the act of setting someone free from a debt, penalty, or obligation.

- Offering (Strong's #4376, Greek: προσφορά, prosphora): an offering, sacrifice; it denotes an act of presenting something to God as an expression of worship or to seek His favor.

This verse highlights the unique and central role of Christ's sacrifice in providing forgiveness for sins. It contrasts the temporary nature of Old Testament sacrifices with the permanent and complete forgiveness obtained through Christ. Once sins are forgiven through Him, there is no need for further offerings or sacrifices, as His sacrifice is sufficient for all time.

Verse 19 (King James Version):
> Having therefore, brethren, boldness to enter into the holiest by the blood of Jesus,

Interpretation:
This verse speaks of the believers' access to God's presence, which is made possible through the sacrificial death of Jesus Christ. It emphasizes the confidence and freedom believers have to approach God because of Jesus' atoning sacrifice.

Commentary:
- "Having therefore, brethren, boldness to enter into the holiest": The term "holiest" refers to the inner sanctuary of the tabernacle or temple, representing the very presence of God. In the Old Testament, only the high priest could enter the Holy of Holies, and that only once a year on the Day of Atonement. However, through Christ's sacrifice, all believers now have boldness and confidence to enter into God's presence.

- "By the blood of Jesus": The reference to the blood of Jesus highlights the sacrificial aspect of His death. In the Old Testament, the shedding of blood was necessary for the forgiveness of sins (Hebrews 9:22), and Jesus' blood is seen as the ultimate and perfect sacrifice that enables believers to approach God with confidence.

Concordance:

- Boldness (Strong's #3954, Greek: παρρησία, parrhesia): freedom in speaking, unreservedness in speech; it denotes openness, confidence, and boldness.

- Holiest (Strong's #40, Greek: ἅγιος, hagios): holy, sacred, set apart; it refers to the most sacred or holy place, particularly in reference to the inner sanctuary of the tabernacle or temple.

- Blood (Strong's #129, Greek: αἷμα, haima): blood; it symbolizes life and is often used in the Bible to represent the sacrificial death of Jesus Christ as the means of atonement for sin.

This verse emphasizes the access believers have to God's presence because of Jesus' sacrifice. It highlights the confidence and freedom believers can have in approaching God, knowing that their sins have been forgiven through the shedding of Jesus' blood.

Verse 20 (King James Version):
> By a new and living way, which he hath consecrated for us, through the veil, that is to say, his flesh;

Interpretation:
This verse explains that Jesus has opened a new and living way for believers to approach God. This new way was consecrated, or made holy, by Jesus through His sacrificial death, symbolized by "the veil," which represents His flesh.

Commentary:
- "By a new and living way": The "new and living way" contrasts with the old way of approaching God under the Old Covenant, which was characterized by rituals, sacrifices, and a veil separating the people

from the Holy of Holies. The new way is "living" because it is based on the life-giving sacrifice of Jesus Christ, which brings spiritual life and access to God.

- "Which he hath consecrated for us": Jesus consecrated this new way through His sacrificial death on the cross. His death removed the barrier of sin and opened the way for believers to have direct access to God.

- "Through the veil, that is to say, his flesh": This is a metaphorical reference to the veil in the temple that separated the Holy Place from the Holy of Holies. The tearing of this veil at the moment of Jesus' death symbolized the removal of the barrier between God and humanity. Jesus' flesh represents His human nature, which was offered as a sacrifice for sin, opening the way for believers to approach God directly.

Concordance:
- New (Strong's #2537, Greek: καινός, kainos): new, fresh, unused, novel; it denotes something that is qualitatively new or different from what was before.

- Living (Strong's #2198, Greek: ζάω, zao): to live, breathe, be among the living; it signifies life in its fullness and vitality.

- Way (Strong's #3598, Greek: ὁδός, hodos): a way, road, journey, path; it refers to the means or method by which something is accomplished.

- Consecrated (Strong's #1457, Greek: ἱερόω, hieroo): to make holy, consecrate, dedicate; it signifies setting something apart for sacred use.

- Veil (Strong's #2665, Greek: καταπέτασμα, katapetasma): a veil, curtain; it refers to the curtain in the temple that separated the Holy Place from the Most Holy Place.

- Flesh (Strong's #4561, Greek: σάρξ, sarx): flesh; it can refer to human flesh or, metaphorically, to human nature as weak and sinful.

This verse emphasizes that Jesus has opened a new and living way for believers to approach God, a way that is consecrated through His sacrificial death. His flesh, representing His humanity, was the means by which this new way was established, removing the barrier between God and humanity and providing direct access to God for all believers.

Verse 21 (King James Version):
> And having an high priest over the house of God;

Interpretation:
This verse declares that believers have a high priest, Jesus Christ, who presides over the house of God. In the Old Testament, the high priest was the chief religious leader who represented the people before God. Jesus fulfills this role for believers in a new and greater way.

Commentary:
- "And having an high priest": Jesus is described as a high priest, a title that signifies His role as the mediator between God and humanity. As a high priest, Jesus offers Himself as a sacrifice for the sins of the people and intercedes on their behalf before God.

- "Over the house of God": The "house of God" refers to the community of believers, the church, which is now considered the dwelling place of God. Jesus is the high priest who ministers over this spiritual house, ensuring that believers have access to God and are cared for spiritually.

Concordance:
- High Priest (Strong's #749, Greek: ἀρχιερεύς, archiereus): high priest; it refers to the chief priest in the Jewish religion, who had the primary responsibility for the administration of the religious rituals and ceremonies.

- House (Strong's #3624, Greek: οἶκος, oikos): a house, dwelling; it can refer to a physical house or, metaphorically, to a household, family, or community.

- God (Strong's #2316, Greek: θεός, theos): God; it denotes the supreme being, the creator and ruler of the universe.

This verse highlights the unique role of Jesus as the high priest over the spiritual house of God, the community of believers. He ministers on behalf of believers, offering Himself as a sacrifice and interceding for them before God. This role emphasizes the intimate relationship believers have with God through Jesus, who ensures their access to God and their spiritual well-being.

Verse 22 (King James Version):
> Let us draw near with a true heart in full assurance of faith, having our hearts sprinkled from an evil conscience, and our bodies washed with pure water.

Interpretation:

This verse encourages believers to approach God with sincerity and confidence, based on their faith in Jesus Christ. It speaks of the cleansing of the heart from guilt and the purification of the body, symbolized by water, which represents spiritual cleansing and renewal.

Commentary:

- "Let us draw near with a true heart": Believers are urged to approach God sincerely, with genuine intentions and without hypocrisy. This indicates the importance of authenticity and honesty in one's relationship with God.

- "In full assurance of faith": Believers are encouraged to approach God confidently, trusting in the finished work of Christ and the promises of God. This assurance comes from faith in Jesus as the means of reconciliation with God.

- "Having our hearts sprinkled from an evil conscience": This imagery reflects the Old Testament practice of sprinkling blood for purification. In the New Covenant, Jesus' sacrifice cleanses believers' consciences from guilt and sin, allowing them to approach God without fear or shame.

- "And our bodies washed with pure water": This likely symbolizes the spiritual cleansing that occurs through baptism, which signifies the believer's identification with Christ's death and resurrection. It also symbolizes the ongoing process of sanctification, where believers are continually cleansed and renewed by the Holy Spirit.

Concordance:

- True (Strong's #228, Greek: ἀληθινός, alēthinos): real, true, genuine; it emphasizes sincerity and authenticity.

- Full assurance (Strong's #4136, Greek: πληροφορία, plērophoria): full assurance, complete confidence; it denotes a firm and unwavering conviction.

- Faith (Strong's #4102, Greek: πίστις, pistis): faith, belief, trust; it refers to a strong conviction or trust in something or someone, particularly in God or in the truths of the Christian faith.

- Evil (Strong's #4190, Greek: πονηρός, ponēros): evil, wicked, bad; it refers to that which is morally wrong or harmful.

- Conscience (Strong's #4893, Greek: συνείδησις, syneidēsis): conscience, the faculty of moral discernment; it refers to the inner sense of right and wrong.

- Washed (Strong's #3068, Greek: λούω, louō): to wash, cleanse; it signifies purification and cleansing.

- Pure (Strong's #2513, Greek: καθαρός, katharos): clean, pure, uncontaminated; it denotes something that is free from impurity or defilement.

- Water (Strong's #5204, Greek: ὕδωρ, hydōr): water; it can refer to physical water or be used metaphorically to represent cleansing and renewal.

This verse emphasizes the importance of approaching God with sincerity, confidence, and faith, based on the cleansing and purification that comes through Jesus Christ. It highlights the transformative nature of the Christian faith, which cleanses believers from sin and enables them to draw near to God with assurance and confidence.

Verse 23 (King James Version):
> Let us hold fast the profession of our faith without wavering; (for he is faithful that promised;)

Interpretation:
This verse encourages believers to remain steadfast in their faith, without doubting or wavering, because God is faithful to fulfill His promises.

Commentary:
- "Let us hold fast the profession of our faith without wavering": Believers are urged to remain firm and unwavering in their confession of faith in Christ. This implies a steadfast commitment to the Christian faith and its teachings, even in the face of challenges or doubts.

- "(for he is faithful that promised)": This clause provides the basis for the exhortation to hold fast to faith. It emphasizes the faithfulness of God, who is trustworthy and reliable to fulfill His promises. Believers can trust in God's faithfulness, knowing that He will not fail them.

Concordance:
- Hold fast (Strong's #2722, Greek: κατέχω, katechō): to hold fast, to retain; it implies a firm grip or secure hold.

- Profession (Strong's #3671, Greek: ὁμολογία, homologia): confession, profession; it refers to the act of openly acknowledging or declaring one's faith.

- Faith (Strong's #4102, Greek: πίστις, pistis): faith, belief, trust; it refers to a strong conviction or trust in something or someone, particularly in God or in the truths of the Christian faith.

- Without wavering (Strong's #186, Greek: ἀκλινής, aklinēs): without bending, firm, unwavering; it denotes a steadfast and resolute commitment.

- Faithful (Strong's #4103, Greek: πιστός, pistos): faithful, reliable, trustworthy; it describes someone who can be trusted to fulfill their promises.

- Promised (Strong's #1861, Greek: ἐπαγγέλλω, epangellō): to promise, to announce; it refers to a declaration or commitment to do something.

This verse underscores the importance of unwavering faith and commitment to God's promises, grounded in the assurance of God's faithfulness. Believers are encouraged to remain steadfast in their confession of faith, knowing that God is faithful and will fulfill His promises to them.

Verse 24 (King James Version):
> And let us consider one another to provoke unto love and to good works:

Interpretation:
This verse encourages believers to consider and stimulate one another to love and good deeds, emphasizing mutual encouragement and support within the Christian community.

Commentary:

- "And let us consider one another": Believers are urged to pay attention to, think about, and regard one another. This implies a deliberate effort to be mindful of the needs, struggles, and well-being of fellow believers.

- "to provoke unto love and to good works": The purpose of considering one another is to provoke, stir up, or incite each other to love and good works. This highlights the importance of mutual encouragement and edification within the Christian community, motivating each other to live out their faith through acts of love and righteousness.

Concordance:

- Consider (Strong's #2657, Greek: κατανοέω, katanoeō): to perceive, to understand, to consider; it implies careful thought and attention.

- Provoke (Strong's #3948, Greek: παροξυσμός, paroxysmos): to stimulate, to provoke; it suggests an incitement or encouragement to action.

- Love (Strong's #26, Greek: ἀγάπη, agapē): love, benevolence, goodwill; it refers to a selfless, unconditional love, particularly the love that God has for humanity and that believers are called to show towards one another.

- Good works (Strong's #2041, Greek: ἔργον, ergon): works, deeds, actions; it refers to actions that are morally good and beneficial to others, reflecting the character of God.

This verse underscores the importance of mutual encouragement and support among believers, motivating each other to live in a manner that reflects the love of God and produces good deeds. By considering and stimulating one another in this way, believers can strengthen their faith and build up the body of Christ.

Verse 25 (King James Version):

> Not forsaking the assembling of ourselves together, as the manner of some is; but exhorting one another: and so much the more, as ye see the day approaching.

Interpretation:

This verse emphasizes the importance of regular gathering together of believers for worship, fellowship, and mutual encouragement, especially as the return of Christ draws near.

Commentary:

- "Not forsaking the assembling of ourselves together": Believers are urged not to neglect or abandon the practice of meeting together as a community of faith. This underscores the importance of corporate worship and fellowship in the life of a believer.

- "as the manner of some is": Some believers had begun to neglect meeting together, possibly due to persecution, apathy, or other reasons. This serves as a warning against falling away from regular fellowship with other believers.

- "but exhorting one another": Instead of forsaking assembly, believers are encouraged to exhort, encourage, and build one another up. This highlights the role of mutual encouragement and support within the Christian community.

- "and so much the more, as ye see the day approaching": As the return of Christ draws nearer, believers are urged to increase their efforts in gathering together and encouraging one another. This is because the challenges and trials of the end times require strengthened faith and unity among believers.

Concordance:
- Forsaking (Strong's #1459, Greek: ἐγκαταλείπω, egkataleipō): to forsake, to desert, to abandon; it implies a deliberate choice to neglect or leave behind.

- Assembling (Strong's #1997, Greek: ἐπισυναγωγή, episynagōgē): gathering together, assembly, congregation; it refers to the act of coming together for a specific purpose, particularly for worship or fellowship.

- Exhorting (Strong's #3870, Greek: παρακαλέω, parakaleō): to encourage, to urge, to exhort; it involves calling someone to take a particular action or to behave in a certain way.

This verse emphasizes the importance of regular fellowship and encouragement among believers, especially in light of the challenges and trials they may face as the return of Christ approaches. By gathering together and supporting one another, believers can strengthen their faith and be better prepared for the days ahead.

Verse 26 (King James Version):
> For if we sin wilfully after that we have received the knowledge of the truth, there remaineth no more sacrifice for sins,

Interpretation:

This verse warns that if a person who has received knowledge of the truth (presumably the gospel message) intentionally continues to sin, rejecting the sacrifice of Christ, there is no other sacrifice available for their sins.

Commentary:

- "For if we sin wilfully": This phrase indicates a deliberate, intentional choice to sin, especially after one has understood the consequences and significance of their actions.

- "after that we have received the knowledge of the truth": This refers to individuals who have heard and understood the gospel message, acknowledging Jesus Christ as the truth and the sacrifice for sins.

- "there remaineth no more sacrifice for sins": The sacrifice of Jesus Christ on the cross is the ultimate and final sacrifice for sins. If someone rejects or disregards this sacrifice, there is no other means of atonement available to them.

Concordance:

- Wilfully (Strong's #1596, Greek: ἑκουσίως, hekousiōs): voluntarily, willingly, deliberately; it denotes a conscious and intentional decision or action.

- Received (Strong's #2983, Greek: λαμβάνω, lambanō): to take, to receive, to accept; it implies an active and intentional reception or acceptance of something.

- Knowledge (Strong's #1922, Greek: ἐπίγνωσις, epignōsis): knowledge, recognition, full knowledge; it refers to a deep and thorough understanding or recognition of the truth.

- Truth (Strong's #225, Greek: ἀλήθεια, alētheia): truth, reality, sincerity; it denotes the concept of truth in its various aspects, particularly in relation to God and His revelation.

This verse serves as a warning against willful and deliberate sinning, especially for those who have received the knowledge of the truth. It underscores the seriousness of sin and the finality of Christ's sacrifice for sins.

Verse 27 (King James Version):
> But a certain fearful looking for of judgment and fiery indignation, which shall devour the adversaries.

Interpretation:
This verse describes the consequences of willful sinning for those who reject Christ's sacrifice. It speaks of a fearful expectation of judgment and fiery punishment for those who oppose God.

Commentary:
- "But a certain fearful looking for of judgment": This phrase suggests a definite and specific expectation of judgment. It indicates a deep sense of fear or dread regarding the impending judgment of God.

- "and fiery indignation": This phrase describes the intense anger or wrath of God, often symbolized by fire in the Bible. It signifies the severity of God's judgment against sin.

- "which shall devour the adversaries": The judgment and fiery indignation are said to "devour" or consume those who are God's adversaries, referring to those who oppose or rebel against Him.

Concordance:

- Fearful (Strong's #5398, Greek: φοβερός, phoberos): fearful, terrible, dreadful; it emphasizes the intense and overwhelming nature of the fear.

- Looking (Strong's #4329, Greek: ἐκδοχή, ekdochē): expectation, anticipation, looking for; it refers to the state of expecting or anticipating something.

- Judgment (Strong's #2920, Greek: κρίσις, krisis): judgment, decision, justice; it denotes the act of judging or the result of judgment.

- Fiery (Strong's #4448, Greek: πυρός, pyros): fiery, burning; it suggests the idea of fire or burning, often used metaphorically to describe intense anger or punishment.

- Indignation (Strong's #2205, Greek: ὀργή, orgē): anger, wrath, indignation; it signifies the strong displeasure or wrath of God against sin.

- Devour (Strong's #2719, Greek: κατακαίω, katakaio): to burn up, consume; it describes the complete destruction or consumption by fire.

This verse emphasizes the severity of God's judgment against willful sinners, highlighting the fearful expectation of judgment and fiery punishment that awaits those who reject Christ's sacrifice. It serves as a warning against disobedience and rebellion towards God.

Verse 28 (King James Version):

> He that despised Moses' law died without mercy under two or three witnesses:

Interpretation:
This verse compares the consequences of rejecting the Mosaic law with the consequences of rejecting the grace of Christ. Under the Mosaic law, those who disobeyed could be put to death based on the testimony of two or three witnesses. The verse suggests that if disobedience under the Mosaic law had such severe consequences, how much more severe will the consequences be for those who reject Christ's sacrifice and grace?

Commentary:
- "He that despised Moses' law": Refers to someone who disregarded or showed contempt for the commands and requirements of the Mosaic law.

- "died without mercy under two or three witnesses": Under the Mosaic law, capital punishment (death penalty) for certain offenses required the testimony of two or three witnesses to establish guilt beyond doubt (Deuteronomy 17:6; 19:15). This emphasizes the seriousness of disobeying the Mosaic law.

Concordance:
- Despised (Strong's #114, Greek: ἐξουθενέω, exoutheneo): to despise, disdain, regard as nothing; it denotes a strong sense of contempt or disregard.

- Law (Strong's #3551, Greek: νόμος, nomos): law, especially the Mosaic law; it refers to the legal and moral requirements of the Mosaic covenant.

- Died (Strong's #599, Greek: ἀποθνήσκω, apothnesko): to die, be dead; it signifies the cessation of physical life.

- Without mercy (Strong's #3928, Greek: ἄνευ οἰκτιρμῶν, aneu oiktirmōn): without mercy, pitilessly; it indicates the absence of compassion or leniency.

- Witnesses (Strong's #3144, Greek: μάρτυς, martys): a witness, one who testifies; it refers to someone who testifies or provides evidence in a legal context.

This verse underscores the seriousness of rejecting the grace of Christ by contrasting it with the severe consequences of disobeying the Mosaic law. It serves as a warning against rejecting God's grace and emphasizes the need to heed the message of salvation through Christ.

Verse 29 (King James Version):
> Of how much sorer punishment, suppose ye, shall he be thought worthy, who hath trodden under foot the Son of God, and hath counted the blood of the covenant, wherewith he was sanctified, an unholy thing, and hath done despite unto the Spirit of grace?

Interpretation:
The verse discusses the severity of punishment for those who reject Christ's sacrifice. It poses a rhetorical question, suggesting that if disobeying the Mosaic law led to severe punishment, how much greater will the punishment be for those who reject Christ? It describes three actions:
1. "Trodden under foot the Son of God": This refers to treating Christ with contempt or disregarding His significance and authority.

2. "Counted the blood of the covenant... an unholy thing": This means regarding Christ's sacrificial blood, which establishes the new covenant, as something common or unclean.

3. "Done despite unto the Spirit of grace": This indicates showing disrespect or contempt towards the Holy Spirit, who imparts God's grace and reveals the truth of the Gospel.

Commentary:

- "Of how much sorer punishment...": This phrase emphasizes the greater severity of punishment for those who reject Christ compared to those who disobeyed the Mosaic law.

- "Who hath trodden under foot the Son of God": Describes the act of treating Christ with contempt or rejecting His authority.

- "Counted the blood of the covenant... an unholy thing": Indicates the act of regarding Christ's sacrificial blood, which established the new covenant, as insignificant or unclean.

- "And hath done despite unto the Spirit of grace": Refers to showing disrespect or contempt towards the Holy Spirit, who reveals the truth of the Gospel and imparts God's grace.

Concordance:

- Punishment (Strong's #5098, Greek: τιμωρία, timōria): punishment, penalty; it denotes the infliction of a penalty or retribution for wrongdoing.

- Trodden under foot (Strong's #2662, Greek: καταπατέω, katapateō): to trample under foot; it signifies treating something as worthless or insignificant.

- Son of God (Strong's #5207, Greek: υἱός, huios, θεός, theos): Son of God; it refers to Jesus Christ, emphasizing His divine nature.

- Blood (Strong's #129, Greek: αἷμα, haima): blood; it symbolizes Christ's sacrificial death and the establishment of the new covenant.

- Covenant (Strong's #1242, Greek: διαθήκη, diathēkē): covenant, testament; it refers to the new covenant established by Christ's sacrificial death.

- Sanctified (Strong's #37, Greek: ἁγιάζω, hagiazō): to sanctify, make holy; it denotes the act of being set apart or made holy by God.

- Unholy thing (Strong's #2839, Greek: κοινόω, koinoō): to make common, defile; it refers to treating something sacred as common or unclean.

- Despite (Strong's #1796, Greek: ἐνυβρίζω, enubrizō): to insult, outrage; it signifies showing contempt or disrespect towards someone.

- Spirit of grace (Strong's #4151, Greek: πνεῦμα, pneuma, χάρις, charis): Spirit of grace; it refers to the Holy Spirit, who brings God's grace and reveals the truth of the Gospel.

This verse serves as a solemn warning against rejecting Christ and His sacrifice, highlighting the severe consequences of such actions. It underscores the importance of recognizing and honoring the significance of Christ's sacrifice and the work of the Holy Spirit in imparting grace and truth.

Verse 30 (King James Version):

> For we know him that hath said, Vengeance belongeth unto me, I will recompense, saith the Lord. And again, The Lord shall judge his people.

Interpretation:

This verse quotes two passages from the Old Testament to emphasize the principle of divine judgment and retribution. The first quotation, "Vengeance belongeth unto me, I will recompense," is from Deuteronomy 32:35, where God declares that He will repay those who reject Him and His ways. The second quotation, "The Lord shall judge his people," is from Deuteronomy 32:36, where God asserts His role as the righteous judge who will judge His people according to their actions.

Commentary:

- "For we know him that hath said...": The author emphasizes that believers are familiar with the words of God regarding divine vengeance and judgment.

- "Vengeance belongeth unto me, I will recompense, saith the Lord": This quotation underscores God's exclusive right to execute judgment and retribution. It highlights His role as the ultimate arbiter of justice.

- "And again, The Lord shall judge his people": This quotation reinforces the idea that God will judge His people, holding them accountable for their actions.

Concordance:

- Vengeance (Strong's #1557, Greek: ἐκδίκησις, ekdikēsis): vengeance, punishment; it denotes the act of inflicting punishment or retribution in response to wrongdoing.

- Recompense (Strong's #467, Greek: ἀνταπόδοσις, antapodosis): recompense, repayment; it refers to the act of giving back or repaying, often used in the context of divine retribution.

- Saith the Lord (Strong's #3004, Greek: λέγω, legō, κύριος, kyrios): say, speak, Lord; it indicates a statement made by the Lord, emphasizing the authority and certainty of His words.

- Judge (Strong's #2919, Greek: κρίνω, krinō): to judge, decide; it refers to the act of making a judgment or decision based on a standard of righteousness.

- People (Strong's #2992, Greek: λαός, laos): people, nation; it can refer to God's chosen people, the Israelites, or more broadly to believers in Christ.

This verse serves as a reminder of God's role as the ultimate judge and avenger. It underscores the certainty of divine judgment and the importance of living in obedience to God's commands.

Verse 31 (King James Version):
> It is a fearful thing to fall into the hands of the living God.

Interpretation:
This verse highlights the seriousness of encountering God's judgment. Falling into the hands of the living God suggests facing His wrath or justice, which is a daunting prospect.

Commentary:
- "It is a fearful thing": This phrase underscores the gravity and seriousness of the consequences of facing God's judgment. It conveys a sense of awe and dread regarding the power and righteousness of God.

- "To fall into the hands of the living God": Falling into God's hands implies being subject to His judgment and justice. The living God is contrasted with lifeless idols, emphasizing His active and sovereign nature.

Concordance:
- Fearful (Strong's #5398, Greek: φοβερός, phoberos): causing fear, dreadful; it describes something that inspires awe or fear due to its power or severity.
- Fall (Strong's #1706, Greek: ἐμπίπτω, empiptō): to fall into, fall among; it indicates the act of coming under a particular condition or experiencing a certain fate.
- Hands (Strong's #5495, Greek: χείρ, cheir): hand; it symbolizes power, control, or authority.
- Living (Strong's #2198, Greek: ζάω, zaō): living, alive; it emphasizes God's eternal and active existence.

This verse serves as a warning against disobedience and rebellion towards God. It highlights the need for reverence and obedience in our relationship with Him, recognizing His authority and righteousness.

Verse 32 (King James Version):
> But call to remembrance the former days, in which, after ye were illuminated, ye endured a great fight of afflictions;

Interpretation:
The author encourages the readers to remember the early days of their faith when they first believed and were enlightened. Despite facing great suffering and trials, they persevered in their faith.

Commentary:

246

- "Call to remembrance the former days": The author urges the readers to recall and reflect on the early stages of their Christian journey, likely a time of fervor and zeal in their faith.

- "After ye were illuminated": This phrase refers to their conversion or enlightenment to the truth of the gospel, indicating a time when they came to know and understand the light of Christ.

- "Ye endured a great fight of afflictions": Despite facing intense suffering and persecution, the readers remained steadfast in their faith, demonstrating their perseverance and endurance.

Concordance:

- Call (Strong's #3415, Greek: μιμνήσκω, mimnēskō): to remind, remember; it implies an active and intentional act of recalling something to mind.

- Remembrance (Strong's #364, Greek: ἀνάμνησις, anamnēsis): a reminder, remembrance; it signifies the act of remembering or recalling something from the past.

- Former (Strong's #4387, Greek: πρότερος, proteros): former, earlier; it denotes a previous or earlier time.

- Days (Strong's #2250, Greek: ἡμέρα, hēmera): days, time; it refers to a period of time, in this case, the early days of their Christian experience.

- Illuminated (Strong's #5461, Greek: φωτίζω, phōtizō): to enlighten, give light; it signifies the moment of spiritual enlightenment or conversion.

- Endured (Strong's #5297, Greek: ὑπομένω, hupomenō): to endure, remain, persevere; it indicates the readers' perseverance in the face of difficulties.

- Fight (Strong's #73, Greek: ἀθλέω, athleō): to contend, fight; it suggests a struggle or conflict, possibly referring to persecution or hardships.

- Afflictions (Strong's #2347, Greek: θλίψις, thlipsis): affliction, trouble; it denotes suffering or distress, possibly due to persecution or trials.

This verse encourages believers to reflect on their past experiences of God's faithfulness and their perseverance through trials, serving as a reminder of God's sustaining grace in difficult times.

Verse 33 (King James Version):
> Partly, whilst ye were made a gazingstock both by reproaches and afflictions; and partly, whilst ye became companions of them that were so used.

Interpretation:
The author explains that the readers shared in the sufferings of others, both by being publicly shamed and enduring persecution themselves, and by associating with those who faced similar mistreatment.

Commentary:
- "Partly, whilst ye were made a gazingstock both by reproaches and afflictions": This part of the verse refers to the readers' personal experiences of being publicly exposed to shame and enduring various forms of suffering, including verbal abuse and physical afflictions, because of their faith.
- "Partly, whilst ye became companions of them that were so used": The second part of the verse highlights the readers' solidarity with those who were mistreated for their faith. They willingly associated themselves with and supported those who suffered persecution, identifying with their struggles and becoming companions in their suffering.

Concordance:

- Partly (Strong's #3303, Greek: μέρος, meros): a part, share; it indicates that the readers' experiences were only a portion of the overall suffering endured by believers.

- Gazingstock (Strong's #2301, Greek: θέατρον, theatron): a public spectacle; it refers to being exposed to public ridicule or shame, as if on a theater stage for all to see.

- Reproaches (Strong's #3680, Greek: ὀνειδισμός, oneidismos): reproach, insult; it denotes verbal abuse or disgraceful treatment.

- Afflictions (Strong's #2347, Greek: θλίψεις, thlipseis): afflictions, troubles; it refers to suffering or distress, often due to persecution or hardships.

- Became (Strong's #1096, Greek: γίνομαι, ginomai): to become, come into existence; it indicates a change or transformation in their relationship with those who suffered.

- Companions (Strong's #2844, Greek: κοινωνός, koinōnos): partner, companion; it implies a close association or sharing in common experiences.

- Were so used (Strong's #3908, Greek: ἀναστρέφω, anastrephō): to behave, live; it suggests the manner in which they lived or conducted themselves, specifically in the context of suffering persecution.

This verse highlights the readers' personal experiences of suffering and their solidarity with fellow believers who faced persecution. It underscores the challenges they endured for their faith and their willingness to stand with others in the face of adversity.

Verse 34 (King James Version):
> For ye had compassion of me in my bonds, and took joyfully the spoiling of your goods, knowing in yourselves that ye have in heaven a better and an enduring substance.

Interpretation:

The author commends the readers for their compassion towards him while he was imprisoned, and for their joyful acceptance of the confiscation of their possessions, knowing that they have a more valuable and lasting treasure in heaven.

Commentary:

- "For ye had compassion of me in my bonds": This part of the verse acknowledges the readers' empathy and support for the author during his imprisonment, indicating their care and concern for him in his difficult circumstances.

- "And took joyfully the spoiling of your goods": The next part praises the readers for their positive attitude towards the confiscation of their possessions. Despite facing material loss, they maintained a joyful outlook, likely due to their faith and the eternal perspective they held.

- "Knowing in yourselves that ye have in heaven a better and an enduring substance": This phrase explains the reason for their joyful acceptance of material loss. They understood that their true treasure was in heaven, where they possessed a superior and everlasting inheritance, contrasting with the temporary nature of earthly possessions.

Concordance:

- Had compassion (Strong's #4834, Greek: συμπαθέω, sumpatheō): to sympathize, have compassion; it indicates a deep empathy and care for someone else's suffering.

- Bonds (Strong's #1199, Greek: δεσμός, desmos): chains, imprisonment; it refers to being physically bound or imprisoned, suggesting the author's incarceration.

- Took joyfully (Strong's #4328, Greek: χαίρω, chairō): to rejoice, be glad; it indicates a joyful response to a situation, despite its difficulty.

- Spoiling (Strong's #4813, Greek: ἅρπαγμα, harpagma): plunder, robbery; it refers to the confiscation or plundering of possessions.

- Goods (Strong's #5222, Greek: ὑπάρχω, huparchō): possessions, property; it denotes material possessions or belongings.

- Knowing (Strong's #1492, Greek: εἴδω, eidō): to know, understand; it suggests a deep understanding or awareness of a truth or reality.

- In yourselves (Strong's #1438, Greek: ἑαυτοῖς, heautois): in yourselves, within yourselves; it indicates an internal knowledge or conviction.

- Better (Strong's #2909, Greek: κρείσσων, kreissōn): better, more excellent; it refers to something superior in quality or value.

- Enduring (Strong's #3306, Greek: μένω, menō): enduring, lasting; it suggests something that remains and is not subject to decay or loss.

- Substance (Strong's #5223, Greek: ὑπόστασις, hupostasis): substance, assurance; it denotes a firm foundation or basis for confidence.

This verse highlights the readers' remarkable response to suffering and persecution, demonstrating their deep faith and understanding of the eternal treasures that await them in heaven. It serves as an encouragement to endure present hardships in light of the greater reward to come.

Verse 35 (King James Version):
> Cast not away therefore your confidence, which hath great recompence of reward.

Interpretation:

The author urges the readers not to lose their confidence in God and His promises, as it brings a great reward.

Commentary:

- "Cast not away therefore your confidence": This phrase admonishes the readers not to abandon or throw away their confidence in God. Confidence here likely refers to their trust, faith, and assurance in God's promises and faithfulness.

- "Which hath great recompence of reward": The author explains that this confidence brings a great reward. This reward could include blessings, spiritual growth, and ultimately, the eternal reward of salvation.

Concordance:

- Cast not away (Strong's #577, Greek: ἀποβάλλω, apoballō): to throw away, reject; it implies the action of discarding something valuable or important.

- Confidence (Strong's #3954, Greek: παρρησία, parrēsia): confidence, boldness; it refers to a bold and confident demeanor, especially in the context of faith and trust in God.

- Which hath (Strong's #3748, Greek: ὅς, hos): which, who, that; it connects the confidence to the reward, indicating that the reward is associated with the confidence.

- Great (Strong's #3173, Greek: μέγας, megas): great, large; it emphasizes the magnitude or importance of something.

- Recompence of reward (Strong's #3405, Greek: μισθαποδοσία, misthapodosia): recompense, reward; it refers to a reward given in return for something, often used in the context of divine rewards for faithfulness and obedience.

This verse serves as an encouragement for believers to maintain their trust and confidence in God, especially during times of trial and difficulty, as doing so will lead to a great reward.

Verse 36 (King James Version):
> For ye have need of patience, that, after ye have done the will of God, ye might receive the promise.

Interpretation:
The author emphasizes the importance of patience, stating that it is necessary for believers to endure in doing God's will so they can receive the promised blessings.

Commentary:
- "For ye have need of patience": Patience is a key virtue in the Christian life, especially in enduring trials and waiting for God's promises to be fulfilled. It involves enduring with perseverance and steadfastness.
- "That, after ye have done the will of God": The phrase highlights the sequence of events: first, believers are to do the will of God, which involves obedience and faithfulness in following His commands and purposes.
- "Ye might receive the promise": The promise likely refers to the blessings and rewards that God has promised to those who are faithful to Him. These promises are often related to salvation, eternal life, and the blessings of the kingdom of God.

Concordance:
- For ye have need (Strong's #2192, Greek: ἔχω, echō): to have, hold; it indicates a necessity or requirement.

- Patience (Strong's #5281, Greek: ὑπομονή, hupomonē): endurance, steadfastness; it refers to the ability to endure and persevere through trials and challenges.

- After ye have done (Strong's #4160, Greek: ποιέω, poiéō): to do, make; it emphasizes the action of doing or carrying out the will of God.

- The will of God (Strong's #2307, Greek: θέλημα, thelēma): will, desire; it refers to God's purpose, plan, and commands for believers.

- Ye might receive (Strong's #2983, Greek: λαμβάνω, lambanō): to take, receive; it indicates the reception or attainment of something promised or offered.

- The promise (Strong's #1860, Greek: ἐπαγγελία, epangelia): promise; it refers to the specific promises of God, including salvation, eternal life, and the blessings of His kingdom.

This verse underscores the importance of patience in the Christian life, especially in waiting for the fulfillment of God's promises. It encourages believers to persevere in doing God's will, knowing that the promised blessings will come in due time.

Verse 37 (King James Version):
> For yet a little while, and he that shall come will come, and will not tarry.

Interpretation:
The verse suggests that the return of Jesus Christ, who is expected to come again, is imminent and will happen without delay.

Commentary:

- "For yet a little while": This phrase indicates that the time until Christ's return is short or brief from a divine perspective, even though it may seem long to us.

- "And he that shall come will come": This reaffirms the certainty of Christ's return. It emphasizes that He will come back as promised.

- "And will not tarry": This means there will be no delay when Christ returns. When the appointed time arrives, His coming will be prompt and immediate.

Concordance:

- For yet a little while (Strong's #1024, Greek: μικρὸν ὅσον, mikron hoson): a little while, a short time; it suggests that the duration is relatively brief.

- He that shall come (Strong's #2064, Greek: ἔρχομαι, erchomai): to come; it refers to the future return of Jesus Christ.

- Will come (Strong's #2240, Greek: ἔρχομαι, erchomai): to come; it emphasizes the certainty of Christ's return.

- Will not tarry (Strong's #5549, Greek: χρονίζω, chronizō): to delay, tarry; it indicates that there will be no delay or hesitation in Christ's coming.

This verse encourages believers to be ready and watchful for the return of Christ, as it could happen at any moment. It also provides reassurance that Christ's return will happen according to God's timing, without delay.

Verse 38 (King James Version):
> Now the just shall live by faith: but if any man draw back, my soul shall have no pleasure in him.

Interpretation:

This verse emphasizes the importance of faith in the life of a believer. It contrasts the just, who live by faith and please God, with those who draw back from faith, causing displeasure to God.

Commentary:

- "Now the just shall live by faith": This statement is a key theological concept found in several places in the Bible, including the Old Testament (Habakkuk 2:4) and the New Testament (Romans 1:17). It highlights that the righteous or just individuals are those who live their lives in faith, trusting in God's promises and His righteousness rather than relying on their own works.

- "But if any man draw back": This phrase refers to turning away from faith, abandoning or renouncing one's belief in God. It suggests a deliberate choice to reject faith and its principles.

- "My soul shall have no pleasure in him": This indicates that God is displeased with those who turn away from faith. It emphasizes the importance of faith in maintaining a relationship with God and living a life that is pleasing to Him.

Concordance:

- The just shall live by faith (Strong's #1342, Greek: δίκαιος, dikaios; πίστις, pistis): the righteous shall live by faith; it emphasizes that righteousness comes through faith in God.

- But if any man draw back (Strong's #5290, Greek: ὑποστείληται, huposteletai): to draw back, shrink back, withdraw; it denotes a deliberate act of turning away from faith.

- My soul shall have no pleasure in him (Strong's #5590, Greek: εὐδοκέω, eudokeo; ψυχή, psyche): I will not be pleased with him; it signifies God's displeasure with those who reject faith.

This verse serves as an encouragement for believers to remain steadfast in their faith, knowing that living by faith pleases God. It also warns against the serious consequences of turning away from faith, highlighting the importance of perseverance in the Christian journey.

Verse 39 (King James Version):

> But we are not of them who draw back unto perdition; but of them that believe to the saving of the soul.

Interpretation:

This verse contrasts two groups: those who draw back from faith and face destruction (perdition), and those who believe and are saved.

Commentary:

- "But we are not of them who draw back unto perdition": Here, the writer asserts that believers are not among those who turn away from faith and face destruction. This emphasizes the assurance of salvation for those who remain faithful.

- "But of them that believe to the saving of the soul": This part of the verse highlights the positive outcome of faith—salvation. Believers are those who continue to trust in God and His promises, leading to the salvation of their souls.

Concordance:

- We are not of them who draw back (Strong's #5288, Greek: ὑποστολή, hupostolē): withdrawal, shrinking back; believers are not characterized by turning away from faith.

- Unto perdition (Strong's #684, Greek: ἀπώλεια, apōleia): destruction, loss; it refers to the ultimate fate of those who reject faith.

- But of them that believe (Strong's #4100, Greek: πιστεύω, pisteuō): to believe, have faith; believers are those who trust in God.

- To the saving of the soul (Strong's #4047, Greek: ψυχή, psychē; σωτηρία, sōtēria): salvation of the soul; faith leads to the salvation of the soul, indicating the ultimate deliverance and preservation of believers.

This verse serves as an encouragement for believers to remain steadfast in their faith, knowing that their faith leads to salvation. It also reinforces the contrast between the destiny of those who reject faith and face destruction and those who believe and are saved.

CHAPTER 11
Faith defined and exemplified

Verse 1 (King James Version):
> Now faith is the substance of things hoped for, the evidence of things not seen.

Interpretation:
This verse defines faith as the assurance or substance of things hoped for, and the evidence of things not seen. Faith provides a tangible reality to things hoped for and unseen.

Commentary:
- "Now faith is the substance of things hoped for": Faith is described as the underlying assurance or reality of things that are hoped

for. It gives substance or essence to our hopes, making them tangible in our minds and hearts.

- "The evidence of things not seen": Faith is also the evidence or conviction of things that are not visible or apparent to our physical senses. It provides a certainty that goes beyond what can be seen or proven empirically.

Concordance:
- Faith (Strong's #4102, Greek: πίστις, pistis): belief, trust, confidence; it denotes a firm persuasion or conviction based on hearing.
- Is the substance (Strong's #5287, Greek: ὑπόστασις, hupostasis): essence, assurance, confidence; it refers to a confidence or assurance regarding things hoped for.
- Of things hoped for (Strong's #1679, Greek: ἐλπίζω, elpizō; Strong's #4229, Greek: πρᾶγμα, pragma): expected, hoped-for things; faith provides a substantial basis for our hopes and expectations.
- The evidence (Strong's #1650, Greek: ἔλεγχος, elegchos): conviction, evidence; it implies a proof or conviction regarding things not seen.
- Of things not seen (Strong's #991, Greek: βλέπω, blepō; Strong's #3700, Greek: ὁράω, horaō): unseen things; faith provides a certainty regarding things that are not visible or apparent.

This verse highlights the central role of faith in the Christian life. It is the foundation of our hope and the conviction of the reality of unseen things. Faith enables believers to trust in God's promises and to live with confidence in His existence and His power, even when His workings are not immediately visible.

Verse 2 (King James Version):
> For by it the elders obtained a good report.

Interpretation:

This verse suggests that the elders, or people of old, were commended or received approval because of their faith.

Commentary:

- "For by it": Referring to faith, indicating that it was through their faith that the elders received approval.

- "The elders obtained a good report": This implies that the elders, or the people of old mentioned in Hebrews 11, were commended or approved for their faith. Their faith was not just a personal conviction but something that was recognized and acknowledged by God.

Concordance:

- Elders (Strong's #4245, Greek: πρεσβύτερος, presbuteros): elders, older people, ancestors; it refers to those who lived in ancient times, especially those mentioned in Hebrews 11 as examples of faith.

- Obtained a good report (Strong's #3140, Greek: μαρτυρέω, martureō; Strong's #3141, Greek: μαρτύριον, martyrion): to bear witness, to obtain a good testimony; it suggests that the elders received a favorable testimony or approval because of their faith.

This verse emphasizes the importance of faith as a means of receiving God's approval. The examples of faith in Hebrews 11 serve as a testimony to the power and significance of faith in the lives of believers.

Verse 3 (King James Version):

> Through faith we understand that the worlds were framed by the word of God, so that things which are seen were not made of things which do appear.

Interpretation:

This verse asserts that faith enables us to understand that the universe was created by the word of God, and that the visible world was formed from the invisible.

Commentary:

- "Through faith we understand": Faith is presented as the lens through which we comprehend or perceive certain truths about the creation of the world.

- "That the worlds were framed by the word of God": This indicates that the universe, or the "worlds," were created by God's spoken word, as described in the Genesis account of creation.

- "So that things which are seen were not made of things which do appear": This suggests that the visible, material world was not created from pre-existing visible substances but from the invisible, indicating a supernatural act of creation by God.

Concordance:

- Worlds (Strong's #165, Greek: αἰών, aiōn): ages, universe, world; it refers to the created order or the universe.

- Framed (Strong's #2675, Greek: καταρτίζω, katartizō): to complete thoroughly, to repair, to adjust; it implies the idea of the universe being perfectly ordered or fashioned by God's word.

- Word of God (Strong's #3056, Greek: λόγος, logos; Strong's #2316, Greek: θεός, theos): the creative utterance or command of God; it refers to God's divine word or command that brought the universe into existence.

- Things which are seen (Strong's #991, Greek: βλεπτός, bleptos): visible things, things that can be seen; it refers to the material world.

- Things which do appear (Strong's #991, Greek: βλέπω, blepō): to look at, to see; it suggests that the visible world was not made from visible substances but from the invisible, indicating a divine and supernatural act of creation.

This verse emphasizes the foundational role of faith in understanding the creation of the world as a divine act brought about by God's word, not through natural processes.

Verse 4 (King James Version):
> By faith Abel offered unto God a more excellent sacrifice than Cain, by which he obtained witness that he was righteous, God testifying of his gifts: and by it he being dead yet speaketh.

Interpretation:
This verse highlights Abel's act of offering a sacrifice to God by faith, which was regarded as more excellent than Cain's. Through this act, Abel was recognized as righteous, and even though he is dead, his faith and righteousness continue to speak.

Commentary:
- "By faith Abel offered unto God a more excellent sacrifice than Cain": Abel's sacrifice was deemed more excellent not because of the nature of the offering itself, but because it was offered in faith, with a right heart attitude.
- "By which he obtained witness that he was righteous": Abel's act of faith testified to his righteousness before God, indicating that his faith was genuine and sincere.
- "God testifying of his gifts": God accepted Abel's sacrifice, signifying His approval of Abel's faith and righteousness.

- "And by it he being dead yet speaketh": Despite Abel's death, his faith and the righteousness it produced continue to speak or testify to others, serving as an example of true faith.

Concordance:
- Faith (Strong's #4102, Greek: πίστις, pistis): belief, trust, confidence; it refers to a firm conviction or belief in something unseen or unproven.
- Sacrifice (Strong's #2378, Greek: θυσία, thysia): an offering, especially a religious offering; it refers to something offered as an act of worship or devotion to God.
- Righteous (Strong's #1342, Greek: δίκαιος, dikaios): just, upright, righteous; it denotes one who is in accordance with God's standards of righteousness.
- God testifying (Strong's #3140, Greek: μαρτυρέω, martyreō): to testify, bear witness; it indicates God's approval or confirmation of something.
- Gifts (Strong's #1435, Greek: δῶρον, dōron): a gift, present; it likely refers to Abel's sacrifice, which was an expression of his faith and devotion to God.
- Being dead yet speaketh (Strong's #435, Greek: λαλέω, laleō; Strong's #599, Greek: ἔτι, eti): to talk, speak; even though Abel is physically dead, his faith and righteous example continue to speak to others.

This verse underscores the importance of genuine faith in our relationship with God, showing that our actions and offerings are meaningful when they stem from a sincere heart of faith.

Verse 5 (King James Version):

> By faith Enoch was translated that he should not see death; and was not found, because God had translated him: for before his translation he had this testimony, that he pleased God.

Interpretation:

This verse speaks of Enoch, who was taken by God without experiencing death. It emphasizes that Enoch's life pleased God, and this pleasing relationship with God was the result of his faith.

Commentary:

- "By faith Enoch was translated that he should not see death": Enoch's translation refers to his being taken up to heaven without experiencing physical death. This event is a testament to Enoch's close relationship with God and his faith.

- "And was not found, because God had translated him": Enoch's disappearance from earth was due to God's direct intervention, indicating a unique and special relationship between Enoch and God.

- "For before his translation he had this testimony, that he pleased God": Enoch's life was characterized by pleasing God, which implies that his faith was genuine and his actions were in accordance with God's will.

Concordance:

- Faith (Strong's #4102, Greek: πίστις, pistis): belief, trust, confidence; it refers to a firm conviction or belief in something unseen or unproven.

- Translated (Strong's #3346, Greek: μετατίθημι, metatithēmi): to transfer, transport, remove; it indicates Enoch's removal from earth to heaven without experiencing death.

- Pleased (Strong's #2100, Greek: εὐαρεστέω, euaresteō): to be well-pleasing, to be acceptable; it suggests that Enoch's life and actions were pleasing or acceptable to God.

- Testimony (Strong's #3141, Greek: μαρτυρία, martyria): testimony, witness; it refers to the witness or evidence of Enoch's pleasing relationship with God.
- God (Strong's #2316, Greek: θεός, theos): God, the Creator and Supreme Being; in this context, it signifies God's role in Enoch's translation and his pleasure with Enoch's life.

Enoch's story illustrates the close relationship that faith can cultivate between believers and God. It shows that a life lived in faith and obedience can lead to a pleasing relationship with God, ultimately resulting in divine favor and blessings.

Verse 6 (King James Version):
> But without faith it is impossible to please him: for he that cometh to God must believe that he is, and that he is a rewarder of them that diligently seek him.

Interpretation:
This verse emphasizes the central role of faith in pleasing God. It states that those who approach God must believe in His existence and His willingness to reward those who earnestly seek Him.

Commentary:
- "But without faith it is impossible to please him": This statement underscores the foundational importance of faith in the relationship between humans and God. Faith is not just one aspect of pleasing God; it is the essential prerequisite.
- "For he that cometh to God must believe that he is": Belief in the existence of God is fundamental. It's not merely a belief in the concept of God but a deep conviction that God truly exists.

- "And that he is a rewarder of them that diligently seek him": Faith also involves trust in God's character—that He is not only real but also just and loving, rewarding those who earnestly seek Him.

Concordance:
- Faith (Strong's #4102, Greek: πίστις, pistis): belief, trust, confidence; it signifies a strong conviction or trust in something or someone.
- Please (Strong's #2100, Greek: εὐαρεστέω, euaresteō): to be well-pleasing, to be acceptable; it indicates the act of bringing joy, satisfaction, or approval to someone.
- Believe (Strong's #4100, Greek: πιστεύω, pisteuō): to believe, have faith in, trust; it signifies a firm conviction or trust in the truth or reliability of something.
- Rewarder (Strong's #3406, Greek: μισθαποδότης, misthapodotēs): one who pays wages, a recompenser; it refers to God as the One who gives a just recompense or reward.

This verse highlights the relationship between faith and the nature of God. It suggests that faith involves not just a belief in God's existence but also a trust in His character and a reliance on His promises. This trust leads to a life that seeks after God diligently, knowing that He rewards such seekers.

Verse 7 (King James Version):
> By faith Noah, being warned of God of things not seen as yet, moved with fear, prepared an ark to the saving of his house; by the which he condemned the world, and became heir of the righteousness which is by faith.

Interpretation:

This verse highlights the faith of Noah, who, despite not yet seeing the flood, obeyed God's warning and built an ark. His faith not only saved his family but also served as a condemnation of the world's unbelief. Through his faith, Noah was considered righteous before God.

Commentary:
- "By faith Noah, being warned of God of things not seen as yet": Noah's faith was based on God's warning about the coming flood, which Noah had not yet witnessed.
- "Moved with fear": Noah's response to God's warning was one of reverence and obedience, demonstrating his faith.
- "Prepared an ark to the saving of his house": Noah's obedience to God's instructions in building the ark resulted in the salvation of his family from the flood.
- "By the which he condemned the world": Noah's faith stood in stark contrast to the unbelief of the world around him, highlighting their condemnation for rejecting God's warning.
- "And became heir of the righteousness which is by faith": Noah's faith made him a recipient of God's righteousness, which comes through faith.

Concordance:
- Faith (Strong's #4102, Greek: πίστις, pistis): belief, trust, confidence; it signifies a strong conviction or trust in something or someone.
- Warned (Strong's #5537, Greek: χρηματίζω, chrēmatizō): to give information to, to instruct, to warn; it indicates a divine communication or instruction.

- Things not seen (Strong's #3361, Greek: μὴ, mē + ὁράω, horaō): unseen things, invisible things; it refers to things that are not visible or apparent.

- Moved with fear (Strong's #2125, Greek: εὐλαβέομαι, eulabeomai): to take heed, to be cautious, to show reverence; it indicates a reverent and cautious response to a warning or instruction.

- Prepared (Strong's #2680, Greek: κατασκευάζω, kataskeuazō): to prepare, to make ready; it refers to the action of building or constructing.

- Saving (Strong's #4991, Greek: σωτηρία, sōtēria): salvation, deliverance, preservation; it signifies the act of being rescued or saved from harm.

- Condemned (Strong's #2632, Greek: κατακρίνω, katakrinō): to judge against, to condemn; it indicates a judgment of guilt or disapproval.

- Righteousness (Strong's #1343, Greek: δικαιοσύνη, dikaiosunē): righteousness, justice, integrity; it refers to the state of being morally right or just.

Noah's faith is celebrated in this verse as an example of obedience and trust in God's word, even when it required actions that seemed unusual or contrary to human experience. His faith not only secured his own salvation but also served as a testament to the world of God's righteous judgment.

Verse 8 (King James Version):
> By faith Abraham, when he was called to go out into a place which he should after receive for an inheritance, obeyed; and he went out, not knowing whither he went.

Interpretation:

This verse speaks of Abraham's faith when God called him to leave his homeland and go to a place that God would later reveal to him as his inheritance. Abraham obeyed God's call, even though he did not know where he was going.

Commentary:
- "By faith Abraham": Abraham's faith is emphasized as the motivation for his actions.
- "When he was called to go out into a place": God called Abraham to leave his homeland and go to a place that God would later reveal to him.
- "Which he should after receive for an inheritance": Abraham was promised by God that the place he was going to would be his inheritance.
- "Obeyed": Abraham's response to God's call was obedience, demonstrating his faith.
- "Not knowing whither he went": Despite not knowing the specific destination, Abraham trusted God and embarked on the journey.

Concordance:
- Faith (Strong's #4102, Greek: πίστις, pistis): belief, trust, confidence; it signifies a strong conviction or trust in something or someone.
- Called (Strong's #2564, Greek: καλέω, kaleō): to call, to summon; it indicates a divine calling or invitation.
- Go out (Strong's #1831, Greek: ἐξέρχομαι, exerchomai): to go out, to depart; it refers to physically leaving a place.
- Inheritance (Strong's #2817, Greek: κληρονομία, klēronomia): inheritance, possession; it signifies something received as a possession or heritage.

- Obeyed (Strong's #5219, Greek: ὑπακούω, hypakouō): to obey, to hear, to listen; it indicates a response of compliance to a command or instruction.

- Not knowing (Strong's #3361, Greek: μὴ, mē + οἶδα, oida): not knowing, unaware; it indicates a lack of knowledge or information.

- Whither he went (Strong's #4226, Greek: ποῦ, pou + ὁδός, hodos): where, way, road; it refers to the destination or path of travel.

Abraham's faith is celebrated in this verse as an example of obedience and trust in God's guidance, even when the destination was unknown to him. His willingness to follow God's call without fully understanding demonstrates his deep faith and reliance on God's promises.

Verse 9 (King James Version):
> By faith he sojourned in the land of promise, as in a strange country, dwelling in tabernacles with Isaac and Jacob, the heirs with him of the same promise.

Interpretation:
This verse refers to Abraham's faith as he lived in the promised land, which was unfamiliar to him, dwelling in tents along with Isaac and Jacob, who were also heirs of the promise made to Abraham.

Commentary:
- "By faith he sojourned in the land of promise": Abraham lived in the land that God had promised to give to him and his descendants.
- "As in a strange country": Even though the land was promised to him, Abraham lived there as a foreigner or stranger because he did not possess it as his own.
- "Dwelling in tabernacles": Abraham, Isaac, and Jacob lived in tents or temporary shelters, emphasizing their nomadic lifestyle.

- "With Isaac and Jacob, the heirs with him of the same promise": Isaac and Jacob were also partakers in the promise given to Abraham, that their descendants would inherit the land.

Concordance:
- Faith (Strong's #4102, Greek: πίστις, pistis): belief, trust, confidence; it signifies a strong conviction or trust in something or someone.
- Sojourned (Strong's #3939, Greek: παροικέω, paroikeō): to dwell as a stranger, to sojourn; it refers to residing in a place where one is not a native.
- Land of promise (Strong's #1869, Greek: γῆ, gē + ἐπαγγελία, epangelia): land, promise; it refers to the territory that God promised to give to Abraham and his descendants.
- Strange country (Strong's #245, Greek: ξένος, xenos + γῆ, gē): foreign land, strange country; it denotes a land that is not one's own.
- Dwelling (Strong's #4637, Greek: σκηνόω, skēnoō): to tent or encamp, to dwell; it indicates residing in temporary accommodations.
- Tabernacles (Strong's #4633, Greek: σκηνή, skēnē): tent, tabernacle; it refers to a temporary dwelling or shelter.
- Heirs (Strong's #2818, Greek: κληρονόμος, klēronomos): heir, possessor; it signifies one who receives an inheritance or possession.
- Same promise (Strong's #846, Greek: αὐτός, autos + ἐπαγγελία, epangelia): same, promise; it refers to the promise of God to give the land as an inheritance.

This verse highlights Abraham's faith as he lived in the promised land, trusting in God's promise even though he did not possess the land himself. His lifestyle as a nomad in tents underscored his recognition that his true inheritance was not in this world but in the future fulfillment of God's promise.

Verse 10 (King James Version):

> For he looked for a city which hath foundations, whose builder and maker is God.

Interpretation:

This verse speaks of Abraham's anticipation and longing for a city that God had designed and built, emphasizing his faith in God's promises.

Commentary:

- "For he looked for a city": Abraham anticipated or expected a city, indicating his forward-looking faith.

- "Which hath foundations": This city was not a temporary or earthly city but one with solid, lasting foundations, indicating permanence and stability.

- "Whose builder and maker is God": Abraham understood that this city was not constructed by human hands but by God Himself, emphasizing its divine origin and eternal nature.

Concordance:

- Looked for (Strong's #4327, Greek: προσδοκάω, prosdokaō): to expect, look for; it denotes an eager anticipation or expectation.

- City (Strong's #4172, Greek: πόλις, polis): city; it signifies a place of habitation, community, and civilization.

- Foundations (Strong's #2310, Greek: θεμέλιος, themelios): foundation; it refers to the base or groundwork upon which something is built.

- Builder (Strong's #5045, Greek: τεχνίτης, technitēs): craftsman, builder; it denotes one who constructs or creates something.

- Maker (Strong's #5045, Greek: δημιουργός, dēmiourgos): maker, creator; it signifies one who brings something into existence or forms it.

This verse underscores Abraham's faith in God's promise of a future city, symbolizing the eternal and heavenly inheritance awaiting believers. It also reflects the Christian's perspective of looking beyond the earthly and temporary to the heavenly and eternal.

Verse 11 (King James Version):
> Through faith also Sara herself received strength to conceive seed, and was delivered of a child when she was past age, because she judged him faithful who had promised.

Interpretation:
This verse highlights Sarah's faith in God's promise to give her and Abraham a child, despite her advanced age. It emphasizes her trust in God's faithfulness to fulfill His word.

Commentary:
- "Through faith also Sarah herself received strength to conceive seed": Sarah's ability to conceive a child in her old age was a result of her faith in God's promise. Her faith enabled her to overcome the natural limitations of her age.
- "And was delivered of a child when she was past age": This refers to the birth of Isaac, which occurred when Sarah was well beyond the typical childbearing years, highlighting the miraculous nature of his birth.
- "Because she judged him faithful who had promised": Sarah's faith was rooted in her conviction that God was faithful and would

fulfill His promise to give her and Abraham a child. Her belief in God's faithfulness was the foundation of her faith.

Concordance:

- Received strength (Strong's #1412, Greek: ἐνδυναμόω, endynamoo): to empower, enable; it indicates the divine enablement or empowerment Sarah received to conceive.

- Conceive seed (Strong's #4690, Greek: σπέρμα, sperma): to conceive seed; it refers to the conception of a child.

- Delivered (Strong's #1080, Greek: τίκτω, tiktō): to bring forth, bear; it signifies the act of giving birth.

- Past age (Strong's #5544, Greek: παράκειμαι, parakeimai): to be past the age, to be advanced in years; it denotes being well beyond the typical age for childbearing.

- Judged (Strong's #2233, Greek: ἡγέομαι, hēgeomai): to consider, regard; it indicates Sarah's estimation or assessment of God's faithfulness.

This verse highlights Sarah as an example of faith, emphasizing her trust in God's faithfulness and His ability to fulfill His promises, even in seemingly impossible circumstances. It encourages believers to trust in God's promises, knowing that He is faithful to fulfill them.

Verse 12 (King James Version):
> Therefore sprang there even of one, and him as good as dead, so many as the stars of the sky in multitude, and as the sand which is by the sea shore innumerable.

Interpretation:
This verse refers to the fulfillment of God's promise to Abraham regarding his descendants. Despite Abraham's old age and Sarah's barrenness, God enabled them to have a son, Isaac, who became

the ancestor of a great multitude, fulfilling God's promise to make Abraham the father of many nations.

Commentary:
- "Therefore sprang there even of one, and him as good as dead": This phrase emphasizes the miraculous nature of Isaac's birth. Abraham, who was as good as dead in terms of his ability to father a child due to his advanced age, became the father of many nations through Isaac.

- "So many as the stars of the sky in multitude, and as the sand which is by the sea shore innumerable": This imagery illustrates the vast number of descendants that God promised to Abraham. It emphasizes the fulfillment of God's promise to make Abraham the father of a great nation, a promise that was realized through Isaac and his descendants.

Concordance:
- Sprang there even of one (Strong's #1537, Greek: ἐκ, ek; and #3391, Greek: μία, mia): out of one; it signifies the miraculous birth of Isaac, who was born from Abraham and Sarah, who were both beyond the age of bearing children.

- As good as dead (Strong's #3499, Greek: νενεκρωμένου, nenekrōmenou): to be deadened; it describes Abraham's condition in terms of his ability to father a child, highlighting the impossibility of natural conception at his age.

- Stars of the sky (Strong's #798, Greek: ἀστήρ, astēr): stars; it symbolizes the multitude of Abraham's descendants, emphasizing their vast number.

- Sand which is by the sea shore (Strong's #285, Greek: ἄμμος, ammos): sand; it also symbolizes the multitude of Abraham's descendants, indicating their countless number.

This verse underscores the miraculous nature of Isaac's birth and the fulfillment of God's promise to Abraham regarding his descendants. It highlights the faithfulness of God in fulfilling His promises, even when they seem impossible from a human perspective.

Verse 13 (King James Version):
> These all died in faith, not having received the promises, but having seen them afar off, and were persuaded of them, and embraced them, and confessed that they were strangers and pilgrims on the earth.

Interpretation:
This verse refers to the faith of the patriarchs and other faithful individuals mentioned in Hebrews 11. Despite not seeing the fulfillment of God's promises in their lifetimes, they believed in them, embraced them, and acknowledged that their true home was not on earth but in heaven.

Commentary:
- "These all died in faith": This phrase emphasizes that the individuals mentioned in Hebrews 11, including Abraham, Sarah, and others, died while still trusting in God's promises, even though they had not yet been fully realized.

- "Not having received the promises": Despite God's promises to them, such as the promise of a land for their descendants, they did not see these promises fulfilled during their lifetimes.

- "But having seen them afar off": This indicates that these individuals had a forward-looking faith. They were able to envision the fulfillment of God's promises in the future, even though it had not yet come to pass.

- "And were persuaded of them": They were fully convinced of the certainty of God's promises, even though they had not yet experienced them.

- "And embraced them": They eagerly accepted God's promises as true and reliable, even though they had not yet come to fruition.

- "And confessed that they were strangers and pilgrims on the earth": This refers to their acknowledgment that their true citizenship and home were in heaven, not on earth. They understood that this world was not their permanent dwelling place, but rather a temporary residence.

Concordance:

- Died (Strong's #599, Greek: ἀποθνῄσκω, apothnēskō): to die; it emphasizes that these individuals passed away without seeing the fulfillment of God's promises in their lifetimes.

- Faith (Strong's #4102, Greek: πίστις, pistis): conviction of the truth of anything, belief; it denotes the unwavering trust these individuals had in God and His promises.

- Not having received (Strong's #3361, Greek: μή, mē; and #2865, Greek: λαμβάνω, lambanō): not yet received; it highlights that the promises had not yet been realized by these individuals.

- Promises (Strong's #1860, Greek: ἐπαγγελία, epangelia): promise; it refers to the assurances given by God to these individuals.

- Seen them afar off (Strong's #4207, Greek: πόρρωθεν, porrōthen; and #3708, Greek: ὁράω, horaō): to see from afar; it indicates that they had a vision of the fulfillment of God's promises, even though it had not yet occurred.

- Persuaded (Strong's #3982, Greek: πείθω, peithō): to persuade, to have confidence; it denotes their firm conviction and confidence in the certainty of God's promises.

- Embraced them (Strong's #782, Greek: ἀσπάζομαι, aspazomai): to greet, to embrace; it signifies their enthusiastic acceptance and welcome of God's promises.

- Confessed (Strong's #3670, Greek: ὁμολογέω, homologeō): to confess, to acknowledge; it indicates their acknowledgment that they were temporary residents on earth, looking forward to their eternal home in heaven.

This verse highlights the faith of the Old Testament saints who trusted in God's promises even though they did not see them fulfilled in their lifetimes. It serves as an encouragement to believers to maintain faith in God's promises, even when they seem distant or delayed.

Verse 14 (King James Version):
> For they that say such things declare plainly that they seek a country.

Interpretation:
This verse refers to the patriarchs and faithful individuals mentioned in Hebrews 11 who, through their words and actions, made it clear that they were seeking a heavenly country, not an earthly one.

Commentary:
- "For they that say such things": This indicates that the individuals mentioned in the previous verses (Abraham, Sarah, and others) expressed their faith and longing for a heavenly homeland.
- "Declare plainly": Their words and actions clearly indicated their desire for a heavenly country. They were not seeking an earthly, temporal dwelling but a heavenly, eternal one.
- "That they seek a country": This country refers to the heavenly city or homeland promised by God to those who believe in Him. It is a place where God dwells, and believers will dwell with Him for eternity.

Concordance:

- Declare (Strong's #1718, Greek: ἐμφανίζω, emphanizō): to manifest, to make known; it emphasizes that their words and actions clearly showed their desire for a heavenly country.

- Plainly (Strong's #3956, Greek: πᾶς, pas; and #3954, Greek: παρρησία, parrēsia): all, openly; it indicates that their declaration was clear and unambiguous.

- Seek (Strong's #1934, Greek: ἐπιζητέω, epizēteō): to seek after, to search for; it denotes their earnest desire and pursuit of a heavenly homeland.

- Country (Strong's #3968, Greek: πατρίς, patris): a fatherland, a native country; it refers to the heavenly city or homeland that believers are seeking, where God dwells and where they will dwell with Him for eternity.

This verse underscores the faith and hope of the Old Testament saints, who looked beyond the earthly realm to a heavenly homeland promised by God. It encourages believers to also set their sights on the eternal promises of God and to live with a heavenly perspective, knowing that this world is not their final home.

Verse 15 (King James Version):
> And truly, if they had been mindful of that country from whence they came out, they might have had opportunity to have returned.

Interpretation:
This verse suggests that if these faithful individuals had been thinking about the country they had left behind, that is, their earthly homeland, they would have had the opportunity to return to it.

Commentary:

- "And truly, if they had been mindful of that country": This indicates that if these individuals had been focused on their earthly homeland, if their hearts and minds had been set on returning there, they would have had the opportunity to do so.

- "From whence they came out": This refers to the physical places they had left behind, such as Ur for Abraham or Egypt for Moses. It represents their past lives before they embarked on their journey of faith.

- "They might have had opportunity to have returned": This suggests that had their hearts been set on returning to their previous lives, they could have done so. However, their focus was on a greater promise—the heavenly country.

Concordance:

- Mindful (Strong's #3421, Greek: μνημονεύω, mnēmoneuō): to remember, to think of; it implies a continual focus or preoccupation with something.

- Country (Strong's #3968, Greek: πατρίς, patris): a fatherland, a native country; it refers to their earthly homeland, the place they had left behind.

- Opportunity (Strong's #2117, Greek: ἔχω, echō): to have, to hold; it suggests the possibility or capability of returning to their previous life.

This verse highlights the single-mindedness and faith of these Old Testament saints, who, despite the challenges and difficulties they faced, remained focused on the heavenly promise rather than being drawn back to their former way of life. It serves as an encouragement for believers to remain steadfast in their faith and to keep their eyes fixed on the eternal promises of God.

Verse 16 (King James Version):

> But now they desire a better country, that is, an heavenly: wherefore God is not ashamed to be called their God: for he hath prepared for them a city.

Interpretation:
This verse contrasts the earthly homeland the faithful could have returned to with the heavenly country they actually desire. Because they seek a heavenly home, God is proud to be called their God and has prepared a city for them.

Commentary:
- "But now they desire a better country, that is, an heavenly": This highlights the shift in focus from an earthly homeland to a heavenly one. The faithful long for a better, heavenly country, indicating their desire for the promises of God's kingdom.
- "Wherefore God is not ashamed to be called their God": This signifies God's approval and pride in these faithful individuals. Their faith and desire for heavenly things are pleasing to Him.
- "For he hath prepared for them a city": God has a special reward for those who seek Him with faith. He has prepared a heavenly city for them, symbolizing the ultimate fulfillment of their longing for a better country.

Concordance:
- Desire (Strong's #3713, Greek: ὀρέγομαι, oregomai): to stretch oneself out in order to touch or grasp something; it denotes a strong desire or longing.
- Better (Strong's #2908, Greek: κρείττων, kreitton): stronger, more excellent; it suggests superiority in quality or nature.

- Heavenly (Strong's #2032, Greek: ἐπουράνιος, epouranios): heavenly, celestial; it refers to things pertaining to heaven or the divine realm.

- Ashamed (Strong's #1870, Greek: ἐπαισχύνομαι, epaischynomai): to be ashamed, to feel shame; in this context, it implies God's pride and approval.

- Prepared (Strong's #2090, Greek: ἑτοιμάζω, hetoimazō): to make ready, to prepare; it indicates that God has made the necessary arrangements for their heavenly dwelling.

- City (Strong's #4172, Greek: πόλις, polis): a city; it represents the heavenly dwelling or the eternal kingdom of God.

This verse emphasizes the superior nature of the heavenly country compared to the earthly one. It underscores the idea that God rewards those who seek Him diligently and have faith in His promises. It serves as an encouragement for believers to set their hearts and minds on heavenly things rather than earthly ones.

Verse 17 (King James Version):
> By faith Abraham, when he was tried, offered up Isaac: and he that had received the promises offered up his only begotten son,

Interpretation:
This verse recounts the story of Abraham's remarkable act of faith when he was tested by God to sacrifice his son Isaac. Despite having received the promises of God through Isaac, Abraham was willing to obey God's command and offer his son as a sacrifice, demonstrating his profound faith and obedience.

Commentary:
- "By faith Abraham, when he was tried, offered up Isaac": This refers to the account in Genesis 22 where God tested Abraham's faith

by commanding him to sacrifice Isaac, his beloved son. Abraham's willingness to obey God's command, even in the face of such a difficult request, demonstrated his unwavering faith.

- "And he that had received the promises offered up his only begotten son": Abraham had received the promises of God regarding Isaac, through whom God had promised to bless all nations. Despite this, Abraham was willing to sacrifice Isaac, trusting in God's ability to fulfill His promises even if Isaac were to die.

Concordance:

- Faith (Strong's #4102, Greek: πίστις, pistis): faith, belief, trust; it denotes a firm conviction, assurance, or trust in something or someone.

- Tried (Strong's #3985, Greek: πειράζω, peirazō): to test, try, tempt; it refers to a trial or testing of one's faith or character.

- Offered up (Strong's #4374, Greek: προσφέρω, prospherō): to offer, present; it indicates Abraham's act of offering Isaac as a sacrifice.

- Only begotten (Strong's #3439, Greek: μονογενής, monogenēs): only, unique, one of a kind; it emphasizes the special relationship between Isaac and Abraham as his unique son.

- Promises (Strong's #1860, Greek: ἐπαγγελία, epangelia): promise, announcement; it refers to the promises God made to Abraham regarding his descendants and blessings.

- Son (Strong's #5207, Greek: υἱός, huios): son, descendant; it denotes Isaac as Abraham's offspring and heir of the promises.

This verse showcases Abraham's extraordinary faith and obedience to God, even in the face of a seemingly impossible request. It serves as a powerful example of faith for believers, demonstrating the kind of trust and obedience God desires from His people.

Verse 18 (King James Version):
> Of whom it was said, That in Isaac shall thy seed be called:

Interpretation:
This verse refers to the promise God made to Abraham regarding his descendants, stating that his offspring would be called through Isaac.

Commentary:
- "Of whom it was said": This phrase indicates that the promise was made concerning Isaac, through whom God had promised to bless Abraham's descendants.
- "That in Isaac shall thy seed be called": This is a reference to Genesis 21:12, where God reaffirms His covenant with Abraham and specifies that it is through Isaac that his descendants will be called. This promise underscores the significance of Isaac in God's plan for Abraham's descendants and the fulfillment of His covenant promises.

Concordance:
- Isaac (Strong's #2464, Greek: Ἰσαάκ, Isaak): Isaac, the son of Abraham and Sarah; he was the child of promise through whom Abraham's descendants would be called.
- Seed (Strong's #4690, Greek: σπέρμα, sperma): seed, offspring, descendant; it refers to the descendants or posterity of Abraham that would come through Isaac.
- Called (Strong's #2564, Greek: καλέω, kaleō): to call, summon, name; it denotes the act of naming or calling someone, in this case, the calling or naming of Abraham's descendants through Isaac.

This verse reinforces the importance of Isaac in the fulfillment of God's promises to Abraham and highlights the lineage through which God's covenant blessings would be passed down. It emphasizes the faithfulness of God in fulfilling His promises, even in situations that seem impossible from a human perspective.

Verse 19 (King James Version):
> Accounting that God was able to raise him up, even from the dead; from whence also he received him in a figure.

Interpretation:
This verse refers to Abraham's faith in God's promise, believing that even if he sacrificed Isaac, God would raise him from the dead. It also suggests that Abraham received Isaac back from the brink of death as a foreshadowing or symbol of resurrection.

Commentary:
- "Accounting that God was able to raise him up, even from the dead": Abraham believed that God had the power to raise Isaac from the dead if he sacrificed him, showing his unwavering faith in God's ability to fulfill His promises even in seemingly impossible situations.
- "From whence also he received him in a figure": This phrase suggests that Abraham figuratively received Isaac back from the dead when God provided a ram for the sacrifice instead. This event served as a symbolic representation or prefiguring of resurrection, illustrating God's provision and faithfulness.

Concordance:
- Accounting (Strong's #3049, Greek: λογίζομαι, logizomai): to reckon, count, consider; it denotes a deliberate and reasoned conclusion, emphasizing Abraham's thoughtful and intentional belief in God's power.

- Able (Strong's #1415, Greek: δύναμαι, dynamai): to be able, have power; it signifies God's inherent ability and power to perform miraculous acts, including raising the dead.

- Received (Strong's #2865, Greek: κομίζω, komizō): to bear, carry, receive; it indicates Abraham's reception of Isaac back from the brink of death, either literally or symbolically.

- Figure (Strong's #3844, Greek: παραβολή, parabolē): a parable, illustration, symbol; it suggests that the event of Abraham offering Isaac was symbolic or illustrative of greater spiritual truths, including the concept of resurrection.

This verse highlights Abraham's profound faith in God's power and faithfulness, demonstrating that he believed in the resurrection long before it was explicitly taught in Scripture. It also points to the symbolic nature of the event, illustrating spiritual truths related to God's provision and the promise of resurrection.

Verse 20 (King James Version):
> By faith Isaac blessed Jacob and Esau concerning things to come.

Interpretation:
This verse highlights Isaac's act of blessing his sons, Jacob and Esau, based on his faith in God's promises regarding their future.

Commentary:
- "By faith Isaac blessed Jacob and Esau": Isaac, despite his physical blindness and old age, blessed his sons based on his faith in God's promises. This act of blessing was not merely a formality but a significant event with spiritual implications, indicating Isaac's trust in God's covenantal promises.

- "Concerning things to come": Isaac's blessings were not just for the present but also included prophetic elements regarding the future destinies of Jacob and Esau. This demonstrates Isaac's belief in God's sovereignty over future events and his role in fulfilling His promises.

Concordance:
- Blessed (Strong's #2127, Greek: εὐλογέω, eulogeō): to speak well of, praise, bless; it signifies Isaac's act of invoking divine favor and bestowing a prophetic blessing upon his sons.
- Concerning things to come (Strong's #3195, Greek: μέλλω, mellō): about to happen, future; it indicates that Isaac's blessings included prophetic elements regarding the future destinies of Jacob and Esau, showing his faith in God's promises for their future.

Isaac's blessing of Jacob and Esau by faith illustrates his trust in God's plan and his role in fulfilling His promises. It also underscores the importance of faith in receiving and imparting blessings in accordance with God's will.

Verse 21 (King James Version):
> By faith Jacob, when he was a dying, blessed both the sons of Joseph; and worshipped, leaning upon the top of his staff.

Interpretation:
This verse recounts Jacob's act of blessing Joseph's sons, Ephraim and Manasseh, and his act of worship while leaning on his staff, all done in faith.

Commentary:

- "By faith Jacob, when he was a dying, blessed both the sons of Joseph": Despite his impending death, Jacob trusted in God's promises and blessed Joseph's sons, Ephraim and Manasseh. This blessing was significant, as it indicated the transfer of the birthright to Ephraim, the younger son, in accordance with God's will (Genesis 48:14-20).

- "And worshipped, leaning upon the top of his staff": Jacob's act of worship while leaning on his staff symbolizes his trust in God's faithfulness and his reliance on Him for support, even in his old age and frailty. It demonstrates Jacob's acknowledgment of God's sovereignty and his unwavering faith in His promises.

Concordance:

- By faith (Strong's #4102, Greek: πίστις, pistis): faith, belief, trust; it signifies Jacob's reliance on God's promises and his confident expectation of their fulfillment.

- Leaning upon the top of his staff (Strong's #4637, Greek: σκῆνος, skēnos): tent, dwelling; it metaphorically represents Jacob's acknowledgment of his temporary dwelling on earth and his anticipation of the eternal promises of God.

Jacob's actions in blessing Joseph's sons and worshiping God while leaning on his staff exemplify his faith in God's promises and his recognition of God's faithfulness throughout his life. This serves as a reminder of the importance of trusting in God's plan and worshiping Him in all circumstances.

Verse 22 (King James Version):
> By faith Joseph, when he died, made mention of the departing of the children of Israel; and gave commandment concerning his bones.

Interpretation:

This verse highlights Joseph's faith as he made provisions for the departure of the Israelites from Egypt and gave instructions regarding the burial of his remains in the Promised Land.

Commentary:

- "By faith Joseph, when he died, made mention of the departing of the children of Israel": Joseph's faith was evident in his prophetic declaration regarding the departure of the Israelites from Egypt. This reflects his belief in God's promise to bring the Israelites out of Egypt and into the land of Canaan, as foretold to Abraham (Genesis 15:13-14).

- "And gave commandment concerning his bones": Joseph's instructions regarding the burial of his bones in the Promised Land (Genesis 50:24-26) demonstrated his faith in God's covenant with Abraham, Isaac, and Jacob, ensuring that even in death, he would be a partaker in the future fulfillment of that promise.

Concordance:

- By faith (Strong's #4102, Greek: πίστις, pistis): faith, belief, trust; Joseph's actions were driven by his unwavering trust in God's promises.

- Made mention (Strong's #3417, Greek: μνημονεύω, mnēmoneuō): to be mindful of, to remember; Joseph's remembrance of the departure of the children of Israel showed his confidence in the fulfillment of God's plan.

- Commandment (Strong's #1785, Greek: ἐντέλλομαι, entellomai): to order, to command; Joseph's instructions regarding his bones were a testament to his faith in God's promise to bring the Israelites to the Promised Land.

- Concerning his bones (Strong's #3747, Greek: ὀστέον, osteon): bones, remains; Joseph's desire to have his bones buried in the Promised

Land symbolizes his hope in the future resurrection and inheritance of the land promised by God.

Joseph's faith in God's promises was evident in his actions even as he faced death. His provision for the departure of the Israelites and his commandment concerning his bones reflect his belief in the fulfillment of God's covenant with Abraham, Isaac, and Jacob.

Verse 23 (King James Version):
> By faith Moses, when he was born, was hid three months of his parents, because they saw he was a proper child; and they were not afraid of the king's commandment.

Interpretation:
This verse highlights the faith of Moses' parents, Amram and Jochebed, who hid Moses for three months after his birth, defying Pharaoh's command to kill all Hebrew male babies.

Commentary:
- "By faith Moses, when he was born, was hid three months of his parents": Moses' parents acted in faith by hiding him, trusting in God's protection and possibly sensing God's calling on his life.
- "Because they saw he was a proper child": The phrase "proper child" in the King James Version is translated from the Greek word "ἀστεῖον" (asteion), which can also mean "beautiful" or "fair." This suggests that Moses' parents saw something special in him, possibly a divine purpose.
- "And they were not afraid of the king's commandment": Despite the danger of disobeying Pharaoh's order, Moses' parents trusted in God's plan for their son's life, showing their faith in God's protection and provision.

Concordance:

- By faith (Strong's #4102, Greek: πίστις, pistis): faith, belief, trust; Moses' parents' actions were driven by their trust in God's plan for their son.

- Was hid (Strong's #2928, Greek: κρύπτω, krypto): to hide, conceal; Moses' parents hid him to protect him from harm, trusting in God's protection.

- Three months (Strong's #5150, Greek: τρίμηνος, trimēnos): three months; the duration for which Moses was hidden, demonstrating his parents' commitment to protecting him.

- Proper child (Strong's #791, Greek: ἀστεῖον, asteion): beautiful, fair, proper; Moses' parents recognized something special about him, which may have been a divine calling or purpose.

Moses' parents' faith in God's plan for their son's life led them to defy Pharaoh's command and hide Moses after his birth. This act of faith played a crucial role in preserving Moses' life and setting the stage for his future role as the deliverer of the Israelites.

Verse 24 (King James Version):
> By faith Moses, when he was come to years, refused to be called the son of Pharaoh's daughter;

Interpretation:
This verse highlights Moses' faith when he reached adulthood, choosing to identify with his Hebrew heritage rather than remain in the privilege of being considered a son of Pharaoh's daughter.

Commentary:

- "By faith Moses, when he was come to years": This indicates that Moses, upon reaching adulthood, made a deliberate and conscious decision based on his faith.

- "Refused to be called the son of Pharaoh's daughter": Despite being raised in the Egyptian palace, Moses chose to reject the identity associated with his upbringing and instead align himself with his Hebrew heritage.

Concordance:

- By faith (Strong's #4102, Greek: πίστις, pistis): faith, belief, trust; Moses' decision was based on his trust in God's plan and his identity.

- When he was come to years (Strong's #1096, Greek: γίνομαι, ginomai + ἀνήρ, anēr): to become, to come into being + man; Moses' decision came as he matured into adulthood, indicating a thoughtful and intentional choice.

- Refused (Strong's #720, Greek: ἀρνέομαι, arneomai): to deny, disown, reject; Moses rejected the identity and privileges associated with being Pharaoh's daughter's son.

Moses' decision to identify with his Hebrew roots rather than enjoy the privileges of Egyptian royalty demonstrated his faith in God's promises to his ancestors and his commitment to God's plan for the deliverance of the Israelites.

Verse 25 (King James Version):
> Choosing rather to suffer affliction with the people of God, than to enjoy the pleasures of sin for a season;

Interpretation:

In this verse, Moses is portrayed as intentionally choosing to endure suffering alongside the Israelites, God's people, rather than indulging in the temporary pleasures of sin.

Commentary:
- "Choosing rather to suffer affliction with the people of God": This emphasizes Moses' deliberate choice to share in the hardships of the Israelites, aligning himself with their struggles and identifying himself as one of them.

- "Than to enjoy the pleasures of sin for a season": Moses recognized the fleeting nature of sinful pleasures and prioritized his commitment to God and His people over momentary gratification.

Concordance:
- Choosing (Strong's #138, Greek: ἐκλέγομαι, eklegomai): to choose, select, prefer; Moses made a conscious decision, showing his commitment to God's people.

- Suffer affliction (Strong's #4778, Greek: συμπάσχω, sumpaschō): to suffer together with, share in suffering; Moses opted to share in the hardships of the Israelites rather than enjoy personal comfort.

- With the people of God (Strong's #2992, Greek: λαός, laos + θεός, theos): the people, nation, crowd + God; Moses aligned himself with God's chosen people, identifying with their struggles and challenges.

- Pleasures (Strong's #2237, Greek: ἡδονή, hēdonē): pleasure, enjoyment, delight; Moses recognized the temporary nature of sinful pleasures.

- For a season (Strong's #4340, Greek: πρόσκαιρος, proskairos): temporary, transient, fleeting; Moses understood that sinful pleasures are short-lived and not worth sacrificing his commitment to God and His people.

Moses' choice reflects a deep commitment to God and His people, prioritizing eternal values over temporary pleasures, and setting an example of faithfulness and endurance.

Verse 26 (King James Version):
> Esteeming the reproach of Christ greater riches than the treasures in Egypt: for he had respect unto the recompence of the reward.

Interpretation:
This verse highlights Moses' perspective, valuing the disgrace or reproach associated with identifying with Christ more highly than the wealth and status he could have enjoyed in Egypt. His focus was on the future reward God would provide.

Commentary:
- "Esteeming the reproach of Christ greater riches than the treasures in Egypt": Moses considered the shame or disgrace that came from identifying with Christ to be more valuable than the wealth and treasures of Egypt. This reflects his deep commitment to his faith and his willingness to prioritize spiritual values over material wealth.
- "For he had respect unto the recompence of the reward": Moses looked ahead to the future reward that God would give him for his faithfulness. This indicates his strong belief in God's promises and his conviction that following God's path, even if it meant suffering, would ultimately lead to a greater reward.

Concordance:

- Esteeming (Strong's #2233, Greek: ἡγέομαι, hēgeomai): to lead, think, consider, regard; Moses valued or considered the reproach of Christ to be greater than the treasures of Egypt.

- Reproach (Strong's #3680, Greek: ὀνειδισμός, oneidismos): reproach, reviling, disgrace; Moses was willing to endure the disgrace or shame associated with identifying with Christ.

- Riches (Strong's #4149, Greek: πλοῦτος, ploutos): riches, wealth; Moses saw the reproach of Christ as more valuable than the wealth of Egypt.

- Treasures (Strong's #2344, Greek: θησαυρός, thēsauros): treasure, storehouse, repository; Moses viewed the reproach of Christ as more valuable than the treasures stored in Egypt.

- Egypt (Strong's #125, Greek: Αἴγυπτος, Aigyptos): Egypt; Moses chose to endure the reproach of Christ over the wealth and status he could have enjoyed in Egypt.

- Respect (Strong's #4308, Greek: προσέχω, prosechō): to hold to, turn the mind to, pay attention to; Moses focused his attention on the future reward God would provide.

- Recompence (Strong's #3405, Greek: μισθαποδοσία, misthapodosia): recompense, reward; Moses looked forward to the reward God would give him for his faithfulness.

Moses' choice illustrates his deep faith and commitment to God, valuing spiritual riches over earthly wealth, and anticipating the future reward that God had promised to those who remained faithful.

Verse 27 (King James Version):
> By faith he forsook Egypt, not fearing the wrath of the king: for he endured, as seeing him who is invisible.

Interpretation:

This verse refers to Moses' departure from Egypt, which he did by faith, without fear of Pharaoh's anger. He did so because he saw God, who is invisible, with spiritual eyes, trusting in Him.

Commentary:

- "By faith he forsook Egypt": Moses left Egypt, including its wealth and status, relying on his faith in God's guidance and promises.

- "Not fearing the wrath of the king": Despite Pharaoh's potential anger and reprisal, Moses was not afraid because he trusted in God's protection and plan.

- "For he endured, as seeing him who is invisible": Moses endured the challenges and uncertainties of leaving Egypt because he had spiritual insight, seeing God's presence and guidance even though God is invisible.

Concordance:

- Faith (Strong's #4102, Greek: πίστις, pistis): faith, belief, trust; Moses' decision to leave Egypt was based on his faith in God.

- Forsake (Strong's #620, Greek: ἀπολείπω, apoleipō): to leave behind, abandon; Moses abandoned Egypt, its wealth, and its comforts.

- Fear (Strong's #5399, Greek: φοβέομαι, phobeomai): to fear, be afraid; Moses did not fear Pharaoh's wrath because of his trust in God.

- Wrath (Strong's #3709, Greek: ὀργή, orgē): anger, wrath; Moses was not afraid of Pharaoh's anger.

- Endured (Strong's #5278, Greek: ὑπομένω, hupomenō): to endure, bear patiently; Moses patiently endured the challenges of leaving Egypt.

- Seeing (Strong's #3708, Greek: ὁράω, horaō): to see, perceive, discern; Moses saw God's presence and guidance with spiritual eyes, trusting in Him.

This verse demonstrates Moses' faith in action, showing his courage to leave Egypt based on his trust in God's guidance and protection, even when faced with the potential wrath of Pharaoh.

Verse 28 (King James Version):
> Through faith he kept the passover, and the sprinkling of blood, lest he that destroyed the firstborn should touch them.

Interpretation:
This verse refers to the actions of the Israelites during the Passover in Egypt. They kept the Passover by faith, following God's instructions to sprinkle the blood of the lamb on their doorposts, so that the destroyer, a reference to the angel of death, would pass over their houses and not harm their firstborn.

Commentary:
- "Through faith he kept the passover": The Israelites, led by Moses, observed the Passover as an act of faith, trusting in God's promise of protection.
- "And the sprinkling of blood": This refers to the specific instruction God gave for the Israelites to sprinkle the blood of the Passover lamb on their doorposts as a sign of their faith and obedience.
- "Lest he that destroyed the firstborn should touch them": By following God's command to keep the Passover and apply the blood, the Israelites were saved from the plague that struck the firstborn in Egypt.

Concordance:
- Faith (Strong's #4102, Greek: πίστις, pistis): faith, belief, trust; the Israelites kept the Passover by faith, trusting in God's protection.

- Passover (Strong's #3957, Greek: πάσχα, pascha): the Passover feast, the lamb slain and eaten during the feast; the Israelites observed the Passover feast as an act of faith.

- Sprinkling (Strong's #4473, Greek: ῥαντισμός, rhantismos): sprinkling, spattering; the Israelites sprinkled the blood of the lamb on their doorposts.

- Blood (Strong's #129, Greek: αἷμα, haima): blood; the blood of the Passover lamb was a sign of protection.

- Destroy (Strong's #622, Greek: ἀπόλλυμι, apollymi): to destroy, put to death; the destroyer refers to the angel of death who killed the firstborn in Egypt.

- Firstborn (Strong's #4416, Greek: πρωτότοκος, prōtotokos): firstborn; the plague targeted the firstborn in Egypt.

- Touch (Strong's #680, Greek: ἅπτω, haptō): to touch, reach, lay hold of; the Israelites were spared from the plague touching them because of the blood.

This verse highlights the importance of faith and obedience in God's instructions, as demonstrated by the Israelites during the Passover in Egypt. Their faith saved them from the plague that struck Egypt, emphasizing the significance of the Passover lamb's blood as a foreshadowing of the ultimate sacrifice of Jesus Christ.

Verse 29 (King James Version):
> By faith they passed through the Red sea as by dry land: which the Egyptians assaying to do were drowned.

Interpretation:
This verse recounts the event when the Israelites crossed the Red Sea on dry land, a miraculous event attributed to their faith in God. The Egyptians, attempting to do the same, were drowned as the waters returned.

Commentary:

- "By faith they passed through the Red sea as by dry land": This refers to the miraculous crossing of the Red Sea by the Israelites, led by Moses, as recorded in Exodus 14. They trusted in God's power to part the waters and make a way for them.

- "Which the Egyptians assaying to do were drowned": The Egyptians, seeing the Israelites' path, attempted to cross the Red Sea as well. However, when they were in the midst of the sea, the waters returned and drowned them.

Concordance:

- Faith (Strong's #4102, Greek: πίστις, pistis): faith, belief, trust; the Israelites crossed the Red Sea by faith in God's power.

- Passed through (Strong's #1224, Greek: διαπορεύομαι, diaporeuomai): to pass through; the Israelites passed through the Red Sea.

- Red Sea (Strong's #2063, Greek: ἐρυθρά θάλασσα, erythra thalassa): the Red Sea; the location of the miraculous crossing.

- Dry land (Strong's #3584, Greek: ξηρός, xēros): dry, dry land; the Israelites crossed on dry land, indicating the miraculous nature of the event.

- Assaying (Strong's #3984, Greek: πειράζω, peirazō): to try, attempt; the Egyptians attempted to cross the Red Sea.

- Drowned (Strong's #2666, Greek: καταπίνω, katapinō): to drown, swallow up; the fate of the Egyptians when the waters returned.

This verse illustrates the power of faith in God to accomplish the miraculous. The Israelites' faith enabled them to pass through the Red Sea safely, while the lack of faith led to the destruction of the pursuing Egyptians. It serves as a reminder of God's faithfulness to His people and the importance of trusting in Him even in the face of seemingly insurmountable obstacles.

Verse 30 (King James Version):
> By faith the walls of Jericho fell down, after they were compassed about seven days.

Interpretation:
This verse recalls the event when the walls of Jericho, a fortified city in Canaan, fell down after the Israelites, led by Joshua, marched around the city for seven days, as commanded by God.

Commentary:
- "By faith the walls of Jericho fell down": This highlights the power of faith in God's promises. The Israelites believed in God's command that the walls of Jericho would fall, and they obeyed, demonstrating their faith.
- "After they were compassed about seven days": The Israelites marched around Jericho once a day for six days, led by priests carrying the Ark of the Covenant. On the seventh day, they marched around the city seven times, and at the sound of the priests' trumpets and the people's shout, the walls collapsed.

Concordance:
- Faith (Strong's #4102, Greek: πίστις, pistis): faith, belief, trust; the Israelites' faith in God's promise.
- Walls (Strong's #5038, Greek: τεῖχος, teichos): a wall, city wall; the walls of Jericho that fell down.
- Jericho (Strong's #2410, Greek: Ἰεριχώ, Ierichō): Jericho, a city in Canaan; the location of the miraculous event.
- Fell down (Strong's #4098, Greek: πίπτω, piptō): to fall, fall down; the walls of Jericho fell down as a result of God's power.

This event demonstrates the effectiveness of faith combined with obedience. The Israelites' faith in God's promise, coupled with their obedience in following His instructions, led to the miraculous destruction of Jericho's walls. It serves as a reminder of the power of faith and obedience in God's plans and purposes.

Verse 31 (King James Version):
> By faith the harlot Rahab perished not with them that believed not, when she had received the spies with peace.

Interpretation:
This verse references Rahab, a harlot from Jericho, who believed in the God of Israel and hid the Israelite spies who came to scout the city. As a result of her faith and actions, she and her family were saved when Jericho was conquered.

Commentary:
- "By faith the harlot Rahab perished not with them that believed not": Despite being a harlot and a Canaanite, Rahab believed in the God of Israel and acted on that belief by hiding the spies and helping them escape. Because of her faith, she and her household were spared when Jericho was destroyed.
- "When she had received the spies with peace": Rahab welcomed the spies into her home and protected them from the authorities in Jericho. This act of hospitality and cooperation with God's people demonstrated her faith.

Concordance:

- Harlot (Strong's #4204, Greek: πόρνη, pornē): a prostitute, harlot; Rahab's former profession, highlighting God's grace and mercy in redeeming her.

- Rahab (Strong's #4477, Greek: Ῥαάβ, Rhaab): Rahab, a harlot from Jericho; known for her faith and for hiding the Israelite spies.

- Perished not (Strong's #622, Greek: ἀπόλλυμι, apollymi): to destroy, die; Rahab and her family were saved from destruction.

- Believed not (Strong's #544, Greek: ἀπειθέω, apeitheō): to disobey, be disobedient; those who did not believe in God perished.

Rahab's story is a powerful example of God's mercy and grace extended to all who repent and turn to Him in faith. Her faith not only saved her life but also earned her a place in the lineage of Jesus Christ (Matthew 1:5).

Verse 32 (King James Version):
> And what shall I more say? for the time would fail me to tell of Gedeon, and of Barak, and of Samson, and of Jephthae; of David also, and Samuel, and of the prophets:

Interpretation:
The author of Hebrews is acknowledging the limitations of time in recounting all the examples of faith from the Old Testament. He mentions several individuals briefly, including Gideon, Barak, Samson, Jephthah, David, Samuel, and the prophets, highlighting their acts of faith.

Commentary:
- "And what shall I more say?": The author is expressing the impossibility of fully recounting all the examples of faith due to the limitations of time and space.

- "For the time would fail me": The author recognizes that time is insufficient to recount all the examples of faith in detail.

- "To tell of Gedeon, and of Barak, and of Samson, and of Jephthae": These are all Old Testament figures known for their acts of faith and courage in various situations.

- "Of David also, and Samuel, and of the prophets": David, Samuel, and the prophets are also mentioned as examples of faith, highlighting their trust in God and obedience to His word.

Concordance:

- Gideon (Strong's #1066, Greek: Γεδεών, Gedeōn): Also known as Jerubbaal, Gideon was a judge and military leader of Israel who relied on God's guidance to defeat the Midianites.

- Barak (Strong's #913, Greek: Βαράκ, Barak): A military commander who, with the prophetess Deborah, led the Israelites to victory over the Canaanites.

- Samson (Strong's #4546, Greek: Σαμψών, Sampson): Known for his great strength, Samson was a judge of Israel who, despite his flaws, demonstrated faith in God.

- Jephthah (Strong's #2422, Greek: Ἰεφθάε, Iephthae): A judge of Israel who made a vow to God before battle, demonstrating his faith.

- David (Strong's #1138, Greek: Δαυίδ, Dauid): The renowned king of Israel known for his faith in God and many Psalms expressing trust in Him.

- Samuel (Strong's #4545, Greek: Σαμουήλ, Samouēl): A prophet and judge of Israel known for his obedience and faithfulness to God.

- Prophets (Strong's #4396, Greek: προφήτης, prophētēs): Refers to the various prophets of the Old Testament who proclaimed God's word and often demonstrated faith through their actions.

These individuals are cited as examples of faith in Hebrews 11, showcasing how faith has been a hallmark of God's people throughout history.

Verse 33 (King James Version):
> Who through faith subdued kingdoms, wrought righteousness, obtained promises, stopped the mouths of lions,

Interpretation:
This verse continues to list the achievements of individuals who demonstrated faith. It highlights their ability, through faith, to conquer kingdoms, practice righteousness, receive promises from God, and even face dangers like lions.

Commentary:
- "Who through faith subdued kingdoms": This refers to individuals in the Old Testament who, through their faith in God, were able to conquer and establish kingdoms, such as David and his conquests (2 Samuel 8).
- "Wrought righteousness": These individuals lived righteously before God, following His commandments and displaying upright behavior in their lives.
- "Obtained promises": They received the promises of God by believing in His word and trusting in His faithfulness to fulfill what He had promised (Genesis 12:2-3, Hebrews 6:15).
- "Stopped the mouths of lions": This likely refers to the story of Daniel in the lion's den (Daniel 6), where Daniel's faith in God protected him from harm when he was thrown into a den of lions for his faithfulness in prayer.

Concordance:

- Subdued (Strong's #2616, Greek: καταβάλλω, kataballō): Means to cast down, overthrow, or subdue.

- Kingdoms (Strong's #932, Greek: βασιλεία, basileia): Refers to ruling powers or dominions.

- Wrought (Strong's #2038, Greek: ἐργάζομαι, ergazomai): Means to work, accomplish, or achieve.

- Righteousness (Strong's #1343, Greek: δικαιοσύνη, dikaiosunē): Refers to the quality of being morally right or just.

- Obtained (Strong's #2013, Greek: λαμβάνω, lambanō): Means to take, receive, or obtain.

- Promises (Strong's #1860, Greek: ἐπαγγελία, epangelia): Refers to declarations or assurances of what is to be given or done, especially by God.

These examples of faith demonstrate the power and impact of believing in God's promises and following His ways. They serve as inspiration for believers to trust in God in all circumstances.

Verse 34 (King James Version):
> Quenched the violence of fire, escaped the edge of the sword, out of weakness were made strong, waxed valiant in fight, turned to flight the armies of the aliens.

Interpretation:
This verse continues to describe the exploits of those who had faith. It mentions their ability, through faith, to extinguish the power of fire, escape death by the sword, gain strength from weakness, show courage in battle, and defeat foreign armies.

Commentary:

- "Quenched the violence of fire": This could refer to instances where individuals, like Shadrach, Meshach, and Abednego (Daniel 3), were miraculously protected from fire because of their faithfulness to God.

- "Escaped the edge of the sword": This likely refers to individuals who were saved from death by the sword, such as David, who escaped death at the hands of Saul (1 Samuel 19-20).

- "Out of weakness were made strong": This could refer to instances where individuals, despite their human weaknesses and limitations, were empowered by God to accomplish great feats.

- "Waxed valiant in fight": This describes individuals who showed great courage and bravery in battle, trusting in God for victory.

- "Turned to flight the armies of the aliens": This likely refers to instances where God's people, through their faith, were able to defeat foreign armies, such as the Israelites under the leadership of Gideon (Judges 7).

Concordance:
- Quenched (Strong's #4570, Greek: σβέννυμι, sbennymi): Means to extinguish or quench.
- Violence (Strong's #2479, Greek: δύναμις, dynamis): Can refer to power or force.
- Fire (Strong's #4442, Greek: πῦρ, pur): Refers to literal fire.
- Escaped (Strong's #1628, Greek: ἀποφεύγω, apopheugō): Means to escape or flee from.
- Edge (Strong's #4750, Greek: στόμα, stoma): Can refer to the mouth or the edge of a sword.
- Sword (Strong's #3162, Greek: μάχαιρα, machaira): Refers to a large knife or sword.
- Weakness (Strong's #769, Greek: ἀσθένεια, astheneia): Refers to weakness, infirmity, or feebleness.

- Made (Strong's #1096, Greek: γίνομαι, ginomai): Means to become, come into existence, or be made.

- Strong (Strong's #1412, Greek: ἰσχυρός, ischuros): Means strong, mighty, or powerful.

- Waxed (Strong's #1096, Greek: γίνομαι, ginomai): Same as above, meaning to become or be made.

- Valiant (Strong's #1415, Greek: ἀνδρεῖος, andreios): Means manly, courageous, or valiant.

- Fight (Strong's #4171, Greek: πόλεμος, polemos): Refers to war, battle, or fight.

- Turned (Strong's #654, Greek: ἀποστρέφω, apostrephō): Means to turn away, turn back, or repel.

- Flight (Strong's #5437, Greek: φυγή, phygē): Refers to flight, fleeing, or running away.

- Armies (Strong's #4753, Greek: στρατός, stratos): Refers to an army or host.

- Aliens (Strong's #245, Greek: ἀλλοτριεπίσκοπος, allotriepiskopos): Can refer to strangers, foreigners, or aliens.

These examples illustrate how faith can lead to miraculous deliverance and victory, even in the face of overwhelming odds. They show that God is able to empower His people to accomplish great things when they trust in Him.

Verse 35 (King James Version):
> Women received their dead raised to life again: and others were tortured, not accepting deliverance; that they might obtain a better resurrection.

Interpretation:

This verse highlights the extraordinary faith of some individuals. It mentions women who saw their dead loved ones raised back to life. It also mentions others who were tortured but refused to accept release, choosing instead to endure suffering in hope of a better resurrection.

Commentary:

- "Women received their dead raised to life again": This likely refers to instances like the widow of Zarephath whose son was raised by Elijah (1 Kings 17:17-24) or the Shunammite woman whose son was raised by Elisha (2 Kings 4:18-37).

- "Others were tortured, not accepting deliverance": This could refer to individuals who were tortured for their faith but chose not to renounce their beliefs in exchange for freedom or relief from suffering.

- "That they might obtain a better resurrection": This suggests that these individuals endured suffering and persecution in the hope of receiving a greater reward in the afterlife, emphasizing the importance of faithfulness and perseverance in the face of trials.

Concordance:

- Women (Strong's #1135, Greek: γυνή, gynē): Refers to women or wives.

- Received (Strong's #2983, Greek: λαμβάνω, lambanō): Means to take, receive, or obtain.

- Dead (Strong's #3498, Greek: νεκρός, nekros): Refers to the dead or a corpse.

- Raised (Strong's #450, Greek: ἐγείρω, egeirō): Means to raise up or awaken.

- Life (Strong's #2198, Greek: ζάω, zaō): Refers to life or living.

- Again (Strong's #3825, Greek: πάλιν, palin): Means again or once more.

- Tortured (Strong's #5178, Greek: μαστιγόω, mastigoō): Refers to being whipped or flogged.

- Not (Strong's #3756, Greek: οὐ, ou): Negative particle indicating denial or negation.

- Accepting (Strong's #286, Greek: ἀποδέχομαι, apodechomai): Means to accept or receive.

- Deliverance (Strong's #629, Greek: λύτρωσις, lytrōsis): Refers to deliverance, redemption, or ransom.

- Might (Strong's #2443, Greek: ἵνα, hina): Conjunction indicating purpose or result.

- Obtain (Strong's #5177, Greek: τυγχάνω, tynchano): Means to obtain or attain.

- Better (Strong's #2909, Greek: κρείττων, kreittōn): Means better, more excellent, or stronger.

- Resurrection (Strong's #386, Greek: ἀνάστασις, anastasis): Refers to a rising or resurrection.

This verse underscores the diverse experiences of those who lived by faith, illustrating both the miraculous interventions of God and the steadfast endurance of believers in the face of suffering. It emphasizes the importance of faith in obtaining God's promises, even in the midst of trials and challenges.

Verse 36 (King James Version):
> And others had trial of cruel mockings and scourgings, yea, moreover of bonds and imprisonment.

Interpretation:
This verse continues to describe the trials endured by those who lived by faith. It mentions some who faced cruel mockings and scourgings, as well as bonds and imprisonment.

Commentary:

- "And others had trial of cruel mockings and scourgings": This indicates that some believers endured verbal and physical abuse, including insults and beatings, because of their faith.

- "Yea, moreover of bonds and imprisonment": In addition to verbal and physical abuse, some believers were also imprisoned or bound, likely for their refusal to renounce their faith.

Concordance:

- Others (Strong's #243, Greek: ἄλλος, allos): Refers to others or another.

- Had trial (Strong's #3985, Greek: πειρασμός, peirasmos): Means a trial, testing, or temptation.

- Cruel (Strong's #2556, Greek: ὠνειδισμός, ōneidismos): Refers to reproach, reviling, or insulting language.

- Mockings (Strong's #3141, Greek: μάστιξ, mastix): Refers to a scourge or whip.

- Scourgings (Strong's #3148, Greek: φυλακή, phylakē): Refers to imprisonment, custody, or being in prison.

- Yea (Strong's #1161, Greek: δέ, de): Conjunction indicating addition or continuation.

- Moreover (Strong's #5037, Greek: τε, te): Also, and, even, or indeed.

- Bonds (Strong's #254, Greek: δέσμη, desmē): Refers to bonds, chains, or imprisonment.

- Imprisonment (Strong's #1201, Greek: δεσμός, desmos): Refers to imprisonment, custody, or being in prison.

This verse highlights the harsh treatment endured by those who remained faithful to God. It demonstrates the courage and endurance of these individuals in the face of persecution, emphasizing the cost of following God wholeheartedly.

Verse 37 (King James Version):
> They were stoned, they were sawn asunder, were tempted, were slain with the sword: they wandered about in sheepskins and goatskins; being destitute, afflicted, tormented;

Interpretation:
This verse continues to describe the hardships endured by those who lived by faith. It mentions various forms of persecution and suffering, including being stoned, sawn asunder, tempted, slain with the sword, and enduring destitution, affliction, and torment.

Commentary:
- "They were stoned": Stoning was a form of execution where the person was pelted with stones until death.
- "They were sawn asunder": This is a historical tradition or legend, not explicitly recorded in the Bible, but traditionally associated with the prophet Isaiah, who was said to have been sawn in half during the reign of King Manasseh.
- "Were tempted": This likely refers to various trials and temptations they faced throughout their lives.
- "Were slain with the sword": This indicates that some believers were killed by the sword, likely as a form of execution.
- "They wandered about in sheepskins and goatskins": This suggests that they were forced to live in harsh conditions, possibly in wilderness areas, wearing animal skins for clothing.
- "Being destitute, afflicted, tormented": This describes their state of extreme poverty, affliction, and suffering.

Concordance:

- They (Strong's #3778, Greek: οὗτος, houtos): Refers to they or these.

- Were stoned (Strong's #3034, Greek: λιθάζω, lithazō): Refers to being stoned or pelted with stones.

- Were sawn asunder (Strong's #636, Greek: δικόμαι, dikomai): Refers to being sawn in two, traditionally associated with the prophet Isaiah.

- Were tempted (Strong's #3985, Greek: πειράζω, peirazō): Refers to being tested or tempted.

- Were slain (Strong's #4969, Greek: κατακόνιζω, katakonizō): Refers to being put to death or killed.

- With the sword (Strong's #3162, Greek: μάχαιρα, machaira): Refers to the sword or a large knife used as a weapon.

- They wandered (Strong's #4105, Greek: πλανάω, planaō): Refers to wandering or being led astray.

- In sheepskins and goatskins (Strong's #4263, Greek: δέρμα, derma): Refers to skins or hides of sheep and goats, used as clothing.

- Being destitute (Strong's #5302, Greek: ὑστερέω, hustereō): Refers to being in need or lacking.

- Afflicted (Strong's #2558, Greek: θλίψις, thlipsis): Refers to affliction, distress, or suffering.

- Tormented (Strong's #3544, Greek: βασανισμός, basanismos): Refers to torment or torture.

This verse highlights the extreme suffering and persecution endured by those who remained faithful to God, emphasizing their unwavering commitment to their faith despite immense hardship.

Verse 38 (King James Version):
> (Of whom the world was not worthy:) they wandered in deserts, and in mountains, and in dens and caves of the earth.

Interpretation:

This verse continues to describe the experiences of those who lived by faith, emphasizing their rejection by the world. It mentions their wandering in desolate places, including deserts, mountains, and caves.

Commentary:

- "(Of whom the world was not worthy:)": This phrase suggests that the world did not recognize or appreciate the value of these faithful individuals, considering them unworthy.

- "They wandered in deserts, and in mountains, and in dens and caves of the earth": This describes their nomadic lifestyle, moving through barren and isolated places, seeking refuge in caves and other remote locations to escape persecution and hardship.

Concordance:

- Of whom (Strong's #3739, Greek: ὅς, hos): Refers to those who lived by faith, mentioned in previous verses.

- The world (Strong's #2889, Greek: κόσμος, kosmos): Refers to the world or the inhabitants of the world.

- Was not worthy (Strong's #514, Greek: ἄξιος, axios): Refers to being worthy or deserving.

- They wandered (Strong's #4105, Greek: πλανάω, planaō): Refers to wandering or being led astray.

- In deserts (Strong's #2048, Greek: ἔρημος, erēmos): Refers to desolate or uninhabited places.

- And in mountains (Strong's #3735, Greek: ὄρος, oros): Refers to mountains or high hills.

- And in dens (Strong's #4693, Greek: σπήλαιον, spēlaion): Refers to dens or caves.

- And caves (Strong's #4693, Greek: σπήλαιον, spēlaion): Refers to caves or caverns.

- Of the earth (Strong's #1093, Greek: γῆ, gē): Refers to the earth or land.

This verse emphasizes the rejection and suffering experienced by those who lived by faith, highlighting their separation from the world and their willingness to endure hardship for the sake of their faith.

Verse 39 (King James Version):
> And these all, having obtained a good report through faith, received not the promise:

Interpretation:
This verse refers to all the people mentioned in the previous verses, who lived by faith and endured various trials. Despite their faithfulness, they did not receive the ultimate fulfillment of the promise—the coming of the Messiah and the establishment of God's kingdom on earth.

Commentary:
- "And these all, having obtained a good report through faith": This phrase acknowledges the commendable faith of the individuals mentioned in the preceding verses. They were commended for their faithfulness and trust in God.

- "Received not the promise": Despite their faith, these individuals did not see the complete fulfillment of God's promises during their lifetimes. They looked forward to the future fulfillment of these promises.

Concordance:

- And these all (Strong's #3778, Greek: οὗτος, houtos): Refers to all the individuals previously mentioned in the chapter who lived by faith.

- Having obtained (Strong's #2013, Greek: λαμβάνω, lambanō): Refers to receiving or obtaining.

- A good report (Strong's #3140, Greek: μαρτυρέω, martyreō): Refers to being attested or commended.

- Through faith (Strong's #4102, Greek: πίστις, pistis): Refers to faith or belief in God.

- Received not (Strong's #2865, Greek: λαμβάνω, lambanō): Refers to not receiving or obtaining.

- The promise (Strong's #1860, Greek: ἐπαγγελία, epangelia): Refers to the promise of God, particularly the promise of the Messiah and the establishment of His kingdom.

This verse underscores the theme of faith that runs throughout Hebrews 11, highlighting the trust and perseverance of those who lived by faith, even though they did not see the complete fulfillment of God's promises in their lifetimes.

Verse 40 (King James Version):
> God having provided some better thing for us, that they without us should not be made perfect.

Interpretation:
This verse suggests that God has provided something better for believers in the New Testament era. The faith heroes of the Old Testament were looking forward to the fulfillment of God's promises, which includes the coming of Christ and the establishment of the new covenant. This verse indicates that their perfection, in terms of the

fulfillment of these promises, is tied to the completion of God's plan in the New Testament era.

Commentary:

- "God having provided some better thing for us": This "better thing" refers to the fulfillment of God's promises through Christ and the establishment of the new covenant, which provides believers with a better relationship with God and a more complete salvation.

- "That they without us should not be made perfect": This phrase indicates that the completion or perfection of God's plan, including the fulfillment of His promises to the faithful of the Old Testament, is connected to the work of Christ and the New Testament believers. Their faith and obedience played a part in God's larger plan that culminated in the work of Christ.

Concordance:

- God having provided (Strong's #4289, Greek: προβλέπω, problepō): Refers to God foreseeing or providing.

- Some better thing (Strong's #2909, Greek: κρείττων, kreittōn): Refers to something superior or better.

- For us (Strong's #2248, Greek: ἡμεῖς, hēmeis): Refers to believers in the New Testament era.

- That they without us (Strong's #846, #2248, Greek: αὐτός, hēmeis): Refers to the Old Testament faithful who did not see the fulfillment of God's promises during their lifetimes.

- Should not be made perfect (Strong's #5048, Greek: τελειόω, teleioō): Refers to being completed or perfected. In this context, it refers to the completion of God's plan through the work of Christ and the New Testament believers.

This verse emphasizes the continuity of God's plan of salvation and the interconnectedness of believers across time, highlighting the role of faith and obedience in God's redemptive work.

318

C H A P T E R   1 2
Christ our example

Hebrews 12 is a rich chapter, especially verse 1, which is often quoted for its encouragement and exhortation. Let's break it down with the King James Bible's references, interpretation, commentary, and the Exhaustive Strong's Concordance.

Verse 1 (KJV):

"Wherefore seeing we also are compassed about with so great a cloud of witnesses, let us lay aside every weight, and the sin which doth so easily beset us, and let us run with patience the race that is set before us,"

References:

- "Cloud of witnesses" may refer to the faithful men and women mentioned in Hebrews 11, often called the "Hall of Faith."

- "Lay aside every weight" implies removing hindrances or distractions.

- "Sin which doth so easily beset us" refers to sins that easily entangle or ensnare us.

- "Run with patience" suggests enduring and persevering in faith.

Interpretation:

- The "cloud of witnesses" can be understood as those who have gone before us in faith, like Abraham, Moses, and others mentioned in Hebrews 11, who serve as examples for us to emulate.

- "Lay aside every weight" implies that we should rid ourselves of anything that hinders our spiritual progress, whether it be sinful behaviors, worldly distractions, or anything else that impedes our walk with God.

- "The sin which doth so easily beset us" likely refers to our tendency to fall into habitual sins or those sins that we are particularly prone to. It's a call to be vigilant and proactive in resisting temptation.

- "Run with patience" encourages us to endure trials and difficulties in our Christian journey with steadfastness and perseverance, knowing that God is faithful and will sustain us.

Commentary:

- This verse serves as an encouragement to believers, reminding them of the faithful examples of those who have gone before and urging them to live similarly faithful lives.

- It highlights the need for active participation in the Christian life, including laying aside hindrances, avoiding sin, and persevering in faith despite difficulties.

- The imagery of running a race suggests that the Christian life is a journey or a marathon that requires endurance and focus.

Exhaustive Strong's Concordance (ESV):

- "Cloud" (G3509): Can mean a dense multitude or throng, possibly alluding to a vast assembly of witnesses.

- "Witnesses" (G3144): Refers to one who testifies or provides evidence, here likely indicating those who testify to the faithfulness of God.

- "Lay aside" (G659): To strip off, lay aside, or cast away, implying a deliberate action on the part of the believer to remove hindrances.

- "Weight" (G3591): Something that is cumbersome or burdensome, suggesting anything that hinders or slows down progress.

- "Sin" (G266): Missing the mark, falling short, or deviating from the right path, indicating any act contrary to God's will.

- "Beset" (G2139): To stand around, meaning to be closely surrounded or encircled, describing how sin can entangle or ensnare us.

- "Run" (G5143): To race or compete, metaphorically used here for the Christian life as a race or journey.

- "Patience" (G5281): Endurance, steadfastness, or perseverance, indicating the need for endurance in the Christian life.

This verse encourages believers to persevere in their faith, drawing strength from the examples of those who have gone before and actively removing hindrances to their spiritual growth.

Verse 2 (KJV):

"Looking unto Jesus the author and finisher of our faith; who for the joy that was set before him endured the cross, despising the shame, and is set down at the right hand of the throne of God."

References:

- "Looking unto Jesus" emphasizes the focus of the believer's attention and faith.

- "Author and finisher of our faith" suggests that Jesus is the pioneer or founder of our faith who perfects it.

- "For the joy that was set before him" indicates the purpose and motivation behind Jesus' endurance of the cross.

- "Endured the cross, despising the shame" describes Jesus' steadfastness and willingness to endure suffering and humiliation.

- "Set down at the right hand of the throne of God" signifies Jesus' exaltation and victory over sin and death.

Interpretation:

- "Looking unto Jesus" encourages believers to keep their eyes fixed on Jesus as the object of their faith and the example to follow.

- "Author and finisher of our faith" implies that Jesus is not only the initiator but also the perfecter or completer of our faith, leading us to maturity and completion in Him.

- "For the joy that was set before him" suggests that Jesus endured the cross because of the ultimate joy of redeeming humanity and fulfilling God's plan of salvation.

- "Endured the cross, despising the shame" emphasizes Jesus' endurance and perseverance in the face of suffering and disgrace, highlighting His perfect obedience to the Father's will.

- "Set down at the right hand of the throne of God" signifies Jesus' exaltation and glorification, indicating His triumph over sin and death and His current position of authority and intercession.

Commentary:

- This verse points to Jesus as the ultimate example of faith and endurance, encouraging believers to follow His example in their own lives.

- It highlights the centrality of Jesus in the Christian faith, emphasizing His role as the founder and perfecter of our faith.

- The reference to Jesus' endurance of the cross and His exaltation serves as a source of encouragement and motivation for believers to persevere in their own faith journey.

Exhaustive Strong's Concordance (ESV):

- "Looking" (G872): To turn the eyes away from other things and fix them on something, implying a deliberate and continuous action.

- "Author" (G747): A pioneer, leader, or founder, indicating Jesus' role as the originator and leader of the Christian faith.

- "Finisher" (G5051): Perfector, completer, or finisher, suggesting that Jesus brings our faith to its intended goal or completion.

- "Faith" (G4102): Conviction, belief, or trust, referring to the Christian faith in Jesus Christ.

- "Joy" (G5479): Gladness, delight, or rejoicing, indicating the joyous outcome that Jesus looked forward to.

- "Endured" (G5297): To remain or persevere under, suggesting patient endurance and steadfastness.

- "Cross" (G4716): The instrument of crucifixion, symbolizing suffering, shame, and death.

- "Despising" (G2706): To think against, i.e., disesteem, slight, or despise, indicating Jesus' attitude toward the shame of the cross.

- "Shame" (G152): Disgrace, ignominy, or reproach, referring to the humiliation associated with the cross.

- "Set down" (G2523): To sit down, implying a position of rest, completion, and authority.

- "Right hand" (G1188): The place of honor and power, indicating Jesus' exaltation and authority.

- "Throne" (G2362): A seat of power, authority, or judgment, symbolizing God's sovereignty and Jesus' rightful place as ruler.

This verse encourages believers to fix their eyes on Jesus as the ultimate example of faith and endurance, who endured the cross and is now exalted at the right hand of God. It emphasizes Jesus' role as the founder and perfecter of our faith, motivating believers to persevere in their own faith journey with endurance and steadfastness.

Verse 3 (KJV):
"For consider him that endured such contradiction of sinners against himself, lest ye be wearied and faint in your minds."

References:
- "Consider him that endured such contradiction of sinners against himself" refers to reflecting on Jesus' endurance of opposition and hostility from sinners.
- "Lest ye be wearied and faint in your minds" warns against becoming discouraged or losing heart in the face of trials and difficulties.

Interpretation:
- "Consider him" encourages believers to meditate on Jesus' sufferings and endurance, drawing strength and encouragement from His example.
- "Contradiction of sinners against himself" describes the opposition and hostility that Jesus faced during His earthly ministry, culminating in His crucifixion.
- "Lest ye be wearied and faint in your minds" warns against the danger of losing spiritual strength and becoming discouraged, emphasizing the importance of maintaining faith and endurance.

Commentary:

- This verse builds on the previous verses, continuing to exhort believers to persevere in their faith by looking to Jesus as their example.

- It underscores the reality of opposition and persecution that believers may face, highlighting Jesus' own experience of facing hostility from sinners.

- By encouraging believers to consider Jesus' endurance, the verse aims to strengthen their resolve and prevent them from becoming discouraged or giving up in the face of trials.

Exhaustive Strong's Concordance (ESV):

- "Consider" (G357): To observe fully, contemplate, or consider attentively, suggesting a thoughtful reflection on Jesus' example.

- "Endured" (G5278): To remain or persevere under, indicating Jesus' steadfastness and endurance in the face of opposition.

- "Contradiction" (G485): Opposition, contradiction, or resistance, referring to the hostility and opposition Jesus faced from sinners.

- "Sinners" (G268): Those who miss the mark or deviate from the right path, indicating those who opposed Jesus.

- "Against himself" emphasizes that the contradiction and opposition were directed specifically at Jesus.

- "Lest ye be wearied" (G1590): To be utterly spiritless, to be wearied out, exhausted, or faint-hearted, suggesting the danger of losing heart or becoming discouraged.

- "Faint" (G1590): To be utterly spiritless, to be wearied out, exhausted, or faint-hearted, indicating a state of spiritual weakness or discouragement.

- "Minds" (G5590): The mind, understanding, or intellect, referring to the inner disposition or attitude.

This verse serves as a warning against spiritual weariness and faint-heartedness, urging believers to reflect on Jesus' endurance in the face of opposition as a source of strength and encouragement. It emphasizes the importance of maintaining faith and perseverance in the Christian journey, especially in the midst of trials and difficulties.

Verse 4 (KJV):
"Ye have not yet resisted unto blood, striving against sin."

References:
- "Ye have not yet resisted unto blood" implies that the readers have not yet faced martyrdom for their faith.
- "Striving against sin" suggests a struggle or conflict against sin and its effects.

Interpretation:
- "Ye have not yet resisted unto blood" acknowledges that the readers have not yet faced the ultimate test of faith through martyrdom.
- "Striving against sin" indicates the ongoing struggle believers face in resisting sin and living according to God's will.

Commentary:
- This verse acknowledges the readers' current situation, recognizing that they have not yet faced the extreme persecution of martyrdom.
- It serves as a reminder that the struggle against sin is ongoing and requires continual vigilance and effort.
- By comparing the readers' current struggles to the ultimate sacrifice of martyrdom, the verse encourages perseverance and faithfulness in the face of trials.

Exhaustive Strong's Concordance (ESV):

- "Ye have not yet" suggests that the readers have not yet experienced a specific event or condition.

- "Resisted" (G478): To stand against, resist, or oppose, indicating a firm stance against something.

- "Unto blood" suggests a level of resistance that results in shedding blood, typically referring to martyrdom.

- "Striving" (G75): To struggle, fight, or contend, indicating a vigorous effort or conflict.

- "Against sin" emphasizes the struggle against sin and its influence in the believer's life.

This verse encourages believers to persevere in their struggle against sin, recognizing that their current trials, though difficult, have not yet reached the level of martyrdom. It underscores the ongoing nature of the Christian life, which requires steadfastness and endurance in resisting sin and living according to God's will.

Verse 5 (KJV):

"And ye have forgotten the exhortation which speaketh unto you as unto children, My son, despise not thou the chastening of the Lord, nor faint when thou art rebuked of him:"

References:

- "Forgotten the exhortation" suggests that the readers have overlooked or neglected to consider a specific instruction.

- "Speaketh unto you as unto children" indicates that the exhortation is given in a manner appropriate for children.

- "Despise not thou the chastening of the Lord" refers to not disregarding or resenting the discipline that the Lord administers.

- "Nor faint when thou art rebuked of him" warns against becoming discouraged or losing heart when corrected by the Lord.

Interpretation:

- The writer admonishes the readers for forgetting an important exhortation, which is presented in a fatherly manner.

- The exhortation emphasizes the importance of accepting and enduring God's discipline without resentment or discouragement.

Commentary:

- This verse highlights the paternal nature of God's discipline, which is meant for the believers' growth and maturity.

- It warns against two negative reactions to God's discipline: despising it or becoming disheartened by it.

- By reminding the readers of this exhortation, the writer encourages them to embrace God's discipline as an expression of His love and care.

Exhaustive Strong's Concordance (ESV):

- "Forgotten" (G1950): To forget, neglect, or overlook, indicating a failure to remember or consider something important.

- "Exhortation" (G3874): A calling near, an admonition or encouragement, suggesting a persuasive appeal.

- "Speaketh" (G2980): To speak or say, indicating the delivery of a message or instruction.

- "Unto you as unto children" emphasizes the manner in which the exhortation is given, as appropriate for children.

- "Despise" (G3643): To regard as insignificant or of little value, indicating a disdainful attitude.

- "Chastening" (G3809): Discipline, correction, or instruction, referring to God's corrective measures for His children.

- "Nor faint" (G1590): To be utterly spiritless, to be wearied out, exhausted, or faint-hearted, suggesting a loss of courage or determination.

- "Rebuked" (G1651): To find fault with, correct, or rebuke, indicating God's corrective action.

- "Of him" emphasizes that the rebuke comes from God Himself.

This verse serves as a reminder to believers not to despise or become discouraged by God's discipline but to accept it as a loving act of correction and instruction. It underscores the need for humility and submission to God's authority, recognizing His fatherly care and concern for His children's spiritual well-being.

Verse 6 (KJV):
"For whom the Lord loveth he chasteneth, and scourgeth every son whom he receiveth."

References:
- "Whom the Lord loveth he chasteneth" indicates that God's discipline is a sign of His love for His children.
- "Scourgeth every son whom he receiveth" suggests that God disciplines every child He accepts into His family.

Interpretation:
- This verse emphasizes the relationship between God's love and discipline, indicating that discipline is a demonstration of His love.
- It also highlights the universality of God's discipline, indicating that all His children can expect to be disciplined.

Commentary:
- The verse draws a parallel between God's discipline and a father's discipline of his children, illustrating the loving nature of God's correction.

- It reassures believers that God's discipline is a sign of their acceptance into His family and His desire for their spiritual growth.

- By understanding God's discipline in this context, believers are encouraged to accept it with gratitude and humility, knowing that it comes from a place of love.

Exhaustive Strong's Concordance (ESV):

- "Loveth" (G5368): To love, indicating a deep, selfless affection or benevolence.

- "Chasteneth" (G3811): To train, educate, or discipline, suggesting corrective instruction.

- "Scourgeth" (G3146): To whip, flog, or beat, indicating a severe form of discipline.

- "Every son" emphasizes that all of God's children, without exception, are subject to discipline.

- "Whom he receiveth" indicates that God disciplines those whom He has welcomed into His family.

This verse teaches that God's discipline is an expression of His love for His children, meant for their instruction and growth. It emphasizes the universality of God's discipline, indicating that all believers can expect to be disciplined by God as a loving father disciplines his children.

Verse 7 (KJV):

"If ye endure chastening, God dealeth with you as with sons; for what son is he whom the father chasteneth not?"

References:

- "If ye endure chastening" suggests that enduring God's discipline is a characteristic of true sons of God.

- "God dealeth with you as with sons" indicates that God's discipline is evidence of His recognition of believers as His children.

- "For what son is he whom the father chasteneth not?" emphasizes the universality of parental discipline as a sign of love and care.

Interpretation:
- This verse highlights the relationship between endurance of discipline and sonship, indicating that enduring discipline is a mark of true sonship.

- It underscores the idea that God's discipline is a distinguishing characteristic of His children, demonstrating His fatherly care and concern.

Commentary:
- The verse presents enduring discipline as a positive attribute, indicating maturity and sonship in God's family.

- It emphasizes that God's discipline is a natural and necessary aspect of the parent-child relationship, demonstrating His love and commitment to His children's growth and well-being.

- By framing God's discipline in the context of fatherly love and care, the verse encourages believers to embrace discipline as a means of spiritual growth and maturity.

Exhaustive Strong's Concordance (ESV):
- "Endure chastening" suggests a patient acceptance or enduring of discipline.

- "God dealeth with you as with sons" indicates that God treats believers as His children when He disciplines them.

- "For what son is he whom the father chasteneth not?" emphasizes the universal nature of parental discipline, indicating that discipline is a normal part of the parent-child relationship.

This verse emphasizes the importance of enduring God's discipline as a mark of true sonship. It highlights the loving and corrective nature of God's discipline, encouraging believers to embrace discipline as a means of spiritual growth and maturity.

Verse 8 (KJV):
"But if ye be without chastisement, whereof all are partakers, then are ye bastards, and not sons."

References:
- "Without chastisement" refers to not experiencing discipline or correction from God.
- "Whereof all are partakers" suggests that all believers share in God's discipline.
- "Bastards, and not sons" contrasts those who do not experience God's discipline with true sons who do.

Interpretation:
- This verse contrasts two groups: those who experience God's discipline as His children and those who do not, indicating that the absence of discipline suggests a lack of true sonship.
- It underscores the idea that discipline is a necessary and universal aspect of the Christian life, demonstrating God's love and care for His children.

Commentary:
- The verse emphasizes the importance of God's discipline in the life of a believer, indicating that it is a sign of true sonship.
- It highlights the idea that discipline is a form of God's love and care, intended for the spiritual growth and maturity of His children.

- By contrasting true sons with "bastards," the verse emphasizes the distinction between those who have a genuine relationship with God and those who do not.

Exhaustive Strong's Concordance (ESV):
- "Without chastisement" suggests a lack of discipline or correction.
- "Whereof all are partakers" indicates that all believers share in God's discipline as a normal aspect of the Christian life.
- "Bastards, and not sons" contrasts those who do not experience God's discipline with legitimate children who do.

This verse emphasizes the universal nature of God's discipline and its importance in the life of a believer. It highlights the idea that discipline is a sign of true sonship and is intended for the spiritual growth and maturity of God's children.

Verse 9 (KJV):
"Furthermore we have had fathers of our flesh which corrected us, and we gave them reverence: shall we not much rather be in subjection unto the Father of spirits, and live?"

References:
- "Fathers of our flesh which corrected us" refers to earthly fathers who disciplined their children.
- "We gave them reverence" indicates that children respected and honored their earthly fathers for their discipline.
- "Father of spirits" refers to God as the source or originator of the spiritual aspect of human beings.

Interpretation:

- This verse draws a comparison between the discipline of earthly fathers and the discipline of God.

- It suggests that if children show respect and obedience to their earthly fathers for their discipline, how much more should they submit to God's discipline, as He is the ultimate source of their spiritual being.

Commentary:

- The verse highlights the natural inclination of children to respect and honor their earthly fathers for their discipline.

- It emphasizes the greater authority and importance of God as the Father of spirits, indicating that His discipline should be even more respected and obeyed.

- By drawing this comparison, the verse encourages believers to submit to God's discipline with reverence and obedience, recognizing His authority and care for them.

Exhaustive Strong's Concordance (ESV):

- "Fathers of our flesh" refers to earthly fathers, indicating a physical or biological relationship.

- "Corrected us" suggests discipline or correction for the purpose of instruction and improvement.

- "We gave them reverence" indicates the response of children to their fathers' discipline, showing respect and honor.

- "Shall we not much rather" emphasizes the greater importance or necessity of something.

- "Be in subjection unto the Father of spirits" indicates the need for submission and obedience to God, who is the source of our spiritual being.

- "And live?" suggests that obedience to God's discipline leads to spiritual life and well-being.

This verse underscores the importance of submitting to God's discipline with reverence and obedience, recognizing His authority and care as the Father of spirits. It highlights the natural respect that children have for their earthly fathers' discipline and suggests that this respect should be even greater for God's discipline, which is ultimately for their spiritual well-being.

Verse 10 (KJV):
"For they verily for a few days chastened us after their own pleasure; but he for our profit, that we might be partakers of his holiness."

References:
- "For they verily for a few days chastened us after their own pleasure" contrasts the discipline of earthly fathers, which is often imperfect and temporary, with God's discipline.
- "But he for our profit" indicates that God's discipline is for our benefit and well-being.
- "That we might be partakers of his holiness" suggests that the purpose of God's discipline is to conform us to His own holy character.

Interpretation:
- This verse contrasts the imperfect and temporary nature of earthly fathers' discipline with the perfect and beneficial nature of God's discipline.
- It emphasizes that God's discipline is ultimately for our good, leading to our participation in His holiness.

Commentary:
- The verse highlights the limitations of earthly fathers' discipline, which is often motivated by their own preferences and may be short-lived.

- It emphasizes the superior nature of God's discipline, which is always for our benefit and aimed at transforming us into His likeness.

- By emphasizing the positive purpose of God's discipline, the verse encourages believers to trust in God's wisdom and goodness, even in the midst of trials and difficulties.

Exhaustive Strong's Concordance (ESV):

- "For they verily for a few days" suggests the temporary nature of earthly fathers' discipline, which is limited to a short period of time.

- "Chastened us after their own pleasure" indicates that earthly fathers' discipline may be motivated by personal preferences or desires.

- "But he for our profit" emphasizes that God's discipline is always for our benefit and well-being.

- "That we might be partakers of his holiness" suggests that the ultimate goal of God's discipline is to conform us to His own holy character, enabling us to share in His holiness.

This verse highlights the positive nature and purpose of God's discipline, contrasting it with the imperfect and temporary nature of earthly fathers' discipline. It emphasizes that God's discipline is always for our benefit, aimed at transforming us into His likeness and enabling us to share in His holiness.

Verse 11 (KJV):

"Now no chastening for the present seemeth to be joyous, but grievous: nevertheless afterward it yieldeth the peaceable fruit of righteousness unto them which are exercised thereby."

References:

- "No chastening for the present seemeth to be joyous, but grievous" acknowledges the painful nature of discipline at the time it is experienced.

- "Nevertheless afterward it yieldeth the peaceable fruit of righteousness" indicates that the ultimate outcome of discipline is positive, leading to righteousness.

- "Unto them which are exercised thereby" suggests that the benefits of discipline are experienced by those who undergo it with a proper attitude and response.

Interpretation:

- This verse acknowledges the initial difficulty and pain that come with God's discipline.

- It emphasizes that, despite the immediate unpleasantness, the ultimate result of discipline is positive, leading to righteousness and peace.

- It also suggests that the benefits of discipline are experienced most fully by those who respond to it with faith and obedience.

Commentary:

- The verse acknowledges the challenging nature of God's discipline, recognizing that it can be painful and difficult to endure.

- It encourages believers to look beyond the immediate discomfort of discipline and focus on the long-term benefits, which include righteousness and peace.

- By highlighting the positive outcome of discipline, the verse provides encouragement and motivation for believers to persevere through difficult times, knowing that God's discipline is ultimately for their good.

Exhaustive Strong's Concordance (ESV):

- "No chastening for the present seemeth to be joyous, but grievous" suggests that discipline is often painful and difficult to bear in the present moment.

- "Nevertheless afterward it yieldeth the peaceable fruit of righteousness" emphasizes that the ultimate outcome of discipline is positive, leading to righteousness and peace.

- "Unto them which are exercised thereby" indicates that the benefits of discipline are experienced by those who undergo it with a proper attitude and response.

This verse encourages believers to endure God's discipline with faith and obedience, knowing that despite the initial pain, it leads to righteousness and peace. It emphasizes the importance of trusting in God's wisdom and goodness, even when His discipline is difficult to understand or bear.

Verse 12 (KJV):
"Wherefore lift up the hands which hang down, and the feeble knees;"

References:
- "Lift up the hands which hang down" suggests encouraging or strengthening those who are discouraged or weak.

- "The feeble knees" refers to those who are physically or spiritually weak and in need of support.

Interpretation:
- This verse is an exhortation to strengthen and support those who are spiritually or emotionally weak.

- It encourages believers to lift up and support one another, especially in times of difficulty or discouragement.

Commentary:

- The imagery of "lifting up the hands which hang down" and "the feeble knees" conveys the idea of providing support and encouragement to those who are struggling.

- It emphasizes the importance of unity and mutual support within the body of believers, encouraging them to care for one another in times of need.

- By exhorting believers to lift up those who are weak, the verse promotes a spirit of compassion, kindness, and solidarity within the Christian community.

Exhaustive Strong's Concordance (ESV):

- "Lift up the hands" suggests raising or supporting those who are weak or discouraged.

- "Which hang down" indicates a posture of defeat or discouragement, needing assistance to be lifted up.

- "The feeble knees" refers to those who are weak or lacking strength, either physically or spiritually, and are in need of support.

This verse encourages believers to support and encourage one another, especially when facing difficulties or struggles. It emphasizes the importance of unity and mutual care within the body of Christ, reminding believers to lift up those who are weak or discouraged, helping them to stand firm in their faith.

Verse 13 (KJV):

"And make straight paths for your feet, lest that which is lame be turned out of the way; but let it rather be healed."

References:

- "Make straight paths for your feet" suggests living a life of integrity and righteousness, avoiding sin and temptation.

- "Lest that which is lame be turned out of the way" warns against causing others to stumble or fall away from the faith.

- "But let it rather be healed" encourages restoring and strengthening those who are weak or struggling.

Interpretation:

- This verse urges believers to live upright lives, avoiding actions or behaviors that could cause others to stumble or fall away from the faith.

- It emphasizes the importance of caring for and restoring those who are spiritually weak or struggling.

Commentary:

- The metaphor of "making straight paths for your feet" conveys the idea of living a life that is morally upright and free from sin.

- It emphasizes the responsibility of believers to consider how their actions and choices may impact others, especially those who are spiritually vulnerable.

- By encouraging believers to prioritize the healing and restoration of those who are weak or struggling, the verse promotes a culture of compassion, empathy, and support within the Christian community.

Exhaustive Strong's Concordance (ESV):

- "Make straight paths" suggests living a life that is morally upright and free from sin, avoiding actions that could lead to stumbling.

- "For your feet" indicates that these paths are for the believers to walk on, emphasizing personal responsibility.

- "Lest that which is lame be turned out of the way" warns against causing others to stumble or fall away from the faith through our actions or behaviors.

- "But let it rather be healed" encourages restoring and strengthening those who are spiritually weak or struggling, rather than causing further harm or damage.

This verse calls believers to live lives of integrity and righteousness, considering how their actions may impact others, especially those who are spiritually vulnerable. It emphasizes the importance of caring for and restoring those who are weak or struggling, promoting a culture of compassion and support within the Christian community.

Verse 14 (KJV):
"Follow peace with all men, and holiness, without which no man shall see the Lord:"

References:
- "Follow peace with all men" encourages believers to pursue peaceful relationships with everyone.
- "Holiness" refers to a state of moral purity and dedication to God.
- "No man shall see the Lord" suggests that holiness is necessary for experiencing a full and close relationship with God.

Interpretation:
- This verse emphasizes the importance of living peacefully with others and pursuing holiness as essential aspects of the Christian life.
- It suggests that holiness is a prerequisite for experiencing a deep and meaningful relationship with God.

Commentary:

- The exhortation to "follow peace with all men" underscores the Christian's responsibility to strive for peaceful and harmonious relationships with others, even in the face of conflict or disagreement.

- The emphasis on holiness highlights the importance of moral purity and devotion to God in the Christian life.

- By linking holiness with the ability to "see the Lord," the verse suggests that living a life of holiness enables believers to experience God's presence and favor in a more profound way.

Exhaustive Strong's Concordance (ESV):

- "Follow peace" suggests actively pursuing or seeking after peace with others, indicating an intentional effort.

- "With all men" emphasizes that believers are called to seek peace with everyone, not just fellow believers.

- "Holiness" refers to a state of moral purity and dedication to God, indicating a separation from sin and dedication to God's will.

- "Without which no man shall see the Lord" suggests that holiness is necessary for experiencing a full and close relationship with God, indicating its importance in the Christian life.

This verse emphasizes the importance of pursuing peace with others and living a life of holiness. It highlights the close relationship between holiness and experiencing God's presence and favor.

Verse 15 (KJV):

"Looking diligently lest any man fail of the grace of God; lest any root of bitterness springing up trouble you, and thereby many be defiled;"

References:

- "Looking diligently" suggests being vigilant and attentive.

- "Fail of the grace of God" warns against falling short of or missing out on God's grace.

- "Root of bitterness" refers to a deep-seated resentment or anger.

- "Springing up trouble you" indicates that such bitterness can cause trouble or harm.

- "Many be defiled" suggests that bitterness can have a negative influence on others.

Interpretation:

- This verse warns believers to be vigilant and attentive to avoid missing out on God's grace.

- It cautions against allowing bitterness to take root in their hearts, as it can lead to trouble and harm, affecting not only themselves but also others.

Commentary:

- The exhortation to "look diligently" underscores the importance of being proactive in guarding against spiritual dangers, such as failing to receive God's grace and allowing bitterness to take root.

- The warning against a "root of bitterness" highlights the destructive nature of unresolved anger or resentment, which can have far-reaching consequences.

- By emphasizing the potential influence of bitterness on others, the verse highlights the importance of maintaining a spirit of forgiveness and grace in all relationships.

Exhaustive Strong's Concordance (ESV):

- "Looking diligently" suggests being vigilant or watchful, indicating an active effort to avoid spiritual pitfalls.

- "Lest any man fail of the grace of God" warns against falling short of or missing out on the fullness of God's grace, indicating the need for continued reliance on God's grace.

- "Lest any root of bitterness springing up trouble you" warns against allowing bitterness to take root in your heart, as it can cause trouble or harm.

- "And thereby many be defiled" suggests that bitterness can have a negative influence on others, spreading and causing harm in the community.

This verse serves as a cautionary warning against complacency in the Christian life. It encourages believers to be vigilant in guarding against spiritual dangers, such as failing to receive God's grace and allowing bitterness to take root. It highlights the importance of maintaining a spirit of forgiveness and grace in all relationships, to avoid negative influences on oneself and others.

Verse 16 (KJV):

"Lest there be any fornicator, or profane person, as Esau, who for one morsel of meat sold his birthright."

References:

- "Fornicator" refers to someone who engages in sexual immorality.

- "Profane person" describes someone who treats sacred things with disrespect or irreverence.

- "Esau" refers to the biblical figure from the Old Testament who sold his birthright for a single meal.

Interpretation:

- This verse warns against immorality and irreverence, using the example of Esau who valued his immediate physical needs over his spiritual birthright.

Commentary:
- The mention of "fornicator" and "profane person" highlights the seriousness of indulging in immoral behavior and treating sacred things lightly.
- By referencing Esau, who traded his birthright for temporary satisfaction, the verse serves as a cautionary tale against prioritizing worldly desires over spiritual blessings.
- It emphasizes the need for believers to value and uphold their spiritual inheritance, even in the face of immediate physical needs or desires.

Exhaustive Strong's Concordance (ESV):
- "Fornicator" refers to someone who engages in sexual immorality, indicating a violation of God's moral standards.
- "Profane person" describes someone who treats sacred things with disrespect or irreverence, indicating a lack of reverence for God and His principles.
- "As Esau" refers to the biblical figure who made a hasty and foolish decision, prioritizing his immediate physical needs over his spiritual birthright.
- "Who for one morsel of meat sold his birthright" refers to Esau's exchange of his birthright, which was his inheritance and spiritual blessing as the firstborn son, for a single meal.

This verse serves as a warning against compromising spiritual values and priorities for the sake of immediate physical desires. It encourages believers to value their spiritual inheritance and to live in a manner that honors God's standards and principles, avoiding immorality and irreverence.

Verse 17 (KJV):
"For ye know how that afterward, when he would have inherited the blessing, he was rejected: for he found no place of repentance, though he sought it carefully with tears."

References:
- "Afterward, when he would have inherited the blessing" refers to the time after Esau had sold his birthright and later sought to receive the blessing from his father Isaac.
- "He was rejected" indicates that Isaac refused to give Esau the blessing intended for the firstborn.
- "He found no place of repentance" suggests that despite his tears and regret, Esau could not change the outcome.

Interpretation:
- This verse reflects on Esau's missed opportunity to receive the blessing due to his earlier decision to sell his birthright, illustrating the consequences of prioritizing immediate desires over spiritual blessings.

Commentary:
- The verse serves as a sobering reminder of the irreversible consequences of certain decisions, even when accompanied by sincere regret and repentance.
- It highlights the importance of making wise and discerning choices, especially in matters of spiritual significance, as the consequences can be permanent.

- By referencing Esau's story, the verse encourages believers to prioritize their spiritual inheritance and blessings over temporary worldly desires.

Exhaustive Strong's Concordance (ESV):
- "Afterward, when he would have inherited the blessing" refers to the time after Esau had sold his birthright and later sought to receive the blessing from his father Isaac, indicating a missed opportunity.
- "He was rejected" indicates that Isaac refused to give Esau the blessing intended for the firstborn, suggesting a permanent decision.
- "He found no place of repentance" suggests that despite his tears and regret, Esau could not change the outcome, indicating the finality of the decision.

This verse serves as a cautionary tale about the consequences of prioritizing immediate desires over spiritual blessings. It underscores the importance of making wise and discerning choices, especially in matters of spiritual significance, as the consequences can be permanent and irreversible.

Verse 18 (KJV):
"For ye are not come unto the mount that might be touched, and that burned with fire, nor unto blackness, and darkness, and tempest,"

References:
- "The mount that might be touched" refers to Mount Sinai, where God gave the law to Moses, and which the Israelites were forbidden to touch.
- "Burned with fire" describes the appearance of Mount Sinai when God descended upon it in fire.

- "Blackness, and darkness, and tempest" describes the terrifying and awe-inspiring appearance of Mount Sinai when God's presence descended upon it.

Interpretation:
- This verse contrasts the terrifying appearance of Mount Sinai, where the law was given, with the approachability and grace of the new covenant through Jesus Christ.

Commentary:
- The mention of Mount Sinai serves to highlight the contrast between the old covenant, characterized by fear and distance from God, and the new covenant, characterized by grace and intimacy with God through Jesus Christ.
- By reminding the readers of what they have not come to, the verse emphasizes the superior nature of the new covenant and the privilege believers have in approaching God through Christ.
- It serves as a reminder of the awe-inspiring nature of God's presence and the importance of approaching Him with reverence and humility.

Exhaustive Strong's Concordance (ESV):
- "The mount that might be touched" refers to Mount Sinai, where God gave the law to Moses, indicating its physical accessibility but also its sanctity and prohibition against touching.
- "Burned with fire" describes the appearance of Mount Sinai when God descended upon it in fire, indicating the presence of God.
- "Blackness, and darkness, and tempest" describes the terrifying and awe-inspiring appearance of Mount Sinai when God's presence descended upon it, indicating the fear and awe inspired by God's presence.

This verse contrasts the fear and awe inspired by the appearance of Mount Sinai with the approachability and grace of the new covenant through Jesus Christ. It emphasizes the superiority of the new covenant and the privilege believers have in approaching God through Christ.

Verse 19 (KJV):
"And the sound of a trumpet, and the voice of words; which voice they that heard intreated that the word should not be spoken to them any more:"

References:
- "The sound of a trumpet" refers to the trumpet blast that accompanied the giving of the law at Mount Sinai, signaling the presence of God.
- "The voice of words" refers to the audible voice of God speaking the Ten Commandments.
- "They that heard intreated that the word should not be spoken to them any more" indicates the fear and awe experienced by the Israelites at the sound of God's voice.

Interpretation:
- This verse describes the fear and awe that accompanied the giving of the law at Mount Sinai, highlighting the strictness and severity of the old covenant.

Commentary:
- The mention of the trumpet blast and the voice of God at Mount Sinai serves to emphasize the fear and awe that characterized the giving of the law.

- It underscores the strictness and severity of the old covenant, in contrast to the grace and accessibility of the new covenant through Jesus Christ.

- The reaction of the Israelites, who begged that the word not be spoken to them any more, highlights the overwhelming nature of God's presence and the law, which stood as a barrier between them and God.

Exhaustive Strong's Concordance (ESV):

- "The sound of a trumpet" refers to the trumpet blast that accompanied the giving of the law at Mount Sinai, indicating the presence of God.

- "The voice of words" refers to the audible voice of God speaking the Ten Commandments, indicating the direct communication of God's law to the people.

- "They that heard intreated that the word should not be spoken to them any more" indicates the fear and awe experienced by the Israelites at the sound of God's voice, suggesting their desire to avoid further communication from God.

This verse describes the fear and awe that accompanied the giving of the law at Mount Sinai, highlighting the strictness and severity of the old covenant. It emphasizes the contrast between the old covenant, characterized by fear and distance from God, and the new covenant, characterized by grace and intimacy with God through Jesus Christ.

Verse 20 (KJV):

"(For they could not endure that which was commanded, And if so much as a beast touch the mountain, it shall be stoned, or thrust through with a dart:)"

References:

- "They could not endure that which was commanded" refers to the Israelites' inability to bear the strict requirements of the law given at Mount Sinai.

- "If so much as a beast touch the mountain, it shall be stoned, or thrust through with a dart" emphasizes the holiness and sanctity of Mount Sinai, such that even animals were not allowed to touch it on pain of death.

Interpretation:

- This verse highlights the seriousness and severity of the law given at Mount Sinai, which even animals were not allowed to transgress upon pain of death.

Commentary:

- The mention of the prohibition against even animals touching the mountain serves to underscore the holiness and sanctity of God's presence and the law given at Mount Sinai.

- It emphasizes the strict requirements of the old covenant, in which even the slightest transgression was met with severe punishment.

- By contrast, the new covenant through Jesus Christ offers grace and forgiveness, showing the superiority of the new covenant over the old.

Exhaustive Strong's Concordance (ESV):

- "They could not endure that which was commanded" refers to the Israelites' inability to bear the strict requirements of the law given at Mount Sinai, indicating the severity of the law.

- "If so much as a beast touch the mountain, it shall be stoned, or thrust through with a dart" emphasizes the holiness and sanctity of Mount Sinai, indicating that even animals were not allowed to touch it on pain of death, indicating the severity of the consequences for transgression.

This verse highlights the seriousness and severity of the law given at Mount Sinai, emphasizing the holiness and sanctity of God's presence and the strict requirements of the old covenant. It serves as a contrast to the grace and forgiveness offered through the new covenant, showing the superiority of the new covenant over the old.

Verse 21 (KJV):
"And so terrible was the sight, that Moses said, I exceedingly fear and quake:)"

References:
- "So terrible was the sight" refers to the awe-inspiring and terrifying appearance of Mount Sinai when God's presence descended upon it.
- "Moses said, I exceedingly fear and quake" indicates Moses' response to the sight of God's presence on Mount Sinai, expressing his fear and trembling.

Interpretation:
- This verse describes the overwhelming fear and awe that Moses experienced when he witnessed the sight of God's presence on Mount Sinai, highlighting the awe-inspiring nature of God's holiness and power.

Commentary:
- The mention of Moses' fear and trembling serves to emphasize the greatness and majesty of God's presence, which inspired such awe in even the most revered figures like Moses.

- It underscores the seriousness and solemnity of the encounter at Mount Sinai, highlighting the reverence and respect due to God's holiness and power.

- This verse serves as a reminder of the difference between the old covenant, characterized by fear and trembling, and the new covenant, characterized by grace and access to God's presence through Jesus Christ.

Exhaustive Strong's Concordance (ESV):

- "So terrible was the sight" refers to the awe-inspiring and terrifying appearance of Mount Sinai when God's presence descended upon it, indicating the overwhelming nature of the experience.

- "Moses said, I exceedingly fear and quake" indicates Moses' response to the sight of God's presence on Mount Sinai, expressing his fear and trembling, indicating the overwhelming nature of the experience for him.

This verse describes the overwhelming fear and awe that Moses experienced when he witnessed the sight of God's presence on Mount Sinai, highlighting the awe-inspiring nature of God's holiness and power. It underscores the seriousness and solemnity of the encounter at Mount Sinai, emphasizing the reverence and respect due to God's holiness and power.

Verse 22 (KJV):

"But ye are come unto mount Sion, and unto the city of the living God, the heavenly Jerusalem, and to an innumerable company of angels,"

References:

- "Mount Sion" or "Zion" refers to the spiritual mount or city of God, representing His presence and kingdom.

- "The city of the living God, the heavenly Jerusalem" refers to the dwelling place of God and the destination of believers, symbolizing the new covenant and the eternal kingdom.

- "An innumerable company of angels" describes the vast multitude of angels in God's presence, emphasizing the majesty and glory of His kingdom.

Interpretation:

- This verse contrasts the old covenant at Mount Sinai with the new covenant in Christ, emphasizing the superior and more glorious nature of the new covenant.

Commentary:

- The mention of "Mount Sion" and "the city of the living God, the heavenly Jerusalem" highlights the spiritual reality of the new covenant, which transcends physical locations and earthly symbols.

- It emphasizes the intimate and direct access that believers have to the presence of God through Jesus Christ, in contrast to the distance and fear experienced under the old covenant.

- By mentioning the "innumerable company of angels," the verse underscores the majesty and glory of God's kingdom and the heavenly realm to which believers now belong through Christ.

Exhaustive Strong's Concordance (ESV):

- "Mount Sion" or "Zion" refers to the spiritual mount or city of God, representing His presence and kingdom, indicating the spiritual reality of the new covenant.

- "The city of the living God, the heavenly Jerusalem" refers to the dwelling place of God and the destination of believers, symbolizing the new covenant and the eternal kingdom, indicating the spiritual nature of the believer's citizenship.

- "An innumerable company of angels" describes the vast multitude of angels in God's presence, emphasizing the majesty and glory of His kingdom, indicating the spiritual realm to which believers now belong through Christ.

This verse contrasts the old covenant at Mount Sinai with the new covenant in Christ, emphasizing the superior and more glorious nature of the new covenant. It highlights the spiritual reality of the believer's relationship with God and citizenship in His kingdom, made possible through Jesus Christ.

Verse 23 (KJV):
"To the general assembly and church of the firstborn, which are written in heaven, and to God the Judge of all, and to the spirits of just men made perfect,"

References:
- "General assembly" or "festal gathering" refers to the gathering of all believers in heaven, symbolizing unity and fellowship.
- "Church of the firstborn" refers to the community of believers who have been redeemed by Christ, emphasizing their status as heirs and firstborn sons in God's family.
- "Written in heaven" indicates that believers' names are recorded in the book of life, signifying their citizenship in heaven.
- "God the Judge of all" emphasizes God's role as the ultimate judge, highlighting His sovereignty and justice.
- "Spirits of just men made perfect" refers to the souls of believers who have died and been perfected in Christ, awaiting the resurrection.

Interpretation:

- This verse describes the glorious assembly of believers in heaven, united in Christ and awaiting the final redemption and resurrection.

Commentary:
- The mention of the "general assembly" and "church of the firstborn" emphasizes the unity and fellowship of believers in heaven, who are all redeemed by Christ and share in His inheritance.
- The reference to believers' names being "written in heaven" highlights their citizenship in heaven and their secure place in God's kingdom.
- By mentioning "God the Judge of all," the verse emphasizes the ultimate justice and sovereignty of God, who will judge all according to His righteous standards.
- The mention of the "spirits of just men made perfect" highlights the reality of believers who have died and been perfected in Christ, awaiting the final resurrection and glorification of their bodies.

Exhaustive Strong's Concordance (ESV):
- "General assembly" or "festal gathering" refers to the gathering of all believers in heaven, symbolizing unity and fellowship, indicating the future unity of all believers in Christ.
- "Church of the firstborn" refers to the community of believers who have been redeemed by Christ, emphasizing their status as heirs and firstborn sons in God's family, indicating the privileged status of believers as God's children.
- "Written in heaven" indicates that believers' names are recorded in the book of life, signifying their citizenship in heaven, indicating the security and permanence of believers' relationship with God.

- "God the Judge of all" emphasizes God's role as the ultimate judge, highlighting His sovereignty and justice, indicating the final judgment that all will face.
- "Spirits of just men made perfect" refers to the souls of believers who have died and been perfected in Christ, awaiting the resurrection, indicating the future glorification of believers' bodies.

This verse describes the glorious assembly of believers in heaven, united in Christ and awaiting the final redemption and resurrection. It emphasizes the unity and fellowship of believers, their secure place in God's kingdom, and the ultimate justice and sovereignty of God as the Judge of all.

Verse 24 (KJV):
"And to Jesus the mediator of the new covenant, and to the blood of sprinkling, that speaketh better things than that of Abel."

References:
- "Jesus the mediator of the new covenant" refers to Jesus Christ, who mediates the new covenant between God and humanity, replacing the old covenant of the law.
- "The blood of sprinkling" refers to the blood of Jesus shed on the cross, which inaugurates the new covenant and brings forgiveness and redemption.
- "That speaketh better things than that of Abel" contrasts the blood of Jesus with the blood of Abel, indicating that Jesus' sacrifice is superior and speaks of forgiveness and reconciliation.

Interpretation:
- This verse highlights the central role of Jesus Christ and His sacrifice in the new covenant, which surpasses the old covenant and brings forgiveness and reconciliation with God.

Commentary:

- The mention of Jesus as the mediator of the new covenant emphasizes His role in establishing a new relationship between God and humanity, based on grace and forgiveness.

- The reference to "the blood of sprinkling" underscores the sacrificial nature of Jesus' death, which brings about the forgiveness of sins and the redemption of humanity.

- By contrasting Jesus' sacrifice with that of Abel, the verse highlights the superior and transformative nature of Jesus' sacrifice, which brings about reconciliation and salvation.

Exhaustive Strong's Concordance (ESV):

- "Jesus the mediator of the new covenant" refers to Jesus Christ, who mediates the new covenant between God and humanity, indicating His role in establishing a new relationship between God and humanity.

- "The blood of sprinkling" refers to the blood of Jesus shed on the cross, which inaugurates the new covenant and brings forgiveness and redemption, indicating the sacrificial nature of Jesus' death.

- "That speaketh better things than that of Abel" contrasts the blood of Jesus with the blood of Abel, indicating that Jesus' sacrifice is superior and speaks of forgiveness and reconciliation, indicating the superior nature of Jesus' sacrifice.

This verse highlights the central role of Jesus Christ and His sacrifice in the new covenant, emphasizing His role as the mediator between God and humanity and the forgiveness and reconciliation that His sacrifice brings. It contrasts Jesus' sacrifice with that of Abel, highlighting the superiority and transformative nature of Jesus' sacrifice.

Verse 25 (KJV):

"See that ye refuse not him that speaketh. For if they escaped not who refused him that spake on earth, much more shall not we escape, if we turn away from him that speaketh from heaven:"

References:

- "Him that speaketh" refers to God, who speaks through His Son Jesus Christ in the new covenant.

- "Him that spake on earth" refers to God speaking through Moses and the prophets in the old covenant.

- "Him that speaketh from heaven" refers to the ongoing revelation of God through Jesus Christ and the Holy Spirit in the new covenant.

Interpretation:

- This verse warns against rejecting the message of God, whether spoken through Moses and the prophets in the old covenant or through Jesus Christ and the Holy Spirit in the new covenant.

Commentary:

- The exhortation to "refuse not him that speaketh" emphasizes the importance of listening to and obeying God's word, which is spoken through Jesus Christ and the Holy Spirit in the new covenant.

- The reference to those who "escaped not" in the old covenant highlights the consequences of rejecting God's word, as seen in the judgment and punishment of those who disobeyed in the past.

- The warning that "much more shall not we escape" underscores the greater responsibility and accountability that comes with the new covenant revelation of God, which surpasses that of the old covenant.

Exhaustive Strong's Concordance (ESV):

- "See that ye refuse not him that speaketh" emphasizes the importance of listening to and obeying God's word, indicating the seriousness of rejecting His message.

- "For if they escaped not who refused him that spake on earth" refers to the judgment and punishment of those who disobeyed God's word in the old covenant, indicating the consequences of rejecting God's message.

- "Much more shall not we escape, if we turn away from him that speaketh from heaven" underscores the greater responsibility and accountability that comes with the new covenant revelation of God, indicating the seriousness of rejecting His message in the new covenant.

This verse warns against rejecting the message of God, whether spoken through Moses and the prophets in the old covenant or through Jesus Christ and the Holy Spirit in the new covenant. It emphasizes the importance of listening to and obeying God's word, highlighting the consequences of rejecting His message and the greater responsibility that comes with the new covenant revelation of God.

Verse 26 (KJV):
"Whose voice then shook the earth: but now he hath promised, saying, Yet once more I shake not the earth only, but also heaven."

References:
- "Whose voice then shook the earth" refers to the event at Mount Sinai when God's presence caused the earth to shake.

- "But now he hath promised" refers to a future event that God has promised to bring about.

- "Yet once more I shake not the earth only, but also heaven" indicates that God will shake not only the earth but also the heavens in a future event.

Interpretation:
- This verse alludes to a future event in which God will shake both the earth and the heavens, indicating a time of great upheaval and change.

Commentary:
- The mention of God's voice shaking the earth at Mount Sinai serves as a reminder of His power and majesty.
- The promise of a future shaking of the earth and heavens suggests a time of great upheaval and change, possibly referring to the final judgment or the renewal of all things.
- This verse underscores the sovereignty of God over all creation and His ability to bring about significant changes in accordance with His purposes.

Exhaustive Strong's Concordance (ESV):
- "Whose voice then shook the earth" refers to the event at Mount Sinai when God's presence caused the earth to shake, indicating the power and majesty of God.
- "But now he hath promised" refers to a future event that God has promised to bring about, indicating a future action of God.
- "Yet once more I shake not the earth only, but also heaven" indicates that God will shake not only the earth but also the heavens in a future event, indicating a time of great upheaval and change.

This verse alludes to a future event in which God will shake both the earth and the heavens, indicating a time of great upheaval and change. It emphasizes the power and sovereignty of God over all creation and His ability to bring about significant changes in accordance with His purposes.

Verse 27 (KJV):
"And this word, Yet once more, signifieth the removing of those things that are shaken, as of things that are made, that those things which cannot be shaken may remain."

References:
- "Yet once more" refers to the future shaking of the earth and heavens mentioned in the previous verse.
- "The removing of those things that are shaken" indicates that the shaking will result in the removal of temporary or earthly things.
- "Those things which cannot be shaken may remain" refers to the enduring and eternal nature of God's kingdom and His promises.

Interpretation:
- This verse explains the significance of the shaking mentioned in the previous verse, indicating that it will result in the removal of temporary or earthly things, leaving only the eternal and unshakeable.

Commentary:
- The shaking mentioned in this verse symbolizes a time of upheaval and change, in which temporary or earthly things will be removed or destroyed.
- The contrast between "those things that are shaken" and "those things which cannot be shaken" highlights the distinction between the temporary and the eternal.
- This verse emphasizes the enduring nature of God's kingdom and His promises, which will remain unshakeable despite the trials and tribulations of the world.

Exhaustive Strong's Concordance (ESV):

- "Yet once more" refers to the future shaking of the earth and heavens mentioned in the previous verse, indicating a future event.

- "The removing of those things that are shaken" indicates that the shaking will result in the removal of temporary or earthly things, indicating a time of upheaval and change.

- "Those things which cannot be shaken may remain" refers to the enduring and eternal nature of God's kingdom and His promises, indicating the permanence of His kingdom.

This verse explains the significance of the shaking mentioned in the previous verse, indicating that it will result in the removal of temporary or earthly things, leaving only the eternal and unshakeable. It emphasizes the enduring nature of God's kingdom and His promises, which will remain unshakeable despite the trials and tribulations of the world.

Verse 28 (KJV):

"Wherefore we receiving a kingdom which cannot be moved, let us have grace, whereby we may serve God acceptably with reverence and godly fear:"

References:

- "Receiving a kingdom which cannot be moved" refers to the eternal and unshakeable nature of the kingdom of God.

- "Let us have grace" emphasizes the need for God's grace to enable us to serve Him acceptably.

- "Serve God acceptably with reverence and godly fear" describes the manner in which believers are called to serve God, with reverence and awe.

Interpretation:

- This verse encourages believers to appreciate and respond to the unshakeable kingdom of God by serving Him with reverence and godly fear, relying on His grace.

Commentary:

- The mention of "receiving a kingdom which cannot be moved" reminds believers of the permanence and stability of God's kingdom, in contrast to the temporary nature of earthly kingdoms.

- The call to "have grace" acknowledges the need for God's enabling grace to serve Him acceptably, recognizing our dependence on Him for spiritual strength and guidance.

- The exhortation to "serve God acceptably with reverence and godly fear" emphasizes the importance of a reverent and humble attitude in our service to God, recognizing His greatness and holiness.

Exhaustive Strong's Concordance (ESV):

- "Receiving a kingdom which cannot be moved" refers to the eternal and unshakeable nature of the kingdom of God, indicating the permanence and stability of God's kingdom.

- "Let us have grace" emphasizes the need for God's grace to enable us to serve Him acceptably, indicating our dependence on God for spiritual strength and guidance.

- "Serve God acceptably with reverence and godly fear" describes the manner in which believers are called to serve God, with reverence and awe, indicating the attitude and approach we should have in our service to God.

This verse encourages believers to appreciate and respond to the unshakeable kingdom of God by serving Him with reverence and godly fear, relying on His grace. It emphasizes the need for humility and dependence on God in our service, recognizing His greatness and holiness.

CHAPTER 13
Warnings and requests

Verse 1 (KJV):
"Let brotherly love continue."

References:
- "Brotherly love" refers to the love and affection that believers are to have for one another as members of the same spiritual family.
- The concept of brotherly love is emphasized throughout the New Testament, including in passages such as John 13:34-35 and 1 Thessalonians 4:9.

Interpretation:
- This verse exhorts believers to maintain and cultivate a spirit of love and unity among themselves, reflecting the love that Christ has shown to them.

Commentary:

- The command to "let brotherly love continue" suggests that brotherly love is not automatic but requires intentional effort and nurturing.

- The term "brotherly love" emphasizes the familial bond that believers share as part of the body of Christ, highlighting the importance of mutual care and support.

- This verse reminds believers that their love for one another is a reflection of God's love for them and is a witness to the world of their identity as disciples of Christ.

Exhaustive Strong's Concordance (ESV):

- "Brotherly love" refers to the love and affection that believers are to have for one another as members of the same spiritual family, indicating the familial bond that exists among believers.

- The command to "let brotherly love continue" suggests that brotherly love is not automatic but requires intentional effort and nurturing, indicating the importance of cultivating and maintaining love among believers.

This verse exhorts believers to maintain and cultivate a spirit of love and unity among themselves, reflecting the love that Christ has shown to them. It emphasizes the importance of intentional effort in nurturing love among believers, as it is a reflection of God's love and a witness to the world.

Verse 2 (KJV):
"Be not forgetful to entertain strangers: for thereby some have entertained angels unawares."

References:

- The command to show hospitality to strangers is found throughout the Bible, such as in Romans 12:13 and 1 Peter 4:9.

- The reference to entertaining angels unawares likely alludes to instances in the Old Testament where angels appeared as ordinary travelers, such as in Genesis 18 when Abraham and Sarah entertained angels who appeared as men.

Interpretation:

- This verse encourages believers to show hospitality and kindness to strangers, as they may be unknowingly interacting with angels or messengers of God.

Commentary:

- The command to "be not forgetful to entertain strangers" emphasizes the importance of hospitality in the Christian life, reflecting God's welcoming and inclusive nature.

- The reference to entertaining angels unawares serves as a reminder that God can work through unexpected means and that showing kindness to others is a way of honoring God.

- This verse encourages believers to be open-hearted and generous in their interactions with others, especially those in need, recognizing that their actions may have deeper spiritual significance.

Exhaustive Strong's Concordance (ESV):

- The command to "be not forgetful to entertain strangers" emphasizes the importance of hospitality in the Christian life, indicating the welcoming and inclusive nature of God.

- The reference to entertaining angels unawares suggests that God can work through unexpected means and that showing kindness to others is a way of honoring God, indicating the potential spiritual significance of acts of hospitality.

This verse encourages believers to show hospitality and kindness to strangers, recognizing that they may be unknowingly interacting with angels or messengers of God. It emphasizes the importance of hospitality in the Christian life and the potential spiritual significance of acts of kindness and generosity towards others.

Verse 3 (KJV):
"Remember them that are in bonds, as bound with them; and them which suffer adversity, as being yourselves also in the body."

References:
- This verse echoes the teaching of Jesus in Matthew 25:36, where He instructs His followers to remember and care for those who are imprisoned.
- It also reflects the broader biblical theme of caring for the oppressed and those in need, as seen in passages like Isaiah 58:6-7 and James 1:27.

Interpretation:
- This verse encourages believers to empathize with and support those who are suffering, whether they are in prison or experiencing other forms of adversity.

Commentary:
- The command to "remember them that are in bonds" underscores the importance of solidarity and empathy with those who are experiencing hardship and persecution.
- By exhorting believers to consider themselves as if they were in the same situation, the verse emphasizes the call to compassionate action and practical support for those in need.

- This verse challenges believers to actively seek out ways to alleviate the suffering of others and to stand in solidarity with those who are oppressed or marginalized.

Exhaustive Strong's Concordance (ESV):
- The command to "remember them that are in bonds" emphasizes the importance of solidarity and empathy with those who are experiencing hardship and persecution, indicating the need for compassion and support for those in need.
- The exhortation to "them which suffer adversity, as being yourselves also in the body" challenges believers to consider themselves as if they were in the same situation, indicating the call to compassionate action and practical support for those in need.

This verse encourages believers to empathize with and support those who are suffering, whether they are in prison or experiencing other forms of adversity. It emphasizes the importance of solidarity, empathy, and practical support for those in need, reflecting the compassionate nature of God's kingdom.

Verse 4 (KJV):
"Marriage is honourable in all, and the bed undefiled: but whoremongers and adulterers God will judge."

References:
- This verse affirms the sanctity and honor of marriage, in line with teachings found throughout the Bible, such as in Genesis 2:24 and Ephesians 5:31-32.
- The warning against sexual immorality and the judgment of God for such behavior is a consistent theme in both the Old and New

Testaments, as seen in passages like Exodus 20:14 and Matthew 5:27-28.

Interpretation:

- This verse emphasizes the importance of honoring marriage and maintaining sexual purity, warning of the judgment that awaits those who engage in sexual immorality.

Commentary:

- The affirmation that "marriage is honourable in all" highlights the value and sanctity of marriage as an institution established by God.

- The statement that "the bed undefiled" emphasizes the purity and exclusivity of the marital relationship, in contrast to the impurity of sexual immorality.

- The warning that "whoremongers and adulterers God will judge" underscores the seriousness of sexual sin and the accountability that individuals have before God for their actions in this area.

Exhaustive Strong's Concordance (ESV):

- The affirmation that "marriage is honourable in all" highlights the value and sanctity of marriage as an institution established by God, indicating the importance of honoring marriage.

- The statement that "the bed undefiled" emphasizes the purity and exclusivity of the marital relationship, indicating the importance of sexual purity within marriage.

- The warning that "whoremongers and adulterers God will judge" underscores the seriousness of sexual sin and the accountability that individuals have before God for their actions in this area, indicating the consequences of sexual immorality.

This verse emphasizes the importance of honoring marriage and maintaining sexual purity, warning of the judgment that awaits those who engage in sexual immorality. It affirms the sanctity of marriage and the purity of the marital relationship, highlighting the accountability that individuals have before God in matters of sexual behavior.

Verse 5 (KJV):

"Let your conversation be without covetousness; and be content with such things as ye have: for he hath said, I will never leave thee, nor forsake thee."

References:

- The command to avoid covetousness is found in the Ten Commandments (Exodus 20:17) and is echoed by Jesus in Luke 12:15.

- The promise that God will never leave or forsake His people is found in various passages in the Bible, such as Deuteronomy 31:6 and Joshua 1:5.

Interpretation:

- This verse encourages believers to avoid greed and covetousness, instead finding contentment in God's provision and the assurance of His presence.

Commentary:

- The command to "let your conversation be without covetousness" underscores the danger of greed and the importance of contentment in the Christian life.

- By exhorting believers to be content with what they have, the verse emphasizes the sufficiency of God's provision and the need to trust in His care.

- The promise that "he hath said, I will never leave thee, nor forsake thee" provides a basis for contentment and security, as believers can trust in God's presence and faithfulness.

Exhaustive Strong's Concordance (ESV):

- The command to "let your conversation be without covetousness" underscores the danger of greed and the importance of contentment in the Christian life, indicating the need to trust in God's provision.

- The exhortation to "be content with such things as ye have" emphasizes the sufficiency of God's provision and the need to trust in His care, indicating the basis for contentment.

- The promise that "he hath said, I will never leave thee, nor forsake thee" provides a basis for contentment and security, as believers can trust in God's presence and faithfulness, indicating the assurance of God's provision and presence.

This verse encourages believers to avoid greed and covetousness, finding contentment in God's provision and the assurance of His presence. It underscores the sufficiency of God's provision and the need to trust in His care, providing a basis for contentment and security in the Christian life.

Verse 6 (KJV):

"So that we may boldly say, The Lord is my helper, and I will not fear what man shall do unto me."

References:

- This verse echoes several Old Testament passages that affirm God as a helper and deliverer, such as Psalm 118:6 and Isaiah 41:10.

- The theme of trusting in God's help and not fearing man is also found in passages like Psalm 56:4 and Proverbs 29:25.

Interpretation:

- This verse encourages believers to trust in God's help and provision, allowing them to confidently declare that the Lord is their helper and to not fear the actions of others.

Commentary:
- The affirmation that "The Lord is my helper" reflects the confidence and trust that believers can have in God's provision and care.
- The declaration that "I will not fear what man shall do unto me" emphasizes the freedom from fear that comes from trusting in God's help and protection.
- This verse encourages believers to rely on God's strength and assistance, enabling them to face challenges and opposition without fear.

Exhaustive Strong's Concordance (ESV):
- The affirmation that "The Lord is my helper" reflects the confidence and trust that believers can have in God's provision and care, indicating the basis for trust in God's help.
- The declaration that "I will not fear what man shall do unto me" emphasizes the freedom from fear that comes from trusting in God's help and protection, indicating the result of trusting in God's help.

This verse encourages believers to trust in God's help and provision, allowing them to confidently declare that the Lord is their helper and to not fear the actions of others. It emphasizes the freedom from fear that comes from trusting in God's help and protection, encouraging believers to rely on God's strength and assistance in all circumstances.

Verse 7 (KJV):

"Remember them which have the rule over you, who have spoken unto you the word of God: whose faith follow, considering the end of their conversation."

References:
- This verse is a call to respect and honor spiritual leaders who teach the Word of God, echoing similar instructions found in passages like 1 Thessalonians 5:12-13 and 1 Timothy 5:17.
- The concept of following the example of faithful leaders is also found in passages like Philippians 3:17 and 1 Corinthians 11:1.

Interpretation:
- This verse encourages believers to remember and honor those who lead and teach them spiritually, following their example of faith and considering the outcome of their conduct.

Commentary:
- The command to "remember them which have the rule over you" emphasizes the importance of respecting and honoring spiritual leaders, recognizing their authority and role in guiding the church.
- The instruction to "follow...whose faith follow" encourages believers to imitate the faith and example of their leaders, learning from their teachings and conduct.
- The phrase "considering the end of their conversation" suggests that believers should reflect on the outcome or result of their leaders' conduct, seeking to emulate their faithful perseverance and ultimate goal.

Exhaustive Strong's Concordance (ESV):
- The command to "remember them which have the rule over you" emphasizes the importance of respecting and honoring spiritual

leaders, recognizing their authority and role in guiding the church, indicating the need for respect and honor toward spiritual leaders.

- The instruction to "follow...whose faith follow" encourages believers to imitate the faith and example of their leaders, learning from their teachings and conduct, indicating the basis for imitation of spiritual leaders.

- The phrase "considering the end of their conversation" suggests that believers should reflect on the outcome or result of their leaders' conduct, seeking to emulate their faithful perseverance and ultimate goal, indicating the reason for reflecting on the conduct of spiritual leaders.

This verse encourages believers to remember and honor those who lead and teach them spiritually, following their example of faith and considering the outcome of their conduct. It emphasizes the importance of respecting and honoring spiritual leaders, learning from their teachings and conduct, and seeking to emulate their faithful perseverance and ultimate goal.

Verse 8 (KJV):
"Jesus Christ the same yesterday, and to day, and for ever."

References:
- This verse emphasizes the unchanging nature of Jesus Christ, echoing similar statements found in passages like Malachi 3:6 and James 1:17.

- The eternal nature of Jesus Christ is a central theme in the New Testament, affirming His deity and unchanging character.

Interpretation:

- This verse declares the eternal consistency and reliability of Jesus Christ, highlighting His unchanging nature across time.

Commentary:
- The statement "Jesus Christ the same yesterday, and to day, and for ever" emphasizes the timeless and unchanging nature of Jesus Christ, highlighting His constancy and reliability.
- This declaration of Christ's unchanging nature provides comfort and assurance to believers, knowing that their Savior remains the same throughout all ages.
- The unchanging nature of Jesus Christ underscores His deity and sovereignty, as He is not subject to the changes and fluctuations of the world.

Exhaustive Strong's Concordance (ESV):
- The statement "Jesus Christ the same yesterday, and to day, and for ever" emphasizes the timeless and unchanging nature of Jesus Christ, highlighting His constancy and reliability, indicating the unchanging nature of Jesus Christ.

This verse declares the eternal consistency and reliability of Jesus Christ, highlighting His unchanging nature across time. It emphasizes the timeless and unchanging nature of Jesus Christ, providing comfort and assurance to believers and underscoring His deity and sovereignty.

Verse 9 (KJV):
"Be not carried about with divers and strange doctrines. For it is a good thing that the heart be established with grace; not with meats, which have not profited them that have been occupied therein."

References:

- The warning against being led astray by false teachings is found throughout the New Testament, such as in Ephesians 4:14 and Colossians 2:8.

- The contrast between the spiritual benefits of grace and the ineffectiveness of dietary regulations is also emphasized in passages like Romans 14:17 and 1 Corinthians 8:8.

Interpretation:

- This verse cautions believers against being swayed by various and strange teachings, emphasizing the importance of establishing their hearts in the grace of God rather than in external practices.

Commentary:

- The warning to "be not carried about with divers and strange doctrines" highlights the danger of being misled by teachings that deviate from the truth of the gospel.

- The statement that "it is a good thing that the heart be established with grace" underscores the importance of grounding one's faith in the grace of God, which is the foundation of salvation and spiritual growth.

- The contrast between "not with meats, which have not profited them that have been occupied therein" highlights the ineffectiveness of relying on external practices, such as dietary regulations, for spiritual benefit.

Exhaustive Strong's Concordance (ESV):

- The warning to "be not carried about with divers and strange doctrines" highlights the danger of being misled by teachings that deviate from the truth of the gospel, indicating the need for discernment and adherence to sound doctrine.

- The statement that "it is a good thing that the heart be established with grace" underscores the importance of grounding one's faith in the grace of God, which is the foundation of salvation and spiritual growth, indicating the importance of establishing one's faith in God's grace.

- The contrast between "not with meats, which have not profited them that have been occupied therein" highlights the ineffectiveness of relying on external practices, such as dietary regulations, for spiritual benefit, indicating the futility of relying on external practices for spiritual growth.

This verse cautions believers against being swayed by various and strange teachings, emphasizing the importance of establishing their hearts in the grace of God rather than in external practices. It warns against being misled by teachings that deviate from the truth of the gospel and underscores the futility of relying on external practices for spiritual benefit.

Verse 10 (KJV):
"We have an altar, whereof they have no right to eat which serve the tabernacle."

References:
- The mention of an altar likely alludes to the sacrificial system of the Old Testament, where offerings were made on the altar as part of the worship practices of the tabernacle and later the temple (Exodus 27:1-8; Leviticus 1:1-17).

- The concept of a new altar or a new way of worship is also mentioned in passages like Psalm 118:27 and Isaiah 56:7, pointing to a spiritual reality beyond the physical altar.

Interpretation:

- This verse suggests a contrast between the old system of worship under the Mosaic Law, where only certain priests had access to the altar and its offerings, and the new system of worship in Christ, where all believers have access to the spiritual benefits of His sacrifice.

Commentary:
- The mention of "an altar" in this verse symbolizes the atoning sacrifice of Christ, which is the basis of the new covenant and the new way of worship for believers.
- The statement that "they have no right to eat which serve the tabernacle" indicates that those who cling to the old system of worship, represented by the tabernacle and its rituals, do not have a share in the spiritual benefits of Christ's sacrifice.
- This verse emphasizes the exclusivity of Christ's sacrifice as the only means of salvation and the only way to access God's grace and forgiveness.

Exhaustive Strong's Concordance (ESV):
- The mention of "an altar" in this verse symbolizes the atoning sacrifice of Christ, which is the basis of the new covenant and the new way of worship for believers, indicating the spiritual significance of Christ's sacrifice.
- The statement that "they have no right to eat which serve the tabernacle" indicates that those who cling to the old system of worship, represented by the tabernacle and its rituals, do not have a share in the spiritual benefits of Christ's sacrifice, indicating the exclusivity of Christ's sacrifice.

This verse suggests a contrast between the old system of worship under the Mosaic Law and the new system of worship in Christ. It emphasizes the atoning sacrifice of Christ as the basis of the new covenant and the exclusivity of His sacrifice as the only means of salvation and access to God's grace.

Verse 11 (KJV):
"For the bodies of those beasts, whose blood is brought into the sanctuary by the high priest for sin, are burned without the camp."

References:
- This verse refers to the sacrificial system under the Mosaic Law, where certain animal sacrifices were offered for sin and their bodies burned outside the camp (Leviticus 4:12; Leviticus 16:27).
- The burning of the sacrificial animals outside the camp symbolized the removal of sin from the community and the need for purification.

Interpretation:
- This verse likely serves as a contrast between the Old Testament sacrificial system, where animals were sacrificed for sin and their bodies burned outside the camp, and the sacrifice of Jesus Christ, whose sacrifice took place outside the city of Jerusalem (Hebrews 13:12).

Commentary:
- The mention of the bodies of the sacrificial animals being burned outside the camp highlights the ritual purity required in the sacrificial system and the separation of sin from the community.
- This verse may also serve as a foreshadowing or typology of Christ's sacrifice, which took place outside the city of Jerusalem, symbolizing the removal of sin from God's people.
- The contrast between the Old Testament sacrificial system and the sacrifice of Christ underscores the superiority and completeness of Christ's sacrifice in dealing with sin.

Exhaustive Strong's Concordance (ESV):

- This verse refers to the sacrificial system under the Mosaic Law, where certain animal sacrifices were offered for sin and their bodies burned outside the camp, indicating the ritual purity required in the sacrificial system.

- The burning of the sacrificial animals outside the camp symbolized the removal of sin from the community and the need for purification, indicating the symbolic significance of the sacrificial system.

This verse likely serves as a contrast between the Old Testament sacrificial system and the sacrifice of Jesus Christ. It highlights the ritual purity required in the sacrificial system and may serve as a foreshadowing of Christ's sacrifice, which took place outside the city of Jerusalem. The contrast underscores the superiority and completeness of Christ's sacrifice in dealing with sin.

Verse 12 (KJV):

"Wherefore Jesus also, that he might sanctify the people with his own blood, suffered without the gate."

References:

- This verse refers to Jesus' crucifixion outside the city of Jerusalem, fulfilling Old Testament prophecies such as Isaiah 53:7-8 and Psalm 22:16.

- The concept of Jesus' blood sanctifying or purifying believers is found in passages like Ephesians 1:7 and 1 Peter 1:18-19.

Interpretation:

- This verse highlights the redemptive work of Jesus Christ, who sanctified or purified believers through His sacrificial death outside the city gates.

Commentary:
- The phrase "that he might sanctify the people with his own blood" emphasizes the sacrificial nature of Jesus' death, which was necessary for the purification of sin.
- The mention of Jesus suffering "without the gate" (outside the city) underscores His identification with outcasts and sinners, as well as the fulfillment of Old Testament types and shadows.
- This verse emphasizes the efficacy and completeness of Christ's sacrifice, which accomplished the sanctification of believers once and for all.

Exhaustive Strong's Concordance (ESV):
- This verse highlights the redemptive work of Jesus Christ, who sanctified or purified believers through His sacrificial death outside the city gates, indicating the redemptive significance of Jesus' death.
- The phrase "that he might sanctify the people with his own blood" emphasizes the sacrificial nature of Jesus' death, which was necessary for the purification of sin, indicating the necessity of Jesus' death for the forgiveness of sin.

This verse highlights the redemptive work of Jesus Christ, who sanctified or purified believers through His sacrificial death outside the city gates. It emphasizes the efficacy and completeness of Christ's sacrifice, which accomplished the sanctification of believers once and for all.

Verse 13 (KJV):

"Let us go forth therefore unto him without the camp, bearing his reproach."

References:
- This verse alludes to the imagery of leaving the camp, which symbolizes leaving behind the old way of life or religious system, and going to Jesus, who was crucified outside the city (Hebrews 13:12).
- The idea of bearing reproach for following Christ is found in passages like Matthew 5:11-12 and 1 Peter 4:14.

Interpretation:
- This verse encourages believers to identify with Christ in His suffering and rejection, being willing to endure reproach and persecution for His sake.

Commentary:
- The exhortation to "let us go forth therefore unto him without the camp" suggests a call to separate from worldly and sinful practices, identifying instead with Christ's sacrificial death and rejection by the world.
- The phrase "bearing his reproach" signifies the willingness to endure shame and rejection for the sake of following Christ, recognizing that such suffering is part of the Christian life.
- This verse challenges believers to embrace a life of discipleship that may involve sacrifice and suffering, yet ultimately leads to a deeper fellowship with Christ.

Exhaustive Strong's Concordance (ESV):
- This verse encourages believers to identify with Christ in His suffering and rejection, being willing to endure reproach and

persecution for His sake, indicating the call to identify with Christ's sacrifice.

- The phrase "bearing his reproach" signifies the willingness to endure shame and rejection for the sake of following Christ, indicating the willingness to endure suffering for the sake of Christ.

This verse encourages believers to identify with Christ in His suffering and rejection, being willing to endure reproach and persecution for His sake. It challenges believers to separate from worldly practices and embrace a life of discipleship that may involve sacrifice and suffering, yet ultimately leads to a deeper fellowship with Christ.

Verse 14 (KJV):
"For here have we no continuing city, but we seek one to come."

References:
- This verse echoes the theme of the temporary nature of earthly things found throughout the Bible, such as in 1 Peter 2:11 and Philippians 3:20.
- The concept of seeking a heavenly or eternal city is also found in passages like Hebrews 11:10 and Revelation 21:2.

Interpretation:
- This verse reminds believers that their ultimate home and citizenship are in heaven, not in this world, and encourages them to live in light of this eternal perspective.

Commentary:
- The statement "here have we no continuing city" emphasizes the transient nature of earthly life and the impermanence of worldly possessions and achievements.

- The phrase "but we seek one to come" highlights the believer's longing for the eternal city of God, where they will dwell forever in the presence of God.

- This verse encourages believers to live with an eternal perspective, prioritizing heavenly values and eternal rewards over temporal pleasures and earthly pursuits.

Exhaustive Strong's Concordance (ESV):

- The statement "here have we no continuing city" emphasizes the transient nature of earthly life and the impermanence of worldly possessions and achievements, indicating the temporary nature of earthly life.

- The phrase "but we seek one to come" highlights the believer's longing for the eternal city of God, where they will dwell forever in the presence of God, indicating the believer's hope for the future.

This verse reminds believers that their ultimate home and citizenship are in heaven, not in this world, and encourages them to live in light of this eternal perspective. It emphasizes the transient nature of earthly life and the believer's hope for the eternal city of God, where they will dwell forever in the presence of God.

Verse 15 (KJV):

"By him therefore let us offer the sacrifice of praise to God continually, that is, the fruit of our lips giving thanks to his name."

References:

- This verse echoes the concept of offering praise and thanksgiving to God found throughout the Bible, such as in Psalm 50:23 and Psalm 100:4.

- The idea of offering spiritual sacrifices is also mentioned in passages like 1 Peter 2:5 and Romans 12:1.

Interpretation:
- This verse encourages believers to offer praise and thanksgiving to God as a spiritual sacrifice, expressing gratitude for His goodness and mercy.

Commentary:
- The phrase "the sacrifice of praise to God continually" suggests that praise and thanksgiving should be a consistent and ongoing part of the believer's life, not just a sporadic or occasional activity.
- The mention of "the fruit of our lips giving thanks to his name" emphasizes that true praise originates from the heart and is expressed through words that acknowledge God's goodness and grace.
- This verse underscores the importance of worship and gratitude in the Christian life, recognizing God's sovereignty and faithfulness.

Exhaustive Strong's Concordance (ESV):
- The phrase "the sacrifice of praise to God continually" suggests that praise and thanksgiving should be a consistent and ongoing part of the believer's life, indicating the continuous nature of praise.
- The mention of "the fruit of our lips giving thanks to his name" emphasizes that true praise originates from the heart and is expressed through words that acknowledge God's goodness and grace, indicating the source of genuine praise.

This verse encourages believers to offer praise and thanksgiving to God as a spiritual sacrifice, expressing gratitude for His goodness and mercy. It emphasizes the importance of worship and gratitude in the Christian life, recognizing God's sovereignty and faithfulness.

Verse 16 (KJV):

"But to do good and to communicate forget not: for with such sacrifices God is well pleased."

References:

- This verse aligns with the broader biblical teaching on the importance of good works and generosity, such as in Matthew 5:16 and 1 Timothy 6:18.

- The idea of pleasing God through acts of kindness and generosity is also found in passages like Hebrews 6:10 and Philippians 4:18.

Interpretation:

- This verse emphasizes the importance of doing good and sharing with others, indicating that these actions are pleasing to God and can be considered as sacrifices offered to Him.

Commentary:

- The exhortation "to do good and to communicate" encourages believers to actively engage in acts of kindness, generosity, and sharing with those in need.

- The phrase "for with such sacrifices God is well pleased" suggests that acts of kindness and generosity are not only beneficial to others but are also pleasing to God, indicating His approval and delight in such actions.

- This verse highlights the idea that our actions toward others can be seen as sacrifices to God, reflecting His love and compassion in tangible ways.

Exhaustive Strong's Concordance (ESV):

- The exhortation "to do good and to communicate" encourages believers to actively engage in acts of kindness, generosity, and sharing with those in need, indicating the importance of good works.

- The phrase "for with such sacrifices God is well pleased" suggests that acts of kindness and generosity are not only beneficial to others but are also pleasing to God, indicating God's approval and delight in such actions.

This verse emphasizes the importance of doing good and sharing with others, indicating that these actions are pleasing to God and can be considered as sacrifices offered to Him. It encourages believers to actively engage in acts of kindness, generosity, and sharing with those in need, reflecting God's love and compassion in tangible ways.

Verse 17 (KJV):

"Obey them that have the rule over you, and submit yourselves: for they watch for your souls, as they that must give account, that they may do it with joy, and not with grief: for that is unprofitable for you."

References:

- This verse is consistent with the biblical teaching on respecting and submitting to authority, such as in Romans 13:1 and 1 Peter 5:5.

- The idea of leaders being accountable for those under their care is also found in passages like James 3:1 and Ezekiel 33:7-9.

Interpretation:

- This verse instructs believers to obey and submit to their spiritual leaders, recognizing their responsibility to watch over their souls and their accountability to God for their leadership.

Commentary:

- The exhortation to "obey them that have the rule over you, and submit yourselves" emphasizes the importance of respecting and honoring spiritual authority, recognizing the role of leaders in guiding and protecting the church.

- The statement that leaders "watch for your souls" highlights the care and concern that spiritual leaders should have for those under their care, indicating the seriousness of their role and the accountability they have to God.

- This verse encourages believers to cooperate with their leaders in a way that brings them joy and not grief, recognizing that disobedience and rebellion are ultimately harmful to the individual and the community.

Exhaustive Strong's Concordance (ESV):

- The exhortation to "obey them that have the rule over you, and submit yourselves" emphasizes the importance of respecting and honoring spiritual authority, indicating the need for submission to spiritual leaders.

- The statement that leaders "watch for your souls" highlights the care and concern that spiritual leaders should have for those under their care, indicating the seriousness of their role and the accountability they have to God.

This verse instructs believers to obey and submit to their spiritual leaders, recognizing their responsibility to watch over their souls and their accountability to God for their leadership. It emphasizes the importance of respecting and honoring spiritual authority, recognizing the care and concern that leaders should have for those under their care.

Verse 18 (KJV):

"Pray for us: for we trust we have a good conscience, in all things willing to live honestly."

References:

- This verse aligns with the biblical teaching on the importance of prayer and maintaining a clear conscience, such as in 1 Thessalonians 5:17 and 1 Peter 3:16.

- The concept of living honestly or with integrity is also emphasized in passages like Proverbs 11:3 and Romans 12:17.

Interpretation:

- This verse is a request for prayer from the author to the recipients of the letter, expressing confidence in their good conscience and desire to live honestly.

Commentary:

- The request to "pray for us" reflects the author's humility and recognition of the need for divine assistance in their ministry and personal life.

- The statement "we trust we have a good conscience" indicates the author's confidence in their integrity and sincerity in their actions and motivations.

- The phrase "in all things willing to live honestly" emphasizes the author's commitment to integrity and transparency in all aspects of life, seeking to live in a way that honors God and others.

Exhaustive Strong's Concordance (ESV):

- The request to "pray for us" reflects the author's humility and recognition of the need for divine assistance in their ministry and personal life, indicating the author's request for prayer.

- The statement "we trust we have a good conscience" indicates the author's confidence in their integrity and sincerity in their actions and motivations, indicating the author's confidence in their integrity.

This verse is a request for prayer from the author to the recipients of the letter, expressing confidence in their good conscience and desire to live honestly. It reflects the author's humility and recognition of the need for divine assistance in their ministry and personal life, as well as their commitment to integrity and transparency in all aspects of life.

Verse 19 (KJV):
"But I beseech you the rather to do this, that I may be restored to you the sooner."

References:
- This verse emphasizes the author's desire for restoration and reunion with the recipients of the letter, reflecting themes of reconciliation and unity found throughout the Bible, such as in 2 Corinthians 13:11 and Ephesians 4:3.
- The concept of earnestly desiring fellowship and communion with believers is also expressed in passages like Romans 1:11-12 and Philippians 1:8-9.

Interpretation:
- This verse is a plea from the author to the recipients of the letter, urging them to pray for his restoration to them, indicating his longing for fellowship and communion with them.

Commentary:

- The phrase "But I beseech you the rather to do this" expresses the author's earnest plea and desire for the recipients of the letter to pray for his restoration to them.

- The statement "that I may be restored to you the sooner" indicates the author's hope that through their prayers, he may be able to return to them more quickly, highlighting his longing for fellowship and unity with them.

- This verse underscores the importance of prayer in fostering unity and reconciliation among believers, as well as the value of earnestly desiring fellowship with other members of the body of Christ.

Exhaustive Strong's Concordance (ESV):

- The phrase "But I beseech you the rather to do this" expresses the author's earnest plea and desire for the recipients of the letter to pray for his restoration to them, indicating the author's request for prayer.

- The statement "that I may be restored to you the sooner" indicates the author's hope that through their prayers, he may be able to return to them more quickly, indicating the author's desire for fellowship and communion with them.

This verse is a plea from the author to the recipients of the letter, urging them to pray for his restoration to them, indicating his longing for fellowship and communion with them. It underscores the importance of prayer in fostering unity and reconciliation among believers, as well as the value of earnestly desiring fellowship with other members of the body of Christ.

Verse 20 (KJV):

"Now the God of peace, that brought again from the dead our Lord Jesus, that great shepherd of the sheep, through the blood of the everlasting covenant,"

References:
- This verse refers to God as the "God of peace," a title found in various places in the Bible, such as Romans 15:33 and Philippians 4:9.
- The mention of Jesus as the "great shepherd of the sheep" aligns with Jesus' own description of Himself in John 10:11 and John 10:14.
- The reference to the "blood of the everlasting covenant" alludes to Jesus' sacrificial death, which established the new covenant, as mentioned in passages like Matthew 26:28 and 1 Corinthians 11:25.

Interpretation:
- This verse acknowledges God as the source of peace and highlights Jesus' role as the shepherd of His people, who secured their redemption through His sacrificial death.

Commentary:
- The designation "God of peace" emphasizes God's character as the one who brings about reconciliation and harmony, especially through the work of Christ.
- The title "great shepherd of the sheep" underscores Jesus' care, guidance, and protection of His followers, likening them to a flock under His watchful care.
- The mention of "the blood of the everlasting covenant" points to the sacrificial death of Jesus as the means by which the new covenant was established, securing eternal redemption for believers.

Exhaustive Strong's Concordance (ESV):
- The designation "God of peace" emphasizes God's character as the one who brings about reconciliation and harmony, indicating God's role in bringing peace.

- The title "great shepherd of the sheep" underscores Jesus' care, guidance, and protection of His followers, indicating Jesus' role as the shepherd of His people.

- The mention of "the blood of the everlasting covenant" points to the sacrificial death of Jesus as the means by which the new covenant was established, indicating the significance of Jesus' sacrifice.

This verse acknowledges God as the source of peace and highlights Jesus' role as the shepherd of His people, who secured their redemption through His sacrificial death. It emphasizes God's character as the one who brings about reconciliation and harmony, underscores Jesus' care and protection of His followers, and points to the sacrificial death of Jesus as the means by which the new covenant was established.

Verse 21 (KJV):

"Make you perfect in every good work to do his will, working in you that which is wellpleasing in his sight, through Jesus Christ; to whom be glory for ever and ever. Amen."

References:

- This verse echoes the prayer for spiritual growth and empowerment found in passages like Philippians 1:6 and Colossians 1:10.

- The concept of doing God's will and pleasing Him is also emphasized in passages like 1 Thessalonians 4:1 and Ephesians 5:10.

- The attribution of glory to Jesus Christ is a common theme in the New Testament, reflecting His exalted status and role in redemption (Philippians 2:9-11; Revelation 5:12-13).

Interpretation:

- This verse is a prayer for God to perfect believers in every good work, enabling them to do His will and pleasing Him, all through the empowering work of Jesus Christ.

Commentary:
- The prayer for God to "make you perfect in every good work" reflects the desire for believers to be mature and complete in their faith, equipped to fulfill God's purposes.
- The phrase "working in you that which is wellpleasing in his sight" highlights the role of God's grace and power in enabling believers to live in a way that honors and pleases Him.
- The attribution of glory "to whom be glory for ever and ever" acknowledges Jesus Christ as the source of all spiritual blessings and the one deserving of eternal praise and honor.

Exhaustive Strong's Concordance (ESV):
- The prayer for God to "make you perfect in every good work" reflects the desire for believers to be mature and complete in their faith, indicating the desire for spiritual growth.
- The phrase "working in you that which is wellpleasing in his sight" highlights the role of God's grace and power in enabling believers to live in a way that honors and pleases Him, indicating the source of spiritual empowerment.

This verse is a prayer for God to perfect believers in every good work, enabling them to do His will and pleasing Him, all through the empowering work of Jesus Christ. It reflects the desire for believers to be mature and complete in their faith, equipped to fulfill God's purposes, and acknowledges Jesus Christ as the source of all spiritual blessings and the one deserving of eternal praise and honor.

Verse 22 (KJV):

"And I beseech you, brethren, suffer the word of exhortation: for I have written a letter unto you in few words."

References:

- The exhortation to "suffer the word of exhortation" is a call to listen attentively to the message being given, which aligns with the biblical emphasis on hearing and heeding God's Word (James 1:19; Luke 8:18).

- The reference to the author having written a letter "in few words" may indicate that the letter of Hebrews is relatively short compared to other New Testament letters.

Interpretation:

- This verse is a plea from the author to the recipients of the letter to receive and accept his exhortation, indicating the importance of the message he has written to them.

Commentary:

- The exhortation to "suffer the word of exhortation" suggests that the recipients should patiently and willingly receive the author's message, even if it contains challenging or uncomfortable truths.

- The phrase "for I have written a letter unto you in few words" indicates that the author has condensed his message into a relatively short letter, yet it contains important and impactful truths that the recipients should take seriously.

- This verse underscores the importance of attentively listening to and obeying the teachings of Scripture, recognizing that God's Word is a source of guidance, correction, and encouragement for believers.

Exhaustive Strong's Concordance (ESV):

- The exhortation to "suffer the word of exhortation" suggests that the recipients should patiently and willingly receive the author's message, indicating the importance of attentively listening to the teachings of Scripture.

- The phrase "for I have written a letter unto you in few words" indicates that the author has condensed his message into a relatively short letter, yet it contains important and impactful truths that the recipients should take seriously, indicating the importance of the message.

This verse is a plea from the author to the recipients of the letter to receive and accept his exhortation, indicating the importance of the message he has written to them. It emphasizes the importance of attentively listening to and obeying the teachings of Scripture, recognizing that God's Word is a source of guidance, correction, and encouragement for believers.

Verse 23 (KJV):

"Know ye that our brother Timothy is set at liberty; with whom, if he come shortly, I will see you."

References:

- Timothy, mentioned in this verse, was a close companion and co-worker of the apostle Paul, as well as a recipient of two New Testament letters written to him.

- The concept of freedom or liberty is a recurring theme in the New Testament, particularly in relation to the freedom believers have in Christ (Galatians 5:1; 2 Corinthians 3:17).

Interpretation:

- This verse informs the recipients of the letter that Timothy has been released from whatever situation was restricting him, and the author hopes to visit them with Timothy soon.

Commentary:
- The mention of Timothy's release may indicate that he was previously unable to travel or minister freely, but now he is at liberty to do so.
- The author's intention to visit with Timothy demonstrates the importance of personal interaction and pastoral care in the early Christian community.
- This verse reflects the close relationships and mutual concern among early Christians, as well as the desire for fellowship and encouragement within the faith community.

Exhaustive Strong's Concordance (ESV):
- The mention of Timothy's release may indicate that he was previously unable to travel or minister freely, but now he is at liberty to do so, indicating Timothy's freedom.
- The author's intention to visit with Timothy demonstrates the importance of personal interaction and pastoral care in the early Christian community, indicating the author's desire for fellowship and encouragement within the faith community.

This verse informs the recipients of the letter that Timothy has been released from whatever situation was restricting him, and the author hopes to visit them with Timothy soon. It reflects the close relationships and mutual concern among early Christians, as well as the desire for fellowship and encouragement within the faith community.

Verse 24 (KJV):

"Salute all them that have the rule over you, and all the saints. They of Italy salute you."

References:
- This verse contains a greeting to the recipients of the letter, instructing them to greet their leaders and fellow believers, which reflects the practice of sending greetings and expressing solidarity in the early church (Romans 16:16; 1 Corinthians 16:20).
- The mention of "They of Italy salute you" suggests that the author and possibly others with him are in Italy, sending their greetings to the recipients of the letter.

Interpretation:
- This verse is a directive for the recipients of the letter to greet their leaders and fellow believers, as well as an indication of the origin of the author and the location from which the letter is sent.

Commentary:
- The instruction to "Salute all them that have the rule over you, and all the saints" emphasizes the importance of showing respect and affection to both leaders and fellow believers within the Christian community.
- The mention of "They of Italy salute you" suggests that the author and possibly other believers in Italy are sending their greetings to the recipients, indicating a sense of connection and unity among believers across different locations.
- This verse reflects the practice of extending greetings and expressing solidarity within the early Christian community, fostering a sense of belonging and shared identity among believers.

Exhaustive Strong's Concordance (ESV):

- The instruction to "Salute all them that have the rule over you, and all the saints" emphasizes the importance of showing respect and affection to both leaders and fellow believers within the Christian community, indicating the importance of unity.

- The mention of "They of Italy salute you" suggests that the author and possibly other believers in Italy are sending their greetings to the recipients, indicating a sense of connection and unity among believers across different locations, indicating a sense of solidarity.

This verse is a directive for the recipients of the letter to greet their leaders and fellow believers, as well as an indication of the origin of the author and the location from which the letter is sent. It emphasizes the importance of showing respect and affection to both leaders and fellow believers within the Christian community, reflecting the practice of extending greetings and expressing solidarity within the early Christian community.

Verse 25 (KJV):
"Grace be with you all. Amen."

References:
- This closing benediction is a common way to conclude New Testament letters, invoking God's grace and blessing upon the recipients (Romans 16:20; 1 Corinthians 16:23).

- The use of "Amen" signifies agreement and affirmation of the prayer for grace and serves as a conclusion to the letter.

Interpretation:
- This verse is a prayer for God's grace to be upon all the recipients of the letter, expressing the author's desire for God's favor and blessing to accompany them.

Commentary:

- The benediction "Grace be with you all" is a fitting conclusion to the letter, emphasizing the central role of God's grace in the Christian life and the importance of relying on His favor and empowerment.

- The use of "Amen" signifies the author's affirmation and agreement with the prayer for grace, indicating that the sentiments expressed are heartfelt and sincere.

- This verse encapsulates the overarching theme of the letter to the Hebrews, which emphasizes the sufficiency of God's grace and the superiority of Christ in all things.

Exhaustive Strong's Concordance (ESV):

- The benediction "Grace be with you all" is a fitting conclusion to the letter, emphasizing the central role of God's grace in the Christian life, indicating the importance of relying on His favor and empowerment.

- The use of "Amen" signifies the author's affirmation and agreement with the prayer for grace, indicating that the sentiments expressed are heartfelt and sincere, indicating the author's sincerity in the prayer for grace.

This verse is a prayer for God's grace to be upon all the recipients of the letter, expressing the author's desire for God's favor and blessing to accompany them. It serves as a fitting conclusion to the letter, emphasizing the central role of God's grace in the Christian life and the importance of relying on His favor and empowerment.

∞

CONCLUSION

The Central Message of Hebrews

Throughout the Book of Hebrews, one resounding theme echoes: the unparalleled supremacy and sufficiency of Jesus Christ. From the opening verses to the closing benediction, the author meticulously crafts an argument, demonstrating how Jesus surpasses all that came before Him in the Old Testament.

Christ's Superiority and Sufficiency:
The author of Hebrews meticulously compares Jesus to various figures and institutions of the Old Testament, showcasing His unparalleled excellence. Jesus is revealed as superior to the angels, greater than Moses, and the ultimate fulfillment of the Levitical priesthood. His sacrifice on the cross is depicted as the perfect and final atonement for sin, rendering the old sacrificial system obsolete. In every aspect, Jesus stands as the pinnacle of God's revelation and the embodiment of His redemptive plan.

The Call to Persevere in Faith:

Embedded within the message of Christ's superiority is a call to perseverance in faith. The author urges readers to hold fast to their confession of Christ, to remain steadfast in the face of trials and persecution. Drawing inspiration from the faith of Old Testament heroes, the author encourages believers to fix their eyes on Jesus, the author and perfecter of faith. In Him, they find the strength and endurance to run the race set before them, knowing that their faith will be richly rewarded.

In conclusion, the Book of Hebrews serves as a powerful reminder of the preeminence of Jesus Christ and the unshakeable foundation He provides for the believer's life. It calls us to anchor our faith in Him alone, to trust in His finished work on the cross, and to persevere with unwavering confidence in His promises. As we heed this call, may we find our hope and assurance in the surpassing greatness of our Savior, who reigns now and forevermore. Amen.